The Time Trap

FOURTH EDITION

Alec Mackenzie

Pat Nickerson

⁴AMACOM

AMERICAN MANAGEMENT ASSOCIATION

New York • Atlanta • Brussels • Chicago • Mexico City • San Francisco
Shanghai • Tokyo • Toronto • Washington, D.C.

Special discounts on bulk quantities of AMACOM books are
available to corporations, professional associations, and other
organizations. For details, contact Special Sales Department,
AMACOM, a division of American Management Association,
1601 Broadway, New York, NY 10019.
Tel.: 800-250-5308.   Fax: 518-891-2372.
E-mail: specialsls@amanet.org
Website: www.amacombooks.org/go/specialsales
To view all AMACOM titles go to: www.amacombooks.org

This publication is designed to provide accurate and authoritative information
in regard to the subject matter covered. It is sold with the understanding that
the publisher is not engaged in rendering legal, accounting, or other professional
service. If legal advice or other expert assistance is required, the services of a
competent professional person should be sought.

Library of Congress Cataloging-in-Publication Data

Mackenzie, R. Alec.
  The time trap / Alec Mackenzie and Pat Nickerson.—4th ed.
      p.   cm.
  Includes bibliographical references and index.
  ISBN-13: 978-0-8144-1338-8
  ISBN-10: 0-8144-1338-2
  1. Time management.   I. Nickerson, Pat.   II. Title.

HD69.T54M33   2009
650.1'1—dc22

                                              2008051597

Printing number

10   9   8   7   6

CONTENTS

Preface   vii

Acknowledgments   xvii

PART ONE
Time Management for the Twenty-First Century

1 Why Time Still Baffles the Best of Us   3

2 Time Traps We've Been Taught   12

3 How to Connect Goals, Objectives, and Priorities   28

4 How to Set Priorities and Hold Them   44

5 How to Tame the Time Log   56

PART TWO
The New Time Traps and Escapes

6 Management by Crisis   71

7 Inadequate Planning,   82

8 Inability to Say No   96

9 Poor Communication   109

10 Poorly Run Meetings   125

11 The World Gone Virtual   139

12 E-Mail Mania   151
13 The Untamed Telephone   163
14 Information Overload and the Paper Chase   175
15 Confused Responsibility and Authority   191
16 Poor Delegation and Training   204
17 Procrastination and Leaving Tasks Unfinished   221
18 Socializing and Drop-In Visitors   238
19 Attempting Too Much   251

PART THREE
Parting Advice

20 Life Lessons in Time Management   263
21 Where Do We Go from Here?   273

PART FOUR
Quick Solutions Summaries for the New Time Traps

Trap 1: Management By Crisis   280
Trap 2: Inadequate Planning   281
Trap 3: Inability to Say No   282
Trap 4: Communication   283
Trap 5: Poorly Run Meetings   284
Trap 6: The World Gone Virtual   285
Trap 7: E-Mail Mania   286
Trap 8: The Untamed Telephone   287
Trap 9: Incomplete Information and the Paper Chase   288
Trap 10: Confused Responsibility and Authority   289
Trap 11: Poor Delegation and Training   290

Trap 12: Procrastination and Leaving Tasks Unfinished   291

Trap 13: Socializing and Drop-In Visitors   292

Trap 14: Attempting Too Much   293

Index   295

PREFACE TO THE FOURTH EDITION

ACKNOWLEDGING ALEC MACKENZIE

When AMACOM Senior Editor Jacquie Flynn invited me to write this new edition of *The Time Trap*, I felt honored to help keep Alec Mackenzie's groundbreaking ideas current. A longtime hero to me, Alec was instrumental in the early success of EBI, Inc., our family-held training company—though he didn't know it until years later.

Why The Time Trap *Inspired Us*

In our first decade in business, based in London, our company came up against stiff competition from the hundreds of organizations flooding the hungry training market there. Our edge? We were marketing the best of American engineering know-how at a time when the British government had mandated training for engineers.

But very soon, political upheaval in Britain caused wildcat strikes that shut down electric power for weeks on end. The next year, the gas industry went out—then the railways. Finally, the Post Office shut down for more than three months, cutting off both direct mail and telephone service—isolating every business in those days before smartphones and laptops. These catastrophes shook everyone . . . our customers, our competitors, ourselves.

Working like demons whenever we could get power for lights and office machinery, we used newspaper ads instead of direct mail advertising. Like every business, we labored to stay afloat. In our own case, forced by circumstance, we opened EBI partnerships in other European countries—

not part of our original plan at all. Those excellent partners taught us that a crisis can sometimes hide a blessing.

During those challenging times, we read Alec Mackenzie's first edition of *The Time Trap*. It gave us new energy, new ideas, new tools and, above all, encouragement to persevere. Recovery took us five years; success took eight.

Thanking Alec Mackenzie "Live"

Well into recovery, with our business going steady at last, my husband and I traveled to Schenectady, New York, to attend a Mackenzie seminar on Team Time Management. Walking across the campus with Alec that day, we thanked him warmly for the helpful influence he had long been in our lives. He was modest and unassuming in accepting our thanks. In person, as in his books and seminars, he stayed totally focused on helping all of us escape from our time traps. To influence so many, so well, he drew on his deep ethical sense for answers that were as pertinent then as they will always be.

MANY VOICES

In this edition, when you read suggestions from "us," or when "we" tell war stories and offer solutions, the messages will be coming from both Alec Mackenzie and me. For this new edition, you'll also glean ideas from dozens of managers and specialists from every walk of business who have escaped their time traps. Of course, you are invited to interact, too, by sending questions and your own ideas for future editions to us at timetamer@sbcglobal.net.

HOW TO USE THIS EDITION

This is a not a book of light reading hints. Many people tell us they have tried for years to apply "helpful hints" gathered from here and there, only to find themselves ensnared again—out of time, out of resources, drowning in a flood of demands. With that in mind, the opening chapters help you focus first on those *human habits* that sabotage everyone's best efforts. If you can examine your day-to-day work habits with some humor and compassion, you'll construct a more dependable escape from whatever practices are keeping you ensnared.

Why We Stay Trapped

In Part I we unravel the tangled pressures that drive us—the many demands imposed by our culture, our workplace, and ourselves. If you read these five chapters thoughtfully, you'll derive a uniquely personal view and build a more reliable exit strategy.

1. Why Time Still Baffles the Best of Us
2. Time Traps We've Been Taught
3. How to Connect Goals, Objectives, Priorities
4. How to Set Priorities and Hold Them
5. How to Tame the Time Log

You'll glean from these chapters a serious probe of root causes, with options for permanently avoiding some of your time traps.

The Time Trap Lists: Old and New Traps:

In Part II of the previous edition, Alec Mackenzie reported on twenty time traps that blocked business people and technologists from achieving their goals. Because so many readers could relate, the book became a best-seller. Here's the list:

The Original Twenty

1. Management by Crisis	11. Meetings
2. Telephone interruptions	12. Paperwork
3. Inadequate planning	13. Leaving tasks unfinished
4. Attempting too much	14. Inadequate staff
5. Drop-in visitors	15. Socializing
6. Ineffective delegation	16. Confused responsibility and authority
7. Personal disorganization	17. Poor communication
8. Lack of self-discipline	18. Inadequate controls and progress reports
9. Inability to say no	19. Incomplete information
10. Procrastination	20. Travel

For our current edition, we took a new survey, sending out the same list, in its original order, knowing that the order would have changed, but wanting respondents to show us precisely how. Respondents soon erased all doubts.

A Glaring Gap   Surveys came back, citing omissions that did not surprise us. The Internet, e-mail (including instant-messaging), and cell phone use/abuse needed to appear on the new list, everyone agreed. But, while respondents spoke of these tools as "all one phenomenon," we needed three separate chapters just to scratch the surface of what's so time-saving, yet time-wasting about our new "virtual" lifestyle.

Reordering the Traps   In twenty years of writing and presenting seminars on time and priority management (first for Dun & Bradstreet and later for American Management Association), I've worked with more than 180,000 time-hungry managers. Their issues and solutions appeared in my earlier AMACOM book *Managing Multiple Bosses*.

In Alec's earlier editions, he repeated his conviction that time traps were enmeshed with one another. We warmed to his conviction that eliminating one trap might cure several at a stroke. So, with Edition Four, the time has come. The new list seeks to untangle and reconnect related traps, offering escape plans for a multiple gain in a single leap. Still, we followed the order proposed by our respondents.

Today's Top Five Traps as Respondents See Them

Trap 1: Management by Crisis—still ranks Number One!

Trap 2: Inadequate Planning—formerly in third place, it now includes the former Trap 8: Lack of Self-Discipline as part of this mix.

Trap 3: Inability to Say No—this has risen from ninth.

Trap 4: Poor Communication—shows a dramatic rise from former slot seventeen.

Trap 5: Poorly Run Meetings—formerly twelfth, it now joins the top irritants.

These top five traps reflect the pressures brought by the rapid, worldwide change that roils every corporation and every government entity. In follow-up discussions, we learned that respondents defined all five traps as corporate or systemic traps, not simply personal issues that people could correct by solo effort.

Communication Took the Steepest Climb   As you see, this trap now enters the top five list, moving from its old rank, seventeenth out of twenty. Many respondents explained its new prominence in their view:

- "We've got great tools: e-mail, voice-mail, IM, etc. But so does everyone else. So we can never get away from the fray. Worse, e-mail style produces message fragments—everything sent in haste, with little forethought."

- "Even small businesses have gone global, so we lack the multicultural awareness and long-distance negotiating skills to connect with people, on the first try. With our partners continents away, we make mistakes, without realizing that we've damaged trust."
- "We isolate ourselves in front of one screen or another for hours per day. Why do we put everything in writing, even to people in the next office?"
- "We're losing our face-to-face skills. We see a lot less patience, tact, insight, compassion. People don't know how to coexist in a room anymore."

It's small wonder that "Poorly Run Meetings" followed "Poor Communications" on the list. If you agree, you'll be interested in the tools we've embedded throughout the book—including many visual tools—to help you get your points across to coworkers, bosses, and customers, with economy and humanity, no matter which medium you use.

Second-Tier Traps: 6–9   Electronics and information issues led off the next group of traps. Though respondents replied from scattered companies and locations and at different times, with no group contact, their rankings produced a consensus.

Interviewees clarified that all felt drowned by information. At whatever level of management—experienced or new to business—everyone now gets easy access to data that would have been out of their reach in the rigid business settings of a decade ago. But this "infoglut" has stretched our critical thinking skills to the max. Which data matters? Which data is correct? How and why should it be used? So the second-tier traps were seen as mixed blessings:

Trap 6: The World Gone Virtual (new)

Trap 7: E-Mail Mania (new)

Trap 8: The Untamed Telephone (new)

Trap 9: Incomplete Information and the Paper Chase (formerly Traps 13 and 19)

The irony of Trap 9's position blew us away! With all our newfound electronic data gathering, how can we lack complete information? Easy: Traps 6, 7, and 8 represent the deluge. Trap 9 represents our failed struggle to wade through it all. More ironically we are still encumbered by paperwork and surrounded by filing cabinets, long after the pundits promised we'd be paperless! Using solo solutions, we can barely dent Traps 6 through 9, so we're going to need an "all-hands" effort, and a systems approach.

Still Buffaloed by Succession Issues   The next two traps were an obvious pair, at least to our survey respondents:

Trap 10: Confused Responsibility or Authority (formerly in sixteenth place)

Trap 11: Poor Delegation and Training (descending from its former sixth position)

Respondents saw a close cause/effect linkage between these two. They intertwine horribly, but our insightful respondents insisted that we must settle Trap 10 before we can do a decent job with Trap 11. In both cases, much of the fault lies with corporate policies that often confuse and confound the best managers' attempts to develop and promote people fairly.

The Final Tier: The Challenges Get Personal   At last, we come to traps we can escape through our own efforts. The final three combine several from the original list, to offer some "winner-take-all" solutions.

Trap 12: Procrastination and Leaving Things Unfinished. Blending former Traps 10 and 11 made sense to all of us.

Trap 13: Socializing and Dealing with Drop-Ins. Combining former Traps 5 and 15, respondents noted that the loss of face-time has dragged socializing to a low spot on the list, making us less adept at handling it when we actually need it.

Trap 14: Attempting Too Much (formerly Trap 4). That this final trap has fallen so low, was a frightening sign. Formerly Trap 4, the habit of "attempting too much" may escape our notice because expectations have grown so unreasonable. Workers productivity is high, but so is unemployment. In America today, earned vacation time piles up until it expires. We now surpass the fabled Japanese in time spent on the job. With massive off-shoring of both manufacturing and service jobs, our audience members tell us: "Unless we stay and do the work—they'll find someone else who will. Warranted or not, that's our fear." Read this chapter carefully, if you feel on the brink of burnout. Regaining your balance is an inside job.

Two Issues No Longer in Play   Garnering so few votes that they dropped off the lists were these two traps:

1. *Inadequate Controls and Reports* (former Trap 18). Thanks to new electronic tools, respondents cited automation as the new source of controls and routine reports, even in small companies. Today, data on a single event, recorded when it occurs, can be "sliced and diced" according to preference; then, transferred to a variety of subsidiary reports, and recalculated, automatically.
2. *Travel* (former Trap 20). Today's "road warriors" seem hardened to security hassles and chaotic flight delays. Fully equipped with our electronic gear, we stay amazingly productive on the road. No matter what the delay, we connect with our companies and our customers more effectively than Alec had dreamed possible when he wrote earlier editions. Still, you'll find some practical comments on controls and travel, dispersed throughout the text wherever they can be helpful.

Life Lessons

Part III: Parting Advice consists of two chapters, the first—Life Lessons in Time Management—offering inspiring personal histories from people who are making more time for their lives as managers, technologists, parents, family members, hobbyists, and community activists. They share the secrets they've learned that continue to inspire them. Perhaps you, too, will recall those people in your own life who've helped you move toward time mastery. The second chapter—Where Do We Go from Here?—provides a brief roadmap of some concrete steps you might take in your struggle to escape the traps you are enmeshed in.

Tools to Fight Hidden Resistance

In Part IV, you'll find a set of Quick Solutions Summaries to help you persevere should your old time habits sneak up on you again. Drawn from our many conversations with intelligent and witty people, these Summary

Charts reveal the ten most common excuses that people use to avoid changing their well-worn habits. We hope you'll smile—and benefit.

Expressed with openness and humor, these "confessions" fill one column per page, while the "recovery tools" fill the opposing side. If you feel a strong tug of resistance when you try a new time practice—turn to these pages for support, before you backslide. They will refresh your resolve to recover.

NEW FEATURES IN THE FOURTH EDITION

Throughout the book, you'll enjoy two new features designed for practicality and fun:

- *Human Comedy:* Ironic confessions from time-taxed people just like us who tried oddball fixes that failed. We hope you'll laugh along with them.
- *Real Voices:* Testimonies and tools from ordinary (and extraordinary) managers who are building new time practices that you might want to borrow. Adopt or adapt the ideas you like, with their blessings.

Previous editions drew comments and scenarios from manufacturing, education, government, and small-to mid-sized businesses. Currently, we meet bigger populations of managers from finance and investment, biotech and health care, energy, aerospace, and information technology.

You'll read their cases and scenarios in every chapter, gaining new solutions from their ideas and insights. Of course, we still work with government and military populations, with public servants, and with small-business owners, so you'll enjoy a wide range of views.

ULTIMATELY, CAN WE ESCAPE OUR TIME TRAPS?

Today, as a manager or technologist, you may boast an excellent education and strong motivation—but you also face unprecedented demands from yourself, your company, your customers, and your community. If the obligations of your work and life are keeping you awake at night—take heart!

Enjoy this book, write in it thoughtfully, try some of the tools, and return to it in thirty days for a self-check. Construct a set of simple time strategies that make sense to you. From the wide array here, you'll be able to select tools you can easily fit into your work and life.

All of us who worked on this book—Alec Mackenzie, my survey respondents, my many mentors and teachers—we all wish you a rewarding return on your investment.

More power to you!

Pat Nickerson
San Diego, 2009

ACKNOWLEDGMENTS

Heartfelt thanks, always . . .

To my husband and business partner, Ken Nickerson, whose patience, wisdom, and good humor have supported every effort, every shared dream for decades.

To MaryEllyn Wyatt, longtime friend, whose wide-ranging tastes let her cast a discerning eye over several chapters.

To Dr. Deborah Smith-Hemphill, friend, colleague, always ahead of the general population on matters both technical and ethical, for her aware and witty advice, especially on technology issues.

To the wonderful "Real Voice" respondents from coast to coast, who took time from their busy lives in business, the professions, and the military, for sharing their ideas about managing time. To Bob Avery, Andrea Cifor, Bart Denison, Vicki Farnsworth, Lindsay Geyer, Ken Mayo, Mel Northey, Roger Nys, Lori Sergent, Richard Shirley, Terry Spenser, Tom Stotesbury, Kris Todisco, and Cathy Wilber, for their practical and inspiring ideas about escaping the Time Traps of work and in life.

Special thanks to Jacquie Flynn, Executive Editor at AMACOM Books, for her sage counsel on this, our second collaboration for AMA-COM, to copyeditor Debbie Posner for her wise consistency, to Editorial Assistant Jennifer Holder for flexible and willing support on this book, and to Associate Editor Mike Sivilli for his expert and energetic support in producing the book.

PART ONE

Time Management for the Twenty-First Century

CHAPTER

Why Time Still Baffles the Best of Us

We've all heard ourselves say it: "There's never enough time!"

Maybe Noah and his family said it, too, as they hurried the paired animals aboard the ark. But, like our forebears of long ago, we all get the same twenty-four hours, the same 1,440 minutes daily. Noah's advantage? His team got a precise deadline, clear consequences, and detailed instructions from a Higher Authority on exactly when and how to proceed.

If you don't feel similarly advantaged, the progress you can make in your allotted time will vary with your culture, your circumstances, and, especially, your choices.

Certainly, having fewer choices would simplify your life. If you've ever lived through a natural disaster, or even a lengthy power outage, you know how it feels to be flung back to fundamentals. Intensely involved, you labor from dawn to dusk on essential survival tasks; you make further progress if you can, by moonlight, firelight, candlelight, or battery power, until well-earned sleep overtakes you. Later, you may remember your effort with pride, but you won't want to repeat it.

DISTRACTIONS, EXPECTATIONS, URGENCY

Why do we seem able to master our time during a crisis, but not on ordinary days? Because of the trio of overarching "supertraps," from which all the other time traps descend. These are:

Trivial Distractions
Undue Expectations
Urgency Trumping Validity

How Distractions Drain Our Time

Let's think about your work/life situation today, especially as it affects your time. If you're like most people, your home, car, and office are loaded with modern tools and data resources. You can stay on top of world news at every moment, reacting quickly to any problem or opportunity that may arise. But, should you?

How Crucial Is Connectivity?

How was it that our forebears, unacquainted with high-speed tools and twenty-four-hour connectivity, were able to research, invent, and achieve so many wonders—from cave paintings to cathedrals, from empire building to electric power, from railroads to radium, from gold panning to trepanning—all between sunlight or candlelight, in the "lands before laptops"? Were they gifted with more grit and intelligence than we? Were they stronger, smarter? Or were they blissfully free of the first great supertrap, Trivial Distractions?

Does Multitasking Save or Waste Time?

Look at your situation today. Everywhere, people try to convince the working public that multitasking is a duty at all times. You've seen those drivers in the next lane, commuting to work. If they're multitasking to save time, they use their GPS and radio traffic alerts to enable a last-minute diagonal dash for the nearest exit. They may try to save even more time by tapping out a text message or returning phone calls, all while slurping their Starbucks and negotiating the off-ramp at 70 mph. Will the time they save by multitasking pay off? Or will it vanish in a cloud of sparks when another driver, similarly engaged, suddenly makes contact? What was their hurry, you wonder, shaking your head as you drive smoothly past.

More and more researchers dispute the notion that multitasking saves time: the human brain cannot actually process two opposing thoughts simultaneously, without loss of quality on both streams of thought. Instead, we do better when we handle mental tasks singly and sequentially. We may improve performance by using visual reminders to stay on track and—with practice—we may accelerate the transit from one task to the next. But even then, focus is easily lost.

REAL VOICES

Here's what Ken Mayo has to say about multitasking. He is Web Coordinator/ Photographer for The Catholic Health Association of the United States.

I have come to believe that multitasking is counterproductive. While striving to get "good" at it, I found the quality of my work suffered greatly. I now try to focus on one task at a time. If I can't complete something, I at least try to divide the task or project into phases. Then when I return to a task or a project, it is easier to remember where to begin again.

Retaining Concentration

You've probably noticed that you make most errors in those closing moments of a task when your mind has moved on, before your fingers can finish the typing, or your hammer can connect with the final nail. Ouch! If we can hold focus on the first thought, wrap it up quickly, and then move on to the next, we may gain some value. If we list our upcoming tasks in writing or on a screen, keeping it always visible before us, we can accelerate when ready. But, meanwhile, we should give each task our single-focus intensity, not split attention, to save time effectively.

HOW WOULD YOU USE THE TIME YOU SAVE?

At our Time Management seminars, we often ask frazzled attendees how they would use the magical gift of a free hour per day. The majority of respondents sing out "Sleep!"

Does that response surprise you? Sadden you? Or sound just like you?

According to studies by various sleep researchers, American adults now average only six hours and forty minutes of sleep per night—not the eight hours recommended to earlier generations. (Indeed, mattress advertisers tell us to maximize a mere six hours by buying better bedding!)

But how do we spend our time preparing for sleep? Many working adults admit to collapsing after dinner, numbly decompressing in front of the TV, while their kids toggle between social web sites, Instant Messaging, combat games, music players, and homework. Ah yes, homework. For too many kids, physical exercise is taken indoors, using only their thumbs! No wonder they're too spent to get up in the morning!

Joking aside, what would most working adults do with that magical twenty-fifth hour? Let's look at some effective escapes from our time traps.

ESCAPE DISTRACTION: FOCUS YOUR TIME ON A GOAL

If you imagine your "gift hour" given to you at a time of your choosing—not when you are fatigued (as might have justified the sleep response) but at a high-energy time—your best time of day—you might have answered differently. Let's ask the energetic you: How would you use your twenty-fifth hour?

- Work on your latest invention?
- Play a sport, or exercise?
- Visit with friends?
- Play ball with your kids?
- Clean up your room?
- Relax?
- Read, study?
- Meditate, pray?
- Paint a picture?
- Visit a gallery?
- Learn guitar?
- Garden?
- Cook?
- Repaint a room?
- Get a spa treatment?
- Volunteer for a cause you care about?

Add yours here.

- _____
- _____

Whatever you selected, one thing is sure: you would hold that gift hour strictly for that goal, not permitting any random distractions or sub-tractions. You'd insist on staying focused on your chosen goal. You'd be clear about your motive for managing that rare gift of time.

If, before going on with this book, you focus on an important personal or life goal currently out of reach, you'll gain a strong impetus to escape any time trap that frustrates you now. So, before proceeding much further, picture that valued goal, keep it modest enough to build or savor in the single saved hour per day . . . something that would keep repaying you with pride or serenity, not just once, but many times over, in the next few weeks or months. Imagine that hour, reliably yours, every day. Keep it in sight.

What About a Gift Hour at Work?

Suppose people in authority gave you the same option at work—the gift of an hour each day—not to handle *their* work priorities but to handle *yours?* What high-value task, important to you or your career, eludes you now be-cause of time demands from customers, colleagues, or bosses? How often have you heard yourself say, "It's just *my* stuff. I'll get to it when everything else quiets down around here."

But that quiet never comes during working hours, so you squeeze in unpaid overtime to work on it, unobstructed. Perhaps as you ponder this book, you can add that task to the list of goals worthy of your best time-management resolves.

Expectations: What Should We Do at Work?

"Choose what to do at work? Who is free to think that way?" you may ask.

You! Yes, you have not only the freedom but the duty to choose what to do at work No matter how sincerely you want to excel at service, no matter how customer-focused your company's policies—everyone must, sooner or later, stake out some criteria that will validate the work they are doing eight to ten hours per day.

Consider the following criteria for accepting a new task, and you may realize that you have been using some or all of these measures, all along. Perhaps these criteria have brought you a modicum of the success you now enjoy.

Picture this: an unusual request comes in when your work schedule is already full. A conflict is apparent. You must consider the following questions:

- What is the *validity* of this new demand? (Its impact or importance, overall?) what would happen if I didn't do this?
- What is its *political sensitivity*? (Is it coming from "on high"?)
- What is the *complexity* of the demand? (Are multiple elements involved?)
- What are the *costs*, *risks*, or *opportunities*?
- What *options* would produce what kinds of distinct outcomes?
- *Whose consultation* must be tapped for approaches or approvals?
- Finally—what is its relative *urgency*, compared with tasks on the front burner?

What you are doing here is making a decision: should this task be allowed to compete for your time against other tasks already booked?

When a request is sent to you because you are the "house expert," or Subject Matter Expert (SME), your expertise may allow you to process those questions so rapidly, easily, and instinctively, that requesters are awed. Soon, however, they'll come to expect your instant response on all topics, familiar or not. Once that happens, you have been typecast; you have stepped unwittingly into the second of the three supertraps, Bowing to Undue Expectations.

ESCAPE EXPECTATIONS: YOURS AND THEIRS

So, how can you pull people's expectation into line with reality? You'd need to figure this out:

1. On what proportion of all incoming work do you need to stop and assess validity?
   - For *senior managers*, who handle mostly decisions and far fewer routines, the sum of incoming tasks that need validating could exceed 80 percent.

- For *mid-level managers* and *specialists* with a lot of precise but repetitive work, some validity questions may have been settled earlier. But you must still reassess incoming tasks when the size of your workload threatens feasibility. If a demand suddenly balloons your workload by more than 20 percent, you need to question the feasibility of that demand. Except in brief emergencies, you cannot add to a full workload by more than 20 percent without risking blind errors. (You'd be talking about moving to a six-day week for the duration of that task—and we know where that leads.)

2. As a second step, answering the other validity questions—political sensitivity, complexity, cost and staffing—will complete your analysis of task validity.

3. Only now, with incoming tasks validated, should you take up the question of urgency. Unless you're running the Emergency Room, the urgency of a task should not influence you as a first consideration. Confirm this, to avoid entering the third of the supertraps, Letting Urgency Upstage Validity.

KEEP URGENCY OUT OF YOUR TRIAGE EQUATION

Only after validating expectations as realistic would you allow urgency to enter your mind. The new rule goes like this:Urgency is a tiebreaker only between two tasks of equal validity.

This is how field hospitals perform triage, not on how fast they can get all patients into surgery but, by determining the seriousness of the damage and the likelihood of each patient's surviving surgery. For example, several wounded are brought in to a field hospital. Two have life-threatening injuries. (They are "A" patients.) Several others have less serious injuries and have been stabilized. (They are "B" patients.) If there is only one surgeon, urgency is now used to break the tie between the two "A" patients: equally serious but with one stronger than the other, the more fragile case will go into surgery first. The stronger patient will go in next. But the "B" cases may have to wait indefinitely, getting attention and care, but not surgery. They are not in the "A" contest at all.

In similar ways, the triage rule follows for business. Urgency is used to tiebreak between two business issues of equal seriousness. If you work to categorize tasks in terms of their objective importance, you will not be overwhelmed by all those requesters who consider themselves to be

"Number One." You'll have a firm grasp on the following rule: Urgency cannot overrule validity. Give some calm thought to this as you review your current and expected workloads.

REAL VOICES

Here's what Richard Shirley has to say about multitasking and triage in military settings. (He's a civilian IT Systems Manager based in San Diego.)

Project prioritization is my favorite method of saving time. I triage the task based on levels of importance and urgency. Keeping multiple tasks from becoming both important and urgent simultaneously keeps me from falling into a reactionary management mode. If I can successfully manage my time then most tasks will be handled as important, before they can become urgent.

I work very hard to hold my focus since I'm being constantly interrupted.

A special request for information or assistance can force everything else to stop. Once again, triage comes into play. If it's a "hot potato"— something that needs immediate attention—I stop what I'm doing and address the issue. Since we are civilians working with the military, this juggling act can come from all sides.

Often, whoever has the most "pull" will get immediate attention. If I'm in the middle of an e-mail, I save a draft copy so I can return to it later, or I set reminders in Outlook. Also, I don't allow an inordinate amount of time to elapse between the interruption and returning to my previous task. (I found that if I fell into this trap, my original focus quickly diminished.) But, the interruptions that I once disliked intensely, I now approach with the understanding that they help me practice time management skills, and develop patience with people.

YOUR CHOICES, YOUR FOCUS, YOUR TIME

Your goal in pursuing better time management is to reach the end of any challenging day, and ask yourself:

- How many minutes or hours was I able to focus, undistracted? (If you were able to beat the average manager's eight minutes of peace and concentration, celebrate!)

- How often did I insist that validity trump apparent urgency? (If your answer makes you proud, celebrate!)
- What proportion of my work added value for those I am here to serve? (If your answer pleases you, celebrate!)
- Was I able to negotiate realistic expectations (quantity, quality and time) in order to validate some tasks? (If yes, then celebrate!)
- How often, today, did my decisions fit my sense of ethics? (Celebrate!)
- Did I work hard, meet a lot of my goals, and have some fun, too? (Celebrate!)

With a clearer sense of your targets posted before you, we wish you good hunting through the welter of ideas and tools presented in the next chapter. May you use them to curtail distractions, adjust expectations (yours and other people's) and find satisfaction in doing work you can validate and celebrate.

It won't be a cakewalk. We're prone to several traps that our traditions have taught us to accept. That's where we're going next.

Time Traps We've Been Taught

Since the earlier editions of *The Time Trap* made the best-seller lists, managers have read dozens of affirming new books and attended management workshops that echoed Alec Mackenzie's practical advice. Perhaps you've heard and heeded some good ideas over the years, trying out a promising new practice for a day or two, but, then—to your surprise—reverting to your old routines.

TOO MANY DEMANDS, TOO MUCH DATA

When too many demands compete for too little time, people naturally feel safer returning to familiar if barely adequate methods. The new practices never take root. (In the training business, we admonish attendees to practice their chosen solutions within seven days, or risk losing them altogether.)

You have plenty of choices, too. Stationers' shelves are stacked with plain and fancy appointment books and pocket organizers. Software developers offer you wonderful applications to integrate meetings, appointments, to-do lists, and projects with your e-mail traffic—automatically, on your instructions. Yet with all these dazzling tools, you still hear people say, "There's never enough time."

That's because information, exploding from worldwide sources, keeps expanding exponentially every day. When you can't keep up with the inflow, software makers and service providers step in to oblige—hiking your personal storage capacity, or holding your info-burden on their own servers, until you tap it or delete it. But to start managing your business overload, you need to tailor your own criteria for opening and retrieving information. The software and service providers will help you stick a finger in the dike, but you must still work out the retrieval logic that will serve you best.

Time for a Tailored Solution?

What you need is a personal set of criteria, a system well-planned to cut through the clutter, ready to retrieve only the data you need at any moment. You need stringent filtering rules tailored to your needs.

"But who has time to think about better criteria!" you may cry. "I've got a live customer standing in front of me every hour of the day!"

Pressure Puts Off Planning

You're right. Cleaning up your personal information system takes planning and decision making—and both of those take time because no one else can do it for you. But you're not alone if you find the prospect daunting and other matters more pressing. Can you relate to the following scenarios?

- You're frustrated when an important job is still not ready at deadline—but you're too exhausted to start hunting for missing data.
- You glance at the clock and realize with a jolt that it's 5:00 P.M., and you haven't even started *your* work while taking care of everyone else's!
- When time-driven projects come up, such as year-end reports, you steel yourself for the long night and weekend hours ahead, and then reach the finish line, afraid that your hasty findings may prove flawed.
- You say yes to a big new assignment even when overloaded, because you dare not delegate to a subordinate with more time but less experience than you.
- Senior requesters tell you, "Drop everything, and do this." But you know they'll return shortly for that "everything" you were told to drop.

Even if you are a time-aware professional—even if you list your priorities in writing, and struggle to maintain them—you can still get sidetracked by two powerful habits, always painted as virtues: responsiveness and randomness. Both of these are spawned by that familiar supertrap, Undue Expectations.

RESPONSIVENESS AND RANDOMNESS: DOUBLE TROUBLE

As a caring professional, you may well have been taught to welcome:

- Walk-in workers with legitimate problems.
  (*The problem is legitimate; the timing may not be.*)
- Unscheduled meetings about other people's priorities.
  (*The solution may lie with them, not with you.*)
- E-mail demands, all tagged "urgent."
  (*You and your team need defensive e-mail protocols.*)
- Lengthy phone calls from "the lonely" or disengaged.
  (*You must redirect without appearing brusque.*)
- A crisis unfolding despite your early warnings.
  (*Politeness forbids saying or thinking "I told you so."*)

When your customers, bosses, or coworkers call upon your natural helpful spirit, you may hasten to oblige, without negotiation. How could a caring person like you allow a hand-wringing associate to suffer discomfort? If you can see a ready solution, you dive right in, "to save time" only to have somebody note, later, that it wasn't really your affair. Sometimes, to hurry an intruder along, you offer some practical advice, then get a series of "yes, buts" in response.

In a last-ditch move, you may shoulder the odious problem yourself, for the sake of peace. You'll earn little or no gratitude, and the upshot is clear: the interrupters will deepen their dependency. They'll be back—and you'll rue your role as rescuer.

Cool Your Itch to Respond

Find a balance that suits you better. When you resist the urge to mend other adults' problems, you give them a chance to extricate themselves on their own. You dampen their appetite for cheap help, and let them expend some effort of their own. Especially for the experienced workers who may report to you, *your* practice of counting to ten may contribute handsomely to *their* development.

In your own defense, you may join the chorus that insists, "Those interruptions are beyond my control. Those people are calling or visiting me for help or leadership. If I'm the senior person (or the Subject Matter Expert), then handling those issues is my job!"

Maybe . . . but is it your job right now?

Reduce Randomness: A Prime Time Robber

To start reversing randomness, consider this simple irony: it's not the interruptions that kill productivity, it's the *randomness* of the interruptions.

Yes, you may accept people's need to get something off their minds by interrupting you at random. But if you can begin reserving small portions of your day as "interruption-free zones" you may improve focus on your own priorities, while remaining accessible and helpful most of the time—just not all of the time. Keep this in mind: when you opt, cheerfully, to take a call or welcome a visitor, you are signaling the following convictions:

- The only good time to handle this is now.
- Being congenial (right now) is more important than completing a priority task.
- This is my last chance to be congenial.
- This may be "that meaningful issue" I was born to solve.
- I dread being left out of the loop.
- Feel free to interrupt me whenever you like.

Forgive Human Nature: Yours and Theirs

Don't be too hard on yourself. It's just "human nature" to be ruled by curiosity, the urge to socialize, and your sense of competence. But each time you accept random interruptions, and undue expectations, that same human nature will nag you, later, into resenting the people who broke your momentum. On those nights when they've all gone home, and you're still working, you'll feel the frustration, realizing that the choice was—and will remain—yours.

REAL VOICES

Here's how Process Manager Andrea Marie Cifor quells the urge to respond to random demand:

If I am "heads-down," I put my communicator (IM) on DND (do not disturb). I do not answer my phone and I only look at e-mail periodically. When doing highly concentrated work, I like to take a break every two hours. When I take a break, I get up and stretch, then briefly triage my e-mail and phone messages.

If someone comes to my desk, I triage them (literally) by telling them I am busy and have a deadline. I let them know when I will have free time. I ask them what they need and assess the priority. If it is urgent, then I address it accordingly; otherwise I slot them in the calendar and get back to work.

WHY TIME WASTERS STILL SURPRISE US

At an early Time Management seminar, Alec Mackenzie asked a group of CEOs to list their biggest time wasters, and to determine where the causes lay. Without exception, they blamed whoever initiated the action, as they listed their five worst wasters:

1. Incomplete information.
2. Employees coming in with problems.
3. Telephone interruptions.
4. Routine tasks bumped back upward to the CEO.
5. Meetings ill-prepared and unmanaged.

These CEOs insisted that the five problems were beyond their power to anticipate or prevent. Later in the course, a video featured a company president making several common mistakes in time management. At that point, our CEO viewers were asked to identify any additional time wasters beyond their original five. Since it was "that other guy" making the mistakes in the video, the CEOs felt detached enough to cite several more time wasters, and they easily laid the blame at the feet of the CEO. The new items included:

6. Attempting too much.
7. Estimating tasks unrealistically.
8. Procrastinating.
9. Poor listening.
10. Failing to say no when necessary.

These seminar attendees came gradually to see that the responsibility for their first five issues had also been theirs, even though other people may have initiated the actions. They came to the conclusion that to make progress with time management, you need to look squarely at your own habits, admitting that the choice to hold focus is yours.

Set Your Boundaries, Not the Other Guy's

Once firm about your own intentions, you can use courtesy and caring in the way you communicate any options you offer to people. You may still protest: "That may be fine for those CEOs. But most of us are mid-managers, supervisors, specialists, service reps. Surely, we don't have the CEO's power to delay or limit response. For us, saying yes to requests is not a habit; it's an obligation." Let's challenge that response.

Will Your Response Habits Stand Up to Scrutiny?

Few of us could explain rationally why we do certain things the way we do—especially with repetitive behaviors. If you doubt this, try a simple test. Notice which shoe you put on first in the morning. Right or left? Tomorrow, try putting on the other shoe first. You'll get a strange, off-kilter sensation. You may even have the absurd urge to stop, take off your shoes, and begin again, the "right" way.

Your working habits can be equally powerful and unconscious. See if you can identify with these workers:

Sam: He reads his e-mail first thing in the morning, and then, checks compulsively, many times per day. He would find it upsetting to turn off the signal that announces new mail. Though few real emergencies arise, he can't control his need to know—even when he's chasing a tight-deadline on a top priority. Or perhaps especially when he's doing an arduous task!

Peg: Keeps two appointment calendars, one at work, and another in an elegant little red leather book that stays in her purse. Occasionally, appointments conflict without her noticing, causing embarrassment at work or at home. Though she could use her electronic calendar to blend both life and work appointments in a seamless day, she can't give up her little red book. It was a gift.

Zhi: Refuses to keep written reminders, either on his computer or on jotted notes. He prides himself on keeping everything in his head. Of course, occasional lapses occur. Wanting to be helpful, he unwittingly says yes to time-consuming tasks in time slots that are already obligated. He needs to write things down, but he denies this. Unconsciously, he equates unaided memory with vigor and competence.

All three workers tend to lose focus because of unconscious habits and the desire to say yes to all demands, random or not.

GO GRAPHIC TO RETOOL YOUR THINKING

To start up your day, jot a simple sticky note with your "Big Three" tasks for the day—those you must accomplish, no matter how many more things you may manage to do. Only then should you open your e-mail to see what else is coming up. Use that visual reminder of priorities to harness the primal power of the eye. (Some people may prefer planning their next day's Big Three the night before, as their last task before leaving the office.)

If there's some new pattern you need to establish, or some old habit you need to break, signal yourself with a visual cue, readable only by you: a note, a key word, a color, an odd object placed deliberately in your line of sight. A sticky note on the edge of your computer screen or dashboard can remind you to repeat and cement a new habit, or enforce a new boundary. You can use a colored dot, a checkmark, a poker chip—anything not translatable by onlookers, but clear to you—to draw you away, repeatedly, from the old behavior toward the new.

Your Work Habits: A Challenging Tapestry

Your work habits have become interwoven with each other, stealthily, by repetition. Many of your habits have been taught to you as virtues, pressed on you by a succession of former bosses and customers. Sometimes, despite everyone's best intentions, your own and your company's interests may have suffered from these enforced distortions. As you set yourself to change any long-term habit, you'll discover an unsettling reality. When you try to dislodge one mental thread, you realize it meshes with another and yet another to hold you captive to the old behavior. For example:

- Unthinkingly, you allow yourself to be roped into every lively break-room conversation with colleagues you enjoy—"for just a minute." You find yourself half an hour late for your next meeting, forgetting that you're moderator today.
- You perform routine tasks yourself, rather than delegate them; then, you regret that your staffers remain untrained.

- You teach subordinates how to perform a task. Then, too rushed to ask for "playback," you authorize the work. When they keep interrupting you with scattered questions, you bite back your annoyance with difficulty.

As many honest managers admit—reform will demand conscious awareness of your ingrained behaviors, firmness about new self-disciplines, and regular, gentle self-affirmation to reinforce your new path.

How the Threads Interconnect

At first, trying to uproot a habit can arouse other alarms. Once you try to correct one bad habit, you uncover a web of related shortcomings entangled with it. For example, you vow to get started on making a particular decision. As you gather your data, you realize that the original specs for that decision are scattered throughout your work space, in your computer archives, even in your car! You haven't cleaned out your incoming e-mail in so long—and everyone's subject lines are so outdated—you can't even locate current files quickly. So you put the decision aside, and then berate yourself for procrastinating.

Now, Let That Interweaving Help You

After decades of helping people to upgrade time management skills, we are convinced that, just as the problems intermesh, so do the solutions. If you choose, for instance, to clean up your e-mail today, you will almost certainly find most of that missing data. If you click on Help in your integration software (Outlook, Lotus Notes, Gmail), you'll get specific advice on keeping your mail files, project notes, and contact files linked and updated automatically—once you have set your preferences.

You and your team can start keeping your subject lines taut, for easier filtering. Will that setup cost you some time? Yes, a little, right now. But you'll make up that time, handsomely, by repetition, using your new system. Are you ready to invest?

SWEEP AWAY FIVE POPULAR ASSUMPTIONS

If, like so many people, you never noticed your human habits impeding your progress, the next few assumptions may sound familiar and even comforting. At first glance, they may seem legitimate, too. But all of them are traps. Eliminating them gradually from your daily practice may accelerate your escape from several of your worst time wasters in a single sweep. Different readers will find different avenues to explore. So here's a workout for you.

- Study the next few common assumptions . . . heartfelt but harmful.
- Use any or all of our logical arguments to sweep them away.
- Then, commit to a new proposition that will win you more satisfying results.

Assumption #1: The "Just Common Sense" Assertion

Time management is simply common sense: most of the time I do quite well just "winging it." Because changes happen so fast around here, I'm able to succeed by adjusting quickly, going on instinct, and breaking some rules.

Sweep Away "Just Common Sense"
- Common sense, unfortunately, is not so common.
- When "winging it" fails, your stress increases.
- As for adjustments, when the volume of your adjustments outpaces the volume of your planned tasks, your job description is no longer valid. Should you be fired, or promoted?
- We sometimes succeed *despite*, not because of, breaking the rules.

New Proposition #1
- Make a written or graphic plan for each day.
- Keep track of instances when you go "off-plan."
- See how often in fact you've been making so-called "adjustments."

Assumption #2: The "Work Best Under Pressure" Pitch

I work best under pressure. Having too much time makes people lazy.

Sweep Away "Best Under Pressure"
- Nobody works better under pressure. They just work faster!
- You certainly work more intensely under pressure. If you keep seeking panic situations, you may be addicted to adrenaline, a

natural stimulant, both legal and lethal in large doses. Have you become a crisis "junkie"?

New Proposition #2

- By starting late, you leave yourself too little time for the planning and consultation that can produce superior results.
- Commit to earlier execution. That way, you can carve out a safe margin to correct flaws, locate elusive data, solicit stakeholder input, and win wider approval for your approach.
- Beware the adrenaline rush that accompanies last-minute miracles. Each time you accept work with unreasonable deadlines, you deny yourself the chance to deliver results that are reliable and reward-worthy.

Assumption #3: The "Loss of Spontaneity" Complaint

Tedious time management rules will dampen my free-wheeling spontaneity.

Sweep Away "Loss of Spontaneity"

- Contrary to common wisdom, discipline buys you freedom in most endeavors. Star athletes or racing drivers practice their moves consistently and repetitively, almost to the point of tedium, so they can show off that "effortless" grace and spontaneity at delivery.
- In the same way, managers need to practice consistent self-discipline, reinforcing time-savvy skills until they appear effortless.
- Discipline (like weight-lifting) helps you build impressive levels of strength and confidence in performance.

REAL VOICES

But self-discipline doesn't come easy. Here's testimony from Cathy Wilber, Pediatric Occupational Therapist and Clinical Manager based in White Plains, New York. She confides:

> Time Management? How important is it? To my boss—extremely important—to me, not enough. Instead, I complain that I can't get it all done. Or I forget to do something and blame it on poor memory. Bottom

line is I am resistant to using time management strategies—resistant to structure and conformity . . . not wanting to be imposed on by authority. Meanwhile I risk unnecessary pain and suffering.

I'm working on it! I find my Outlook calendar extremely helpful. My e-mails get sorted into folders in Outlook. To regain focus when interrupted, I use sticky notes, posted right in front of my face or taped to the table with Scotch tape so they can't get lost. I also send myself e-mail reminders.

New Proposition #3 (for Cathy Wilber and you . . .)

- Better to indulge your free-wheeling spontaneity on innovation, design and development, marketing, sales, and customer service—whatever parts of your work you call creative.
- Then, invest effort in upgrading your administrative skills—managing the flow of repetitive work, storing and retrieving data, setting standards, scheduling, and executing to fulfill your promises.
- Following good rules can build your reputation for reliability and consistency. You might also get home in time for dinner more often without a laptop full of "homework."
- Examine your current workload: Use your creativity to cut the waste and rework that trap you in unpaid overtime. Indulge your spontaneity by having fun, in your newly liberated free time.

Assumption #4: The "Too Busy to Learn" Excuse

Installing the tools of time management looks like a lot of work. I don't have time for all that.

Sweep Away "Too Busy to Learn"
- You may recall the famous tale of the lumberman who argued, "I don't have time to sharpen my axe; I've got this whole forest to cut down!"
- Your prime tool of time management—a written plan—represents visual proof when you have been given too much work for the time available. You can then seek the approval you

need to change the scope of your workloads and adjust deadlines to sensible levels.

- You don't have the time *not* to plan. It's true that writing your daily plan takes a few minutes of serious thought, but this tool, combined with other time management techniques can save you two hours per day. In later chapters, we'll detail your likely return on investment.

New Proposition #4
- First, define time management as self-discipline in pursuit of your goals, not as an imposition from above.
- To work up willingness, envision a measurable reward or process improvement dramatic enough to propel you forward.
- Have another look at your workload: Which pieces could you, or someone else, perform faster or more reliably? Put it in writing and sell it to your boss.

Assumption #5: The "One Tool Is Enough" Constraint

For good time management, I don't need a book, a course, or an array of tools. My daily to-do list has served me for years. (Though, I admit— today's list often bleeds over into tomorrow's.)

Sweep Away "One Tool Is Enough"
- You're right. A written or graphic to-do list is a wonderful tool. We recommend it, especially when it ties to your Calendar, your Project Lists—and your incoming e-mail. That's why today's software integrates these tools, automatically, upon your instructions.
- Whether you rely on electronic tools or you chart the workload by hand on a whiteboard, you are right to focus the power of the eye to capture the load at a glance.
- *But*—if your list continually bleeds to the following day, you are in the supertrap Undue Expectations. That's dangerous for you.

New Proposition #5
- Once you are skilled at integrating your new demands among existing commitments, you can assess your situation—current and future—and negotiate new tasks in a context that's visible to requesters.

- Use that clear, graphic rendering to make realistic commitments, buying more time, shrinking the scope of some projects—or trading off with other tasks.
- Use your graphic to-do lists, later, to document your performance as a planner who meets commitments.

MINIMUM REQUIREMENTS FOR AN INTEGRATED ELECTRONIC TOOLKIT

Whether the company's design or your own, your toolkit should let you:

1. Prioritize tasks according to pre-set rules based on relative risk and value.
2. Estimate standard lead-times for common tasks.
3. Spot the impact of new incoming tasks on tasks previously committed.
4. Link incoming demands with your project lists and schedules, especially if incoming demand is primarily e-mailed (harder to negotiate) rather than walked in (easier to show your reservations).
5. Base your decisions (execute, postpone, rescope, or dismiss tasks) on visual data you can show to requesters now, and to assignees who must perform the work later.

No Computer Wimps Allowed!

If you don't know how to use the integration tools built into your computer software, then take a class with your company, your software retailer, or your local adult education center. At modest cost in time and money, you'll soon become adept. Furthermore, you can build a network of computer-savvy friends from among instructors and fellow learners—a vital asset, especially for small-business owners or stand-alone managers.

ERADICATE ASSUMPTIONS: THE TWO-COLUMN TO-DO LIST

Savvy workers are adopting this tool from our Chaos Management seminars to illustrate the process of taking a new task from "Merely Requested" to "Fully Committed"—and back again, if a crisis should strike. This visual approach disciplines requesters into realizing that a lower priority, accepted today, may get sacrificed to a higher priority tomorrow. They focus on the chart, not on you, as this reality sinks in.

Let Ellen Perry illustrate:

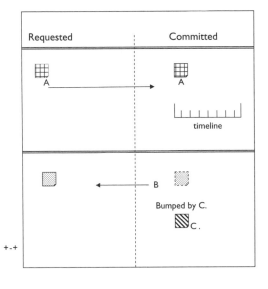

Task A

Customer Service Supervisor Ellen Perry gets a legitimate request with a tight deadline. In the left-hand column, she posts Task A (on a sticky note, actual or virtual). Task A will remain "Requested" until she can estimate and timeline the task. She finds a slot for it on the right-hand "Committed" side of the chart where it stays until completed, most likely performed in segments as indicated on the timeline. Requester A may have access to Ellen's chart, in order to track progress on the task.

Task B

Another legitimate task, B, makes it to the "Committed" side, but it gets bumped, later by more important task C. Ellen does not shield Requester B from the realities. The task returns to the left-hand "merely requested" side for a while. (Incidentally, Ellen has learned by experience that a "bumped" requester will often mobilize, making small upgrades to the "waitlisted" task to render it ready for reinstatement ASAP.)

With practice using the Two-Column To-Do chart, Ellen builds a reputation for making promises she can actually keep!

TIME MANAGEMENT: THE ODDEST ASSUMPTION OF ALL

Do you really manage your hours on earth? Your time is one asset you'd like to consider yours alone, and yet, you can't keep it. You can give it as a gift to your loved ones. You can donate it to worthy causes as a volunteer, and you can lease it out to your employers for an agreed sum. But you can't bank it.

Companies, and institutions, too, tend to think of time as one of their five assets:

1. *Capital:* Funds invested and deployed.
2. *Physical Assets:* Machinery, buildings, land, raw materials and goods for sale or held in inventory.
3. *Information:* Data made meaningful and retrievable; intellectual property for use or sale.
4. *Human Resources:* Workers, recruited, hired, deployed, trained, and motivated.
5. *Time:* Measured, estimated, and spent—but it cannot be banked for future use.

The first three—inanimate resources—can be manipulated, combined, increased or decreased, bought or sold at variable rates by your organization. Those three can be moved about or discarded at will, with varying but mostly predictable consequences. The fourth, human resources, represents the people whose services and skills your company may buy and sell (at agreed hourly or monthly rates). Companies have the power to retain or release people (with foreseeable repercussions). They can train and develop, respect or neglect employees (with attendant benefits and risks). Smart companies choose to keep people enlightened and informed so they can perform at their best.

But the fifth resource—time—remains less subject to human control than we like to admit. It cannot be accelerated or slowed. It must be spent the instant it is received, and at one fixed rate: sixty seconds per minute, sixty minutes per hour. We cannot choose *whether* to use it, only *how.*

SELF-MANAGEMENT FOR GOAL ATTAINMENT

As a human being, you may see your life expectancy as a mystery, a set of numbers in an actuarial table. Once you waste time, you cannot reel it back in. So, in fact, you do not manage time at all. You only manage yourself in relation to it.

We hope this chapter has intrigued you by questioning traditional assumptions about time. In the next few chapters you'll find many more tools for tackling the main task of life: self-management in pursuit of goals that satisfy.

CHAPTER

How to Connect Goals, Objectives, and Priorities

Goals . . . Objectives . . . Priorities. In casual conversation, business people often use the terms interchangeably. This is a mistake with serious consequences. Though the terms are certainly related, they flow in a strict cascading hierarchy, from goals to objectives to priorities. If you attempt to prioritize your daily tasks without a clear picture of the goals and objectives that are driving them, you can invest a lot of time and effort to produce a result that falls short, because the goal never became clear—to you or anyone else. Admit it—it happens all the time.

So before going further, we need to clear up the thinking trap that distorts priority setting for so many managers. This effort may not come easy—because many people actually prefer working on "priorities," those tangible tasks demanded by "live" requesters for immediate action. Working on "live" priorities can seem vivid, real, and possibly even heroic.

Conversely, some people tend to resist setting goals and objectives or even thinking about them. Goals seem far off, hazy and indistinct. Requesters rarely mention them, up front. (Remember those "mission statements" that some companies had engraved onto their lobby walls, way back in the seventies—which haven't been revisited since?) If your company is more serious about mission statements, then consider those to be the overarching principles, set atop any goal statement.

The very idea of setting goals may give us the same vague uneasiness we associate with New Year's resolutions. People tell us we ought to set them, but we recall those many January resolutions that thawed too soon when our intent was only halfhearted.

We admit it: our goals, especially our business goals, tend to fail if they are nonspecific, overambitious or—conversely—short-sighted. For example:

- Written goals such as "Seek success in my job" or "Provide for my children's education" sound laudable but aren't specific enough to drive purposeful action.
- Some people boast an ambitious goal, then abandon it, fearing criticism if they should fall short.
- Other people set out on the first leg of an ambitious goal—without information on its component parts—i.e., objectives—only to find they can't get beyond the first couple of steps. The path has a beginning and an end, but no middle. It's like trying to assemble that Christmas bike without instructions. You know what it should look like, you know what it should do, so you put it together. The result is wobbly, and those leftover screws and bolts that didn't seem to fit anywhere turn out to have been essential.

That's how it feels when a boss or customer gives you that vague order, "Just get on with it . . . I'll explain later." Whatever you may have been thinking about today's priorities can evaporate in a moment.

THE CASCADE FROM GOALS TO OBJECTIVES TO PRIORITIES

Here's how the process is meant to operate in business.

Stage I: Goals

Owners or investors and senior managers commit the research, the funds and the impetus to enter a new market, launch a new product, or offer a new service. They draw up strategic plans that focus on the end point (the goal), citing the advantages or gains that this enterprise offers. They set out the concepts and parameters, add financial and political support, and lay out the goals for management in ways designed to motivate eager sign-up.

Stage 2: Objectives

Next, division and department heads draw up plans detailing all the diverse elements to be managed—design, engineering, finance, manufacturing, marketing, sales, service, and administration. They lay out the programs and processes involved, plan for coordinated results, and deploy the start-up teams, doling out the budgets and setting up precise deliverables and time lines.

Stage 3: Priorities

Now, the actual performers in each department learn about the goals and objectives set by those above them. They accept their assignments and organize the practical task groupings to accomplish them. They make specific plans and schedules to fit this new work into their existing workloads. (Priority setting would be such a cinch if new tasks could enter a relatively light workload. Alas, that's rarely the case.)

In fact, priority setting is not about scheduling—not yet. It's not about *when* to do the new tasks—it's about *whether* these tasks should be allowed to compete with standing obligations. Priority setting aims to make goal-accomplishment feasible—on both old and new goals.

To risk priority setting without knowledge of the overall goals and objectives is foolhardy but frequently assumed. It's what we're expected to do when a boss or customer considers it okay to say, "Just do it! I'll explain the background later."

Goals and objectives are not "background." They are the horizon line and the detailed maps for the trek you're about to take.

GOALS: GET A LOOK AT ASSIGNERS' HORIZONS

Your time is short. That's why you're reading this book. You'll want to avoid waste and frustration by encouraging bosses and customers to let you view their horizon before you take on a batch of tasks to prioritize.

One way to get accord on goals and objectives is to design a "Work Objectives Template" that requires specific data about any assigner's goals and objectives before your team accepts the work. Consider how you would design such a tool: make it easy to fill in, but make sure it will enable you to get the information you need before committing to a major new entrant into your workload.

Project name: _____   **Number:** _____

Overall goal if part of master project: _____

Your objective/purpose: Please state the objectives you need to meet. (Examples: Tighten flange interfaces, reduce shipping weight, prevent fabric folds, etc.)

_____

_____

Parameters: Please specify:

    Quantity Required _____

    Quality _____ (Rough estimate? Draft? Customer-ready?)

    Budget $_____

    Time Estimate for the work: _____ hours? (NOTE: We cannot accept deadlines without an agreed time estimate)

    Deadline: Date: _____   Time: _____

The specific features in this exemplar are mere suggestions. Consider what you would include in a format of your own. Keep it brief and easy to fill out. Test it on the willing, then on your more challenging requesters.

Expect Resistance? Overcome It

It's possible that some requesters may accuse you of arrogance for even asking these questions. If you anticipate that, then try a backdoor approach.

Accept their usual vague orders, then try filling out your template yourself. Show them any "blanks" that need answers. The impetus need not come from them, but the answers must!

How One Team Clarified Requirements

At NASA Houston a few years ago, the team that calculates trajectories to distant planets needed a memorable model to remind requesters that exploring different parts of the solar system would involve vastly different investments of time and expense.

"Isn't that obvious?" you might wonder. "Aren't they all 'rocket scientists'?"

Actually, they're not. The Trajectory Team got many requests from senior people, skilled and gifted in their own specialties, but *not* in astronomy. The one feature they did have in common was their all-too-human proneness to the supertrap Undue Expectations.

A requester might order a calculation for a point fairly near the earth. The team might produce the data quickly and cheaply. Delighted with the good service, that requester now expects the same quick, cheap service on "trajectories to anywhere." Of course, pointing out how "different" one request was from another put the team in constant hot water. Soon, they felt the sting of the statement "Virtue is its own reward."

MAKING REALITY VIVID

So the Trajectory Team needed to produce a simple *Guide to Requesting Trajectories*. They played around with several versions—most with far too much detail to hold the attention of requesters. The process needed boiling down. The team went to the trouble, producing a simple grid with three clearly distinct groupings of destinations in the solar system. They showed the three vastly different requirements on people and computers to run the three families of calculations. (In conversation, the team jokingly referred to the three levels as: "plain vanilla," "tutti-frutti," and "hot fudge sundae with whipped cream and nuts." But the final single-screen graphic illustrated the cost of work in the three areas. (We're paraphrasing here.)

Area A: $1/second to calculate trajectories.
Time required: X hours

Area B: $10/second to calculate
            Time required: Add 50%

Area C: $100/second to calculate.
            Time required: Indeterminate (Minimum: add 200%)

Requesters found that screen very useful. Like all competent people, they felt better "knowing what they were talking about" when dealing with lateral specialties. The Trajectory Team could negotiate comfortably with the chart in plain view.

Your Own Application? Tailor a Tool

Do you deal with internal or external customers who would benefit from some "at a glance" education on the parameters that hem you in? Grab a sketchpad and think it through. Then, simplify. (They don't need to know all your details: they just need to know what they are actually asking for, under changing circumstances.) This tool will save time for both parties in any future negotiation.

HOW MATCHING OBJECTIVES PAYS OFF

Famous chief executives and powerful middle managers earn their lofty reputations because they can articulate a vision (goal) that is highly ambitious, highly motivating, and likely to win support—moral, financial, and political.

Next, they make the objectives tangible, measurable, and visible on a realistic time line to propel understanding and commitment from the teams who must set priorities based on them.

Whatever your management role, you can lead more powerfully when you delineate the goals that are yours to set; then clarify objectives (the practical routes to meeting those goals) and then support the effort of staff members as they set priorities that will directly respond to objectives.

Start Simple, Start at Home

Still not turned on to goal setting? Then, start simple. Take comfort in the fact that you have already used goal-setting skills successfully. And you did it "your way." Think of it—you have already employed an effective goal-setting process to achieve every task you have ever been proud of, at home or at work. When we ask seminar attendees to spend a few minutes thinking about homegrown goals they've met, we see a glow of pride and pleasure steal across many faces. Join them:

- Did you paint the exterior of your house, solo, to save thousands of dollars and get a close-up inspection of your main material asset?
- Did you repair your home computer, aided only by your chat pals on the Internet?
- Did you organize a successful event for your favorite charity?
- Did you coach a Little League team to a winning season?
- Did you plant a garden that fed your household and half the neighborhood?

Think of a recent proud moment at home? Which goal-setting skills had you used?

- You made your goals specific and realistic.
- You built in enough "stretch" to stay motivated.
- You set up objectives and benchmarks to track your progress.
- You set up priorities, and brought the job in on time and on budget.
- You persevered until you reached your goal.

Goals, Actions, Results

Here are some simple "homegrown" goals successfully acknowledged by recent class members:

Goal: Lose five pounds in one month for Class Reunion.

Actions: Bought only low-fat foods; stopped "eating out" for a month.
Restarted exercise program, and walked daily from the far parking lot.

Result: Lost seven pounds. Looked and felt great at the event.

Goal: Take six tennis lessons in April/May before vacation.

Actions: Searched out local tennis coaches and testimonials.
Started saving the fees in February.
Engaged a coach, end of March.

Spruced up last season's tennis wardrobe, rackets, and accessories.

Warned my teenagers about preparing their own lunches on Saturdays.

Result: Now on my fourth lesson. Corrected a few bad habits; won two matches.

Surprise Result: One of my kids made his own written pre-vacation plan; we're "high-five-ing" each other on daily follow-through.

CLEAR PROGRESSION: FROM GOALS TO OBJECTIVES TO PRIORITIES

Some people seem to be born, understanding this continuum. Others make a conscious effect to learn and use it. Here's an example that Alec Mackenzie found inspiring: An energetic young woman—a waitress whom the Mackenzie family met while traveling—told them that she had come to the United States from Germany with a particular career goal in mind.

REAL VOICES

"I want to own my own business within five years, and I've decided that an MBA will help me do that," she said.

"So you're in graduate school now?" Alec asked.

"No, I'm taking math and business classes at the local college; I need to do that before I can get into the grad school I want—and I have just one semester to go. Meanwhile, I'm earning money for my final semester."

She instinctively understood the step process: goals, objectives, priorities.

* She set her overarching goal: business ownership in five years.
* She set her objective: grad school MBA.
* She then set her priorities: take the college prep classes to qualify, and earn enough at the restaurant job to finance the final college semester.

If, like this woman, you've gained skill at meeting personal targets, you can transfer those skills to your next workplace challenge. The stakes may be bigger, involving more players, but you have already demonstrated, instinctively, how to cascade from goals to objectives to priorities.

WORKPLACE GOALS AND OBJECTIVES: OFTEN SET ABOVE YOU

Dictated by your organization's strategic plans, your workplace goals are set, primarily, at levels above you., then conveyed to you through your division or department head. Indeed, most major companies adhere to some form of Management by Objectives, illustrated thus:

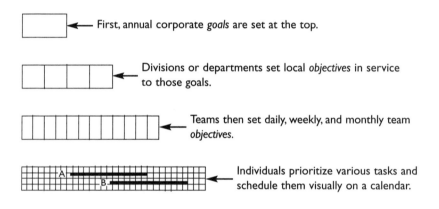

First, annual corporate *goals* are set at the top.

Divisions or departments set local *objectives* in service to those goals.

Teams then set daily, weekly, and monthly team *objectives.*

Individuals prioritize various tasks and schedule them visually on a calendar.

A Large-Scale Industrial Illustration

Let's say a major steel company commits to building a new blast furnace and steel production facility. This huge project will take several years and massive resources to accomplish.

The *goals* statement may specify overall strategic details: acreage needed; environmental impacts; access to shipping, rail and road transport; production capacity: quantities and types of ores to be processed; types of steel to be produced—in short, a mountain of decisions that lay out strategic goals for the project.

Next, detailed *objectives* will be defined in each distinct category of early-stage development: shareholding, borrowing, budgeting, contracting, design, engineering, purchasing, architecture, production, testing—and later, recruitment, hiring, staffing, and day-to-day operating plans.

No matter how carefully the company forecasts such a large-scale, long-range enterprise, these objectives will be challenged and adjusted, as industrial and financial conditions change, during the multiyear life of the start-up. The goals will remain in place, while objectives will be fine-tuned to meet conditions not predicted at the start, despite the expertise available.

Finally, as the plant nears completion, each responsible manager will list department *priorities* and assign tasks to the teams who will execute them. Department progress will be tracked in performance audits and reports—daily, weekly, monthly as the plant reaches capacity. During the year, teams and individuals will receive periodic performance reviews that recognize their achievements and enhance their career plans.

Whether you must manage a vast enterprise like the one just outlined—or you're running a small business, or handling a specialty for a mid-sized company, you need to feel comfortable insisting on clarity when accepting assignments.

FROM CORPORATE GOALS AND OBJECTIVES TO YOURS

Day to day, you should think of your own objectives as specific, time-sensitive tasks or groups of tasks that have cascaded down from longer-term, wider corporate goals and department objectives. At a moment's notice, you should be able to write up your current list of major objectives for the current year.

An Example: Delia Cronin, Chief Financial Officer

Goal: Delia's company wants to expand its Asian reach into two new countries, Singapore and Thailand, in 2011. Conditions in the two countries are totally distinct; so distinct sets of goals are already in place, and merger negotiations with local partners are complete.

Objectives: These have been set up for each business unit: finance, manufacturing, marketing, sales, customer service—the gamut—in both countries. Based on the list of objectives for the finance group, Delia Cronin now lists her objectives for the year, choosing the top eight risks/opportunities that she must manage through others.

- She lists her main task areas randomly, and then numbers them in "survival" order.

CFO Ojectives, January to January: Year: _____	
Top Risks/Opportunities	Survival Order
Currency risk	1
Forecasts	4
Acquistions	2
Audits	8
Budgets	6
Team-building	3
Taxes	7
Cash flow	5

- Tasks 1–4 represent highest orders of risk and value, in Delia's opinion. These top items get the top slots because they are inherently high-impact, long range, unstable, and partially under the control of others (including governments). They will require Delia's most vigilant attention and high-impact decision making during the year. Though she will be accountable for all eight areas, her most intense focus will be on item 1, then 2, 3, 4.
- She assigns lower numbers (5–8) to items that, though important, are more stable, with many current activities automated. They are more controllable by procedures already in place in finance and accounting.
- Furthermore, she has entrusted day-to-day dealings on items 5–8 to managers and specialists, each with a strong track record of managing cash, audits, budgets, and tax compliance.

Chart Objectives for Your Year

Anyone looking at Delia Cronin's list would know she is a financial officer in an international firm. The headings reveal that much, at a glance.

Now, consider your own job for the year beginning this month. Recall the company's goals and the department objectives to which you have committed. Recall the tasks you'll be likely to perform/supervise for the next twelve months and complete the chart below.

My Objectives: Next 12 Months

Task Groups or Risks	Survival Rank #
_____	_____
_____	_____
_____	_____
_____	_____
_____	_____
_____	_____
_____	_____
_____	_____

Randomly list these top responsibilities and risks. Just as you could tell that Delia was a financial officer, any reader should be able to tell what job title you hold. Now number the objectives in survival order. This means that lower-level items might be sacrificed to assure the safe delivery of Number One. Use no duplicate numbers. There can be only one Number One.

Give your high numbers (1–4) to those objectives with the longest-range impacts (both risks and benefits). You will manage these objectives closely because they are less stable, are strongly influenced by events outside your control, or are likely to need more frequent decision making.

You'll give lower numbers (5–8) to objectives that are more stable. You'll tend to accomplish these more easily, almost routinely, or you may delegate portions of them to trusted staffers under your direction.

Prepare to Defend Your Objectives

You'll want to post your Top Eight Objectives chart in a place where you and others can see it. When daily demands mount up that seem disconnected from anything on your Objectives list, you'll now be more careful about saying yes.

Be ready to justify priorities against objectives at any moment, for you never know when a boss, customer, or a competitive move will force you to revise this list, adding in a new high-risk, high-value objective.

For example, a senior manager may change a department objective for some compelling reason. Then, your own list of objectives will undoubtedly change, too. You will need to examine your options, and gauge the trade-offs that would flow from them. You may need to take something *off* your Objectives list—a much bigger deal than simply adjusting day-to-day priorities. With a change in objectives, you can't just "try harder" or "run faster." You'll need to drop one of your top eight off your list—show that the item that has dropped to Number 9 or lower (a subsidiary list)—and possibly jettison a whole train of priorities that were attached to the demoted objective.

Without a doubt, you'll be engaging in some lateral negotiations.

TO LAUNCH A NEW OBJECTIVE WITH YOUR TEAM

With a new objective added to your list you need to plan your own approach, then work with subordinates and lateral teams to get the necessary new commitment. The best tool we know for accomplishing that is SMART charting, which gets its name from the factors it looks at: specifics, measurables, attainables, resources, time line.

So many writers and so many companies have adapted SMART charts as a planning device, that we've been unable to trace the original source. Instead, we use our own adaptation, not only for individual planning, but for team collaboration across different disciplines.

In dozens of companies and government installations, we've seen team leaders communicate quickly and clearly about their plans for achieving an assigned objective. Then, their partners to that operation come alongside, just as quickly and clearly, with their own matching or contrasting views.

Using sticky notes as we recommend—and without any opening discussion—this exercise takes less than ten minutes to write and post. The fun (and real value) comes in the discussion that follows. Using the power of the eye, teams see and grasp immediately:

- *Specifics:* What is expected? By when? Why?
- *Measurables:* Costs, time, space, tonnage, etc.: what numbers really matter?

- *Attainables:* What will it take to overcome specific obstacles?
- *Resources:* Which people or teams, inside and outside, will be needed?
- *Time line:* Illustrate this: When will various resource people enter the timeline?

How a SMART Chart Exercise Begins

Imagine that you are a project manager tasked to move some of your staffers from one location to another. You take the opening vertical column of a SMART chart, and write one sticky note to define each vertical issue:

SMART CHART	**Project Manager**	**Facilities**	**IT**	**Moving Company**	**Engineers**
Specifics (What?)					
Measurables (How much?)					
Attainables (Stoppers?)					
Resources (Who?)					
Timeline (When to when?)					

An Example

Use only one sticky note per letter: S-M-A-R-T.

S: Jot the specifics of the planned move. For example: *"Move 15 computer drafting techs from HQ to Satellite Building on 10/22."* (Don't labor over S details. You will refine them based on your work on M-A-R.)

M: Record only those quantities that matter, for example.: *"Square footage per person drops from 100 square feet to 80. Some current furniture will not fit."*

A: Here, list factors that could stop the show. *"Some engineers will complain who have not seen the new streamlined furniture. Must sell off large drafting tables to stay within budget."*

R: List your resources: *facilities, IT, moving company, drafting techs. Plus cleaners, and caterer for weekend moving day.*

T:

You would simply indicate on the time line—using arrows or colors—which of your resource people would be active on the time line at various points.

Invite Candor Early

Your objective in writing each sticky note is to be as truthful as possible with those whose cooperation you need. Which factors would matter most to them as they try to make a commitment?

As project manager, you would open your meeting by presenting your column of the SMART chart; then invite each of the cooperating parties to fill out and post their own sticky notes in their own columns, alongside. They take ownership immediately: we have never seen it fail.

Expect an unusually honest rendering on their "M" and "A" notes. SMART charting really helps people to quantify the work they'll need to contribute, the costs they may have overlooked, and the threats to attainment that they will need to overcome. They get realistic and honest, right away.

With SMART charting, a revolutionary upgrade occurs—parties really engage, energetically, on Day One, Hour One. They don't just "salute the flag" halfheartedly, stack the task on a pile somewhere, and allow a fatal time lapse before expressing their objections. Instead, they don't just "tell you now." They show you! You'll want to celebrate that!

Allow your SMART charts to stay posted on a shared wall (actual or virtual) for a few days, so people can continue mulling things over and upgrading their solutions.

Caution: Measure First

Most good planners begin with a statement of the objective: "S" on the SMART chart. Then their minds (and those of their followers) go immediately to the steps that will be involved. This seems logical. But discourage it.

The steps must wait until you have validated the main elements (the M-A-R-T). Do not try listing the steps too early: this would waste time if your discoveries at M, A, or R (inaccurate measures, threats to attainment, or inadequate resources) force you to shrink the scope or extend the time of your objective. Some of the steps you imagined taking will not be needed at all.

Instead, focus—as the SMART design requires—on the "M". Take the trouble to calculate the measurables that will matter most.

If You Can't Measure It, You Can't Manage It!

We agree. And we would add that you can't get a team to understand what they're committing to unless you show them:

- How many? (Compare to your usual production run.)
- How fast? (Compare to your usual speed.)
- How big? (Give them the square footage, the tonnage, the mass.)
- How frequently? (Cite required benchmarking meetings, interim inspections, renewed authorizations, . . .)

In short, show them how much harder or easier this task will be, compared or contrasted with the usual. If you, as project manager, know that what you're asking will be twice as much work, twice as fast as usual, you must show it that way, vividly.

HOW CLEAR OBJECTIVES PAY OFF

A team will follow you anywhere if you lead them honorably, show them your map of objectives, and invite them to post theirs. If you give them ownership over their commitments, they will follow you all the way to the end of the challenge. A joint SMART chart uses the power of the eye to assess measurements, achievability, and resources at a glance. Using that team chart of objectives, individuals can then set their own daily priorities, with fewer missteps and frustrations.

Individual priority setting—getting the next steps right—will be our focus of the next chapter.

CHAPTER

How to Set Priorities and Hold Them

Today, you are asked to reset priorities, not daily, but hourly or at the "speed of change." Hundreds of messages can clog your e-mail, voice mail and smart phone. Mergers, acquisitions, and reorganizations can leave your head spinning. On some days, managers or customers can paint even the most absurd demands as valid, urgent, and nonnegotiable. Often, if the requester has enough clout, you accede to the demand, and add a few more hours to your unpaid overtime.

A decade ago, most people reported to one boss, so they knew whom to consult about conflicting priorities. Today, you're just as likely to report to several bosses.

If your business is built upon matrix management and project management, you may perform different roles in different groups: you may supervise one team, serve on a second, and act as internal consultant or SME on a third. Furthermore, your "virtual" colleagues and clients may access you directly across continents and cultures, so your clock never stops.

Hence, you face fuzzier lines of authority and thinner support than ever. As for setting and holding to priorities, you are on your own! You need a good system that suits your style.

MINIMUM REQUIREMENTS FOR PRIORITIZING

There is *no* one best way. But you can build your system on three firm elements:

1. Build your logic on Pareto's Law, the "20/80" Law.
2. Defend your logic with performance criteria.
3. Start each day with a written plan: three bullets, right in front of you, on your task screen, or on a sticky note at eye level.

PRIORITIZE WITH PARETO

Vilfredo Pareto was a European economist who demonstrated, in 1893, a new and surprising ratio: 20 percent of Europe's population now owned 80 percent of its booming wealth. Almost unnoticed, as the industrial revolution had advanced, ownership had shifted from a small, exclusive group of landed nobility to a boisterous population of newly rich industrialists.

In the decades since, Pareto's pronouncements still hold. Despite global upheavals of many kinds, 20/80 still applies on most matters, business, industrial, and political. Twenty percent of campaign contributors donate eighty percent of funds. Twenty percent of driver behaviors cause eighty percent of road accidents. (Run an Internet search on Pareto's Law to find hundreds more examples.) The take-away for you is this:

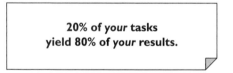

**20% of *your* tasks
yield 80% of *your* results.**

Eureka! Those are your top priorities!

YOUR OVERARCHING EIGHT OBJECTIVES

If you have already written and posted your list of Eight Objectives for this Year (see Chapter 3), then you can more easily rate today's incoming priority contenders against it, reserving the best (most reliable) slots for the top 20 percent of tasks—those that contribute most to your objectives.

What constitutes a "best" slot? Settle upon the time slot when you have excellent focus, energy, privacy, and access to data. Realize that "best" does not mean "earliest."

Why Early Slots May Not Be Best

In many settings, the first hour of the day is the most chaotic, with friends, colleagues, and customers already lining up for service. (They believe in "do it now.") But your top 20 percent tasks often need your best concentration and energy—your best slots.

Secondary items, including urgent ones, should get secondary slots. And these secondary slots may actually occur at early points in your day. You'd be smart to dot a few "urgency slots" into days when you know there will be a lot of turbulence generated. And, yes, it's perfectly OK to clear a lot of small stuff at various points in your schedule—but never at your "prime focus times." Whatever you do, you must assure that no demand of lesser importance ever usurps a time slot already reserved for a task of higher importance and greater risk!

No matter how urgent the intruding task may appear to its owner, it must be bigger and better than today's priorities—*your* priorities—to steal a priority slot.

Pareto Overturns the "Do It Now Delusion"

Once you embrace Pareto's Law, you can seriously oppose the common dictates that say "do it now!" or "handle a piece of paper only once!"

Sure, those rules sound good, but they would only make sense if all incoming tasks had equally high impacts. Pareto is right, so only 20 percent of your tasks deserve attention at the best times on your schedule. Further, of the 80 percent of items clamoring for your attention, only 60 percent may deserve your attention soon—somewhere in the middle 60 percent of your day.

And the lowest 20 percent may not merit your attention ever! Certainly not by comparison with your top 20 percent! Hence, your new rule should be:

**Don't DO It Now—
VALIDATE It Now!**

THE PROCESS OF VALIDATING WORK

Compare new demands against those in your current load. If an issue can really compete in importance and validity, then slot it in and get it done—not "now"—but in a slot that will assure delivery by its deadline.

If it's only a mid-value item, then give it a slot on your schedule that cannot intrude on any slot dedicated to your top 20 percent. Or delay giving it any slot at all—instead, post it in a "holding space" for slotting later.

(In the two-column To-Do List (Chapter 2), you'd post it in the "Requested" column, and not move it to the "Committed" side until ready.)

Invitation: Take a moment right now to list your current "top 20 percent" of tasks—those most likely to drive 80 percent of your results. Compare them against your chart of Eight Objectives for this Year. See how closely your current priorities are serving your objectives.

Look for Patterns

If you see too many items competing for your time, and showing little or no linkage to your objectives list, ask yourself:

- Are these really tied to *someone else's* objectives? Someone lateral? Who wins?
- If they are tied to the objectives of my boss, I need my eyes opened.
- If mine, what new entry must go onto my objectives list?
- What will the new entry bump?
- Have I been promoted, demoted, or just intruded upon?

Once you can see a pattern, you can assess validity. You can question "alien" priorities, accept your new objective (plus all the priorities that will flow from it), or you can negotiate it away.

HOW GRAPHIC MAPS AID TEAM THINKING

Here's how some brilliant aeronautic engineers illustrated their priorities with Pareto's Law during our many seminars with government, military, and private contractors in the satellite and rocketry business.

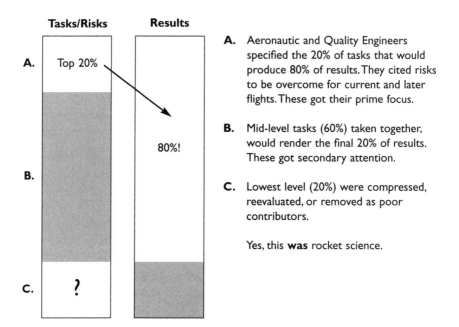

Tasks/Risks   **Results**

A. Top 20%

B.

80%!

C. ?

A. Aeronautic and Quality Engineers specified the 20% of tasks that would produce 80% of results. They cited risks to be overcome for current and later flights. These got their prime focus.

B. Mid-level tasks (60%) taken together, would render the final 20% of results. These got secondary attention.

C. Lowest level (20%) were compressed, reevaluated, or removed as poor contributors.

Yes, this **was** rocket science.

What followed for these engineers were serious discussions about the criteria that a Task/Risk had to meet to merit their best slots, their best attention, their willing sacrifices.

CRITERIA: FOUNDATION FOR PRIORITIES

You may or may not be preparing a manned space flight today, but in either event you will need to choose the tasks that belong in your top 20 percent, and you need to eliminate the risks that might jeopardize your top 20 percent of results. That's why the rocket scientists equated *validating tasks* and *eliminating risks* as the prime process in prioritizing work to get results.

To set up priorities and hold them against all comers you need to base your choices on a set of criteria that others will recognize and respect. Here are some possibilities drawn from many different industrial and service settings:

Sample Risk/ValueCriteria						
	Project A		Project B		Project C	
	Yes	No	Yes	No	Yes	No
Safety threat						
Cost overrun						
Income potential						
Compliance						
Top-tier customer						
Critical path on larger effort						
Specialists needed						

Find Criteria That Fit Your Field

To reduce arguments when time is short, decide what specific features or conditions would justify "bumping" tasks previously validated in favor of a new priority. Invest time in setting these criteria. Arrange them in impact order: apply numerical weights if you like. Then, reap big savings in time and stress by eliminating "ad hoc haggling."

UNIFY YOUR TEAM AROUND OBJECTIVES

When achievement of department objectives must rely on mixed specialties or disciplines, then the team's day-to-day priorities may compete, inevitably, for limited resources—labor, budget, data, materials, and time. Your competing tasks and outcomes must be "readable" not just by you, but by your boss and other lateral groups, all parties to a challenge.

Here's a view from Bart Denison, Software Operations Lead at a firm based in Redmond, Washington.

I meet regularly with my customers and my management to discuss workloads, and to help determine priorities so that I am focused on the right goals. From time to time, there may be a need for more hours spent at work, but I have agreement from most of the customers and managers that none of the team should be working more than 45 hours a week on a regular basis.

Multiple Disciplines? Agree on Priorities

In high-tech companies like Bart's, day-to-day priorities are built upon specific but often exclusive knowledge bases. This means that a threat may arise, unseen by others, but vividly clear to any specialist concerned. If you are that specialist, you must be able, not only to adjust your own priorities, but to inform collateral teams and managers about threats and options. Failing to do so would leave them blind. Doing so in timely fashion builds trust and reduces stress for everyone.

In well-managed companies, this tension among disciplines is so clear that making critical adjustments across disciplines is a valued activity; it is the usual focus of team meetings and the central topic of many "all-hands" announcements. Such companies become skilled at adjusting to new conditions without undue turbulence

Multiple Requesters? Give and Get Political Cover

If you are a project manager, office manager, or administrator, you probably report to multiple bosses, so you need to take initiatives yourself when they cannot easily agree. If you are not using project management software, you can build your own tracking chart to show competing demands, with potential conflicts and recovery options in living color. Use these tools to get your main boss on board early when you know a conflict will arise between requesters at senior levels. Your boss will appreciate getting good heads-up data on your plans and fallback options and will be more likely to support your decisions.

Why Posted Graphics Are a Must

If you've been blessed with a photographic memory and high intelligence, you may handle multitasking brilliantly in your head and blithely neglect charting your tasks. But, remember, your bosses and colleagues can't read your mind. So unless you also have telepathic powers, you must illustrate priority conflicts for them, along with the effects of adjustments. With convenient electronic tools, you can adjust task lists with a keystroke and post them to a shared web page. Similarly, your written and graphic charts can be updated easily with a sticky note on a wall chart.

The technology is so easy—why do we hear so much resistance at our seminars? Because participants—even those who can focus on *whether* to honor a request—can't promise *when* because they can't estimate the task. This brings out the worst in requesters, who now dig in for a higher-priority slot. This causes a stressful condition for both parties that I like to call "Deadline Dementia."

HUMAN COMEDY

How many managers suffer from a chronic condition called Deadline Dementia? That's an odd word—*deadline*. It originated in military prisons, where it referred to a line on the ground beyond which prisoners could not stray—or risk being shot for attempted escape.

The term has continued to mean a forbidden crossing with penalties.

There's nothing funny about *dementia*: the dictionary definition says: *An impairment of mental powers characterized by melancholy, withdrawal and delusions.* The funny part comes at work, when the deadline is the only clear thing about a request: it's the requester who has the delusions—and the performer who suffers melancholy and wants to withdraw!

STANDARD LEAD TIME TOOL: ONE CURE FOR DEADLINE DEMENTIA

Many smart departments publish a list of common tasks they perform, along with realistic time estimates. They post these on a shared site, and encourage requesters to take a look before submitting requests with optimistic deadlines imposed.

For new or unfamiliar work, you can take two differing approaches:

1. You can consult with teams who have had prior experience with this or related tasks. Ask for an average performance time, knocking out any records set by their best and worst performers, and averaging from a middle group of performers.
2. If no such experience is available, you can pre-estimate a task yourself—and then adjust it. Here's how it would work:

When you accept an assignment, ask the requester for an estimate of the time necessary to complete the task. Always do that before accepting a deadline as reasonable. (Mostly, requesters don't have a clue about work time estimates, but ask!) If common sense will let you do an "eyeball" estimate, go ahead. If not, offer to evaluate the job and come back later with an estimate.

Remember: No Deadlines Without Estimates

Only after you have made a thoughtful estimate can you agree on a reasonable deadline. Next time you start to evaluate a job, don't look at the clock or the calendar. Instead, consider the discrete tasks involved, and decide where on a time line they will fall.

Let's say you were tasked to do a report on customer acceptance of a recent product upgrade. You "eyeball" the task, based on prior experience with market research, and estimate your actual labor for 10–12 hours of work, stretched out over an indeterminate period to accommodate participation by others. Now to validate:

Work Estimating Chart

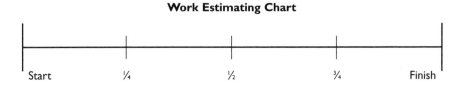

Start   ¼   ½   ¾   Finish

Draw a horizontal task line: decide what activities would comprise the first quarter of work. Decide which work must occur in each of the four segments.

First Quarter Tasks (estimated time: four hours)
- Check customer lists. Pull random sample of X users for mailing list (e-mail or paper).
- Refine existing copy for customer letter.

Second Quarter to Mid Point (estimated time: two hours)
- After "wait time" collect customer e-responses (3% of total mailed).
- Program computer to calculate responses, extrapolate data.

Third Quarter (estimated time: four hours)
- Get approvals from management on interpretation of results.
- Draft text of report.
- Add any further surveying/sampling if required.
- Finalize report.

Fourth Quarter (estimated time: two hours)
- Circulate report to departments concerned.
- Solicit e-reactions from manufacturing, customer service, other departments committed to quick response.
- Finalize findings and recommendations.

Check your estimates as you go. If you find during your first quarter of work that your estimates were too tight (or more rarely, too loose), you can make your own adjustments and give early warning to the other parties involved, so they can adjust, too. Don't join the optimists who keep hoping for the best and wind up making everyone late or narrowing their time windows hopelessly at the final hours. Decision makers insist on early warning.

Publish Your Standard Time Menu

At the end of the exercise, capture what you learned and add it to a "menu" of standard lead times on common tasks. You and your team can publish these, periodically, on a shared site, to help people make more of their requests realistic and timely from the start.

- Imagine the training time this tool will save when you are ready to delegate a task.
- Imagine how useful such a tool will be to your successor when you get promoted!

I've seen this "lead time" process work successfully at Hewlett Packard, Procter & Gamble, and other companies where managers welcomed accurate information on how much they could expect—and how fast—when a sudden sales or customer service opportunity arose. Instead of panic, they got the panache and polish they wanted by keeping their requests realistic.

DON'T MAKE YOUR MANAGERS FLY BLIND

Almost every week, I meet a specialist or manager who expresses doubt about daring to chart risks for their hierarchical superiors. They say, "Who am I to set or change priorities? I've been given my orders. My managers and my customers expect me to comply. That's that!"

It's true that in 80 percent of the cases you will comply, even if it hurts. Business hierarchies are generally designed that way. You will take on new work, without a murmur. You will adjust in silence. You will work late nights and weekends. And you'll be right to do so.

But for a select few tasks—high-impact, high-investment, problem-laden, and assigned at the last minute—you will see a risk and realize that you must negotiate. After all, your bosses or customers may not know, or recall, the state of play for tasks previously assigned. Beware: If you accept a new rush request that will "bump" a major existing task, and you say nothing, you force your requesters to accept a blind risk.

CONCLUSION: Lay out the situation as you see it. Sketch out some options with their various outcomes. But the one thing you cannot do is stay silent.

Avoid Opting Out

Many frustrated specialists have found themselves in a crossfire between two embattled managers whose priorities clash. A few have tried this dangerous ploy: "They're the ones in authority. I'll just let them duke it out. They'll decide. I'll comply and let the chips fall where they may."

Bitter experience has shown that this approach can leave you in a worse position than before. If neither side really understands the volume of work involved, they may cook up an even worse solution. Some harried managers may order you to "just *do* it—get both jobs done." Still others will suggest trade-offs that leave both jobs at risk. You have to stay in the game.

REAL VOICES

Here's how Executive Assistant Vicki Farnsworth handles legitimate priority conflicts at HealthAlliance Hospitals Inc., in Leominster, Massachusetts, where she assists a Physician/Executive, the VP Business Development, a Corporate Quality Officer, and two Directors:

> *As for setting priorities for myself and several executives, I always ask for a specific completion date and then, prioritize accordingly. If several of the people I support approach me for the same time slot, I show them the conflicting workloads, offer options, and then defer to them to make the final priority call.*

SHOW RISKS: OFFER OPTIONS

If, like Vicki, you're the one delivering the final product, never opt out of a discussion on conflicting assignments. Instead, take three tactful steps:

1. Show the risk involved if you attempt clearing both tasks at speed.
2. Show options that make practical sense, with roughly matched trade-offs (pain levels) for either side.
3. State your own preferred solution and the reasons for it.

Then, with a clear conscience, you can accept their joint mandate and perform your best effort. By electing to negotiate, you give both parties the right to examine risks and options, and to accept the honest advice of the one who must deliver the goods: you!

In this chapter, we've given you many different tools for understanding priorities in their relation to risks, rather than urgent deadlines. To see how your new focus on priorities can correct your views about where your time goes, check the next chapter.

CHAPTER

How to Tame the Time Log

How many times a week do you hear yourself or your colleagues say, "I just don't know where the time goes!"?

Most people sigh resignedly, believing there's no remedy. But—since you're reading this book—you are probably determined to find out where your time actually goes. This chapter offers you two sets of remedies: the first to uncover your time killers, the second to protect and maintain your priorities.

Time seems to evaporate when you're very busy. If you can discover where your time actually goes, you can capture more value from it, and control the leaks that rob you by stealth.

HOW LOGGING GOT A BAD NAME

The simplest tool for getting control is a time log. But too many users and authors, by misreading the correct uses of logging, have given it a bad name. What do they fear?

Boredom. Yes, time-logging would be tedious if you kept it up for long. But you won't!

Inaccuracy: People forget to make entries, then try plugging items from memory . . . then abandon the job. But, it's not crucial to write in every entry. In our system, you enter only those distractions that conflict directly with your top priorities.

Guilt: People are shocked when they see their time losses; they berate themselves without mercy. But you can take up logging with the conviction that you're not a machine. While you'll never manage time perfectly, your brief, selective logging exercise will help you to protect your top priorities. That's the whole point.

Right about now, your own denial may kick in, with a further deterrent: "I think I can skip this part," you may say. "I already know pretty much what I do on any given day."

On the contrary: no one has a realistic idea of what happens all day. People who write a log are always surprised. They learn that logging, while not as exhausting, time consuming, or embarrassing as they had feared, does point out—often for the first time in life—what's really happening, and pretty quickly, too. If you choose to log your interruptions (just those that attack your priorities), you'll make fascinating discoveries— in private!

Still Need Convincing?

Realize this: Most of us tend to forget about small interruptions, especially those we enjoy. We especially tend to overlook time spent socializing, unaware how much time this can eat up in the aggregate. (Don't worry that you'll become a hermit; rejoice that you'll get home on time more often.)

Sure, you may admit that you're always looking for things, or playing phone tag, or waiting for essential replies, or deleting useless stuff from your e-mail. But logging helps you to total up the losses from these many small things. With a log, you'll easily spot a pattern of attention switching—and realize with dazzling clarity where your time goes.

Too Busy to Log?

As Alec Mackenzie famously says:

> If you swear you can't find time to do a quick log, you are, ipso facto, the very sort of person who needs to keep one. If you keep your log

sheet close at hand, you'll find it takes almost no time because a well-designed log lets you enter items quickly, with coding known only to you.

Don't Let Denial Delay Your Start

Once you begin, don't be alarmed at the realities you uncover. "Oh, no," you may protest. "I know this looks bad, but today wasn't a normal day."

Frankly, in all our years of teaching people about time management, we have yet to see anyone demonstrate a "normal" day. On the contrary, we see it dawn on the majority just how abnormal our normal days are.

One salesperson, after logging for a day, was stunned to discover that he had spent less than 20 percent of his time on his number-one priority—and was late on deliverables: "If I keep having 'normal days' like this," he cracked, "I'll be out of a job!"

So stay open to keeping a log. To change a habitual pattern takes more conviction than you can build on sheer memory. There's simply no better way than logging to get an accurate picture. More important, you'll get a powerful incentive to start applying remedies on the spot.

SELECTIVITY: THE MOST VITAL SECRET

If you try to log everything you do all day, you'll not only suffer boredom, you'll get nothing else done. But that's not what we have in mind. How did that salesman grasp so clearly that his number-one priority kept getting lost in the shuffle? He focused his log on a short list of his top three priorities. Then he recorded "changes of direction," noting only the items that intruded into time slots reserved for priorities. So here's how to design your log:

1. Start with a simple two-column layout.
2. In the left-hand column—let's call it your "Red Zone"—you list *only* your top-priority tasks with their allotted time slots.
3. You hope the right-hand column will remain blank. Here, you log *only* those incidents that you allow to divert you from Red Zone tasks.

Top 3 Red Zone Tasks (Show times you allocated.)	Diversions from Red Zone Tasks (Note what you allowed to intrude.)
8:00 to 8:45 Get data for report due 2:00 PM.	8:15 Took call: office party. (5 min) 8:30 2nd call re party. (10 min)
9:30 to 10:00 Coach Alan on project	OK. Done.
12:30 to 1:30 Write report.	12:45 Spouse called re errand (10 min) 1:00 pm Checked email (15 min). 1:50 Yikes: I'm rushing to finish!

Highlight Those Top Three Tasks

So, among the many appointments, meetings, and routines in your day, you're only highlighting (as Red Zone items) three top priorities for your day. Allot your best time segments to those three tasks, or to the portions of those tasks that you have scoped out for that day. Some workers dedicate at least 20 percent of any day to making headway on Red Zone priorities, even those with forgiving deadlines. Top priorities go into the left column; your shifts of attention into the right. How hard is that?

Jot down any diversion, no matter how brief or trivial-seeming. Note the source or reason for the interruption. Note how long you spend on diversions. Some will be worthwhile; others not.

With this system, you still have a number of hours every day that are wide open for slotting your second-level priorities. If you stray from those, you need not log the diversions because they do not wreak the same level of damage on your day. This selectivity eliminates the complaint that logging can take up your whole day. You're only interested in diversions that interfere with Red Zone activities.

As for the rest of your day—you're not trying to be perfect. Live and let live! At the end of the day, you will look back and see what proportion of your allotted time actually went to your top priorities. You can then get tougher-minded about the diversions you allow to nibble away at your priorities.

With some clearly visible portions of your day left open for second-level tasks as well as for worthy interrupters, you'll feel more willing to accommodate people. When you are sure that your Red Zone items are getting done, you remain centered and steady in dealing with people, all day.

BRACKETING RED ZONES WITH CONTACT CUSHIONS

You may have noticed, in the simple Red Zone chart above, that the manager tried to allot reasonable time segments to his top three tasks. But you also noticed that, for him, the *best* time of day did not mean the earliest time.

Like him, you can start your day, by protecting your top 20 percent of tasks in slots that represent the best times to get the work done. Next, to assure that would-be interrupters will hold your Red Zones sacred, you can provide them with "contact cushions" on either side of any Red Zone, times they can easily contact you.

Here's a graphic way to represent that:

1. Use a common time chart (laid out in 15 minute segments) to illustrate.
2. Let's say that—on a particular day, you reserve just two hours, total, for your Red Zone tasks.
3. You choose times when you expect some quiet: say, mid-morning and mid-afternoon for these Red Zones.

Block in only your most vital tasks (or segments of tasks) for the day. And don't forget to chart your contact cushions as well.

Let others notice that you have bracketed those Red Zones with "open" contact cushions so that anxious or impatient people can reach you in timely fashion without interrupting deadline work. You've created a visual signal that helps you protect at least 20 percent of your day, and helps others see that they still can reach you most of the time. After a while, you may be able to extend Red Zone time beyond a couple of hours, but for now, get some practice at reserving parts of your day, and getting others to see that as completely reasonable.

Valid Interrupter: New Top Priority Perhaps?

Sometimes, you will decide that an emergency interruption is valid enough to bump a task out of your Red Zone. If you know that it's worth the sac-

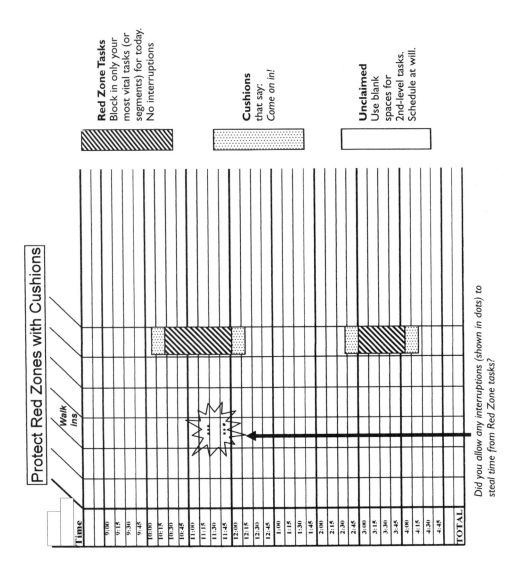

Protect Red Zones with Cushions

Time	Walk ins				
9:00					
9:15					
9:30					
9:45					
10:00					
10:15					
10:30					
10:45					
11:00					
11:15					
11:30					
11:45					
12:00					
12:15					
12:30					
12:45					
1:00					
1:15					
1:30					
1:45					
2:00					
2:15					
2:30					
2:45					
3:00					
3:15					
3:30					
3:45					
4:00					
4:15					
4:30					
4:45					
TOTAL					

Red Zone Tasks
Block in only your most vital tasks (or segments) for today. No interruptions

Cushions
that say:
Come on in!

Unclaimed
Use blank spaces for 2nd-level tasks. Schedule at will.

Did you allow any interruptions (shown in dots) to steal time from Red Zone tasks?

rifice, then give yourself points for good judgment. Be sure to record the task that won the contest. Remember, your credit will come, not from handling tasks that looked more urgent, but tasks that were more valid—higher in risk and value than the Red Zone tasks you had set up for your day.

NOTICE: If such a pattern repeats—if new tasks keep bumping the old—then your job description has changed—often, to handling more valuable tasks.

Provide Two Further Options

Consider adding two more facilities to speed interrupters on their way:

1. You can provide a "drop box" or special e-mail address, with a response intervals guaranteed, so requesters can dump their problem and run, without interrupting you. Give them your explicit assurance as to when they'll get an answer.
2. You can also encourage people to try "self-help" before interrupting you. Here's a typical way to enable this: Whenever you advise or teach a subordinate or colleague how to handle a problem, you can both agree, right then, to post a note to a shared intranet site, outlining the solution so they can handle it, next time, on their own.

LOGGING CHOICES: LOW OR HIGH-TECH

Use whatever medium is easier for you. Keeping a log by hand is quicker than you'd think, especially if you code or abbreviate your jottings. Since no one sees them but you, no one else needs to understand them. Some simple guidelines follow:

- Jot down interruptions as they occur. You may forget, otherwise.
- Invent or tailor some abbreviations.
- Use initials or project numbers to denote people or projects.
- Indicate interruptions with an X or check mark.
- When someone interrupts with a question, use a question mark with the person's initials.
- For calls, you might use a capital C with an arrow pointing to or away from the person's initials. (C>TB might mean you called TB, whereas C<TB might indicate that she called you.)

Prefer Higher-Tech Notes?

If your working life is mostly virtual, you'll be happier creating a time spreadsheet—or you can adapt a tool you already use—Microsoft Outlook, your Gmail, a Lotus Notes application, or a simple Project Management tracker. The main idea is to show yourself any "diversions from priorities" as you track various elements of a day.

(I'm always amazed how many people use only a tiny portion of a software application; but hesitate to click on Help, for additional uses. Your software developers have provided everything you need, if you look for it.)

Otherwise, you can study one of the *For Dummies* or *Idiot's Guide* books to exploit the time-tracking help that your software already offers. You'll get practical shortcuts—illustrated and in plain language.

HIDDEN CLUES: FIVE CAUTIONS

This next example shows you how one manager, Samantha Gregorio, learned where her time was going with a simple, handwritten log. If you can stay open-minded—as she did—you'll discover a few areas where you can make immediate gains.

Before she started, she mulled over some useful cautions:

1. She would not log everything that happened in the day. She would focus only on Red Zone tasks—and the interruptions that might threaten them.
2. She would stick to specifics. If she were to record a ten-minute interruption as simply "Phone Call," she would be unable, later, to judge whether it was a useful or wasteful choice.
3. She would record items like daydreaming, getting coffee, or socializing, even if they seemed minor and even if they seemed "simply human." Her purpose was to grasp the impact of time stolen from Red Zone tasks by minor issues.
4. She would log as she went long, realizing she could not hope to reconstruct details accurately later.
5. She foresaw that the temptation to make herself look good would be nearly irresistible. So, no one would see this log but herself. By writing honestly as she went along, she could self-correct on the spot. That would leave her fewer errors to feel bad about as the day moved on.

What Samantha's Log Revealed

Samantha, a sales manager for a pharmaceutical company, held to her resolve and showed her log to no one, but she recorded her responses to some set questions that night with refreshing honesty.

We've transcribed them with the following key:

Q = Question

A = Answer

D = Defenses

I = Insights (Samantha's views may help the rest of us protect Red Zone time.)

Q: Did you start on your number one goal at the time you had intended?
A: *No. In fact, I never got to it until 4:30 P.M. (Pause . . .)*
    D: But today wasn't a typical day.

Q: What distracted you from starting?
A: *Well, I was interrupted by a customer crisis, starting at 2:00 P.M. (Silence . . .)*
    I: Hmmmm, I should admit I was already late by then. I had put off my number one in favor of my easier number two priority, thinking I'd have plenty of time to catch up later.

Q: How could you have avoided that distraction?
A: *I couldn't, I could not have put off that customer issue! (Silence . . .)*
    I: But I could have stuck to my priority task in the morning, and I'd have been safely ahead when the "bomb" dropped in the afternoon.

Q: Once distracted, how long did it take you to recover?
A: *I never recovered, as far as priority number one went.*

Q: What was your longest period, uninterrupted, in the Red Zone?
A: *Thirty minutes, first thing in the morning.*

Q: What was your most productive period?
A: *First thing this morning: then, briefly, right after lunch.*

I: I'm usually good late in the day, too, but not today. I was too tired and frustrated.

Q: What was your least productive period?

A: *9:30 to 11:30 and 2:45 to 3:30. (Total: 2 hours 45 minutes, least productive.)*

D: These were both pegged for priority work, but my boss called an ad hoc staff meeting that wiped out the mid-morning, and then, the customer issue wrecked the afternoon. So I stayed late, but still didn't finish my priorities. (Silence . . .)

I: I should have seen that the staff meeting would not be productive for me: I could have begged off. Then it overran by 30 minutes more. Finally, because the boss was right there, I stayed 20 minutes longer to get some answers I will be needing tomorrow. I could have done it with e-mail, I suppose—though getting face time with the boss isn't a cinch. Still . . . I sacrificed priorities . . .

We're grateful for Samantha's testimony, and her honest insights, because they show that all of us allow some bits of time to leak away. But the really damaging leaks are those that directly impact our priorities. Be tough about Red Zone tasks. Then, go easy on yourself about lesser leaks throughout your day.

Logging Helps You See Your Situation

Samantha demonstrated a further warning for all of us: we tend to be honest about the damage, but we may still try to rationalize the *causes* of time loss as arising from others' actions. Logging was Samantha's first step in bringing her invisible time problems to the surface, and it can be yours, too.

ANALYZE YOUR LOG TO MAINTAIN MOMENTUM

To get maximum value from your logging exercise, ask yourself the questions that helped Samantha. Do it while studying your completed chart. In fact, keep asking yourself these questions long after you have stopped logging. They'll help you discover insights and maintain your improved habits.

Ten Vital Questions for You

1. Did you start on your number one goal at the time you intended?
   a. Did anything distract you from starting?
   b. How could you have avoided that distraction?
   c. Once distracted, how long did it take you to recover?
2. What was your longest period, totally uninterrupted on priorities?
3. What was your most productive period? Why?
4. Least productive? Why?
5. To what extent did you achieve your main goals? Were your time estimates adequate? Should you adjust for the future? Completing something like the chart below may help you see the big picture.

Priority Goal (or Segment Planned)	% Completed
1.	
2.	
3.	

6. Did you keep any task that could have been delegated?
7. Concerning interruptions:
   a. Were any interruptions actually more valid than the scheduled task? If yes—and if they'll repeat, then add them to your priority list.
   b. What categories of interruptions were heaviest? Phone? . . . Walk-in? . . . Crises? . . . Self-imposed escapes?
   c. Did you needlessly interrupt anyone else?

8. Contacts:
   a. Were your planned contacts aimed at advancing priorities?
   b. Did they take longer than planned? Was your data ready?
   c. Did you get the right person? Was that person ready?
9. Paperwork and E-mail:
   a. Did you spend time checking your e-mail during time slots intended for priorities?
   b. Did you lose time on paper because of clutter, poor filing, missing data?
10. Monitoring:
    a. Did you have an adequate tracker for monitoring progress, especially on elements of your priority tasks?
    b. Did you use or provide a simple template for reporting progress by any teammates assigned to the task?

NOTE: Later, in Part 3, you'll find a quick one-page checklist based on the Ten Vital Questions. Use it and share it with colleagues at work.

Despite your best disciplines, there will always to people and events to interrupt your original plans, so you need to have a recovery strategy ready and waiting.

REAL VOICES

Here's Richard Shirley, a civilian IT System Manager for the military in San Diego, who says it perfectly:

What about those inescapable "X-factors"—the people and events outside our planning curve that can and will impact us? We have to spot the potential; then build some flexibility and readiness into our day. We all have a boss—someone we answer to—who may require a quick response to an unforeseen event.

My department could be running at peak performance, handling issues quickly and efficiently, but if the electricity somehow gets interrupted, we must be able to mitigate this "X-Factor" capably, so that nobody's effectiveness can be completely nullified. No matter how well we manage our time, being able to flex for quick recovery is a constant challenge.

We agree with Richard. To see where you might have to go, you must be able to see where you have been—especially to detect patterns likely to repeat their attacks on your prime time. That's where a selective logging process can help you.

GOING ON FROM HERE

Keep your Red Zone log for three days; analyze what it tells you about your current habits, and gain some benefits from your own deeper insights. Then, select just a few permissive habits for removal or remodeling. Give yourself credit for your good habits—habits like Richard's contingency planning—to assure rapid response and recovery. Reinforce them and rejoice!

That's the groundwork you need for acing the second part of this book: escaping today's time traps!

PART TWO

The New Time
Traps and Escapes

CHAPTER

Management by Crisis

Of all the time concerns mentioned in our original surveys, none had a more devastating effect on morale than the fear that one's company was managing by crisis. A decade later, our current respondents still rank this threat number one. Why do we still fail to see the crisis early enough to stop it? Once acknowledged, crises make front-page news, but they are rarely sudden. Instead, they tend to build stealthily while we're too busy to notice. A thin trickle of minor errors and neglects, occurring systemically throughout an enterprise, can drain resources, the way a pinhole leak can weaken an underground pipe until the floor caves in. Where are the gauges and meters that should be warning us?

IS THIS A CRISIS OR A QUIRK AT WORK?

Are you watching your team's "trickle-meter"? As with death and taxes, none of us can get through life without some chaotic days at work. We all juggle time-gobbling annoyances that block us from accomplishing goals. Singly, these don't qualify as crises; but in the aggregate they can. If your team keeps bouncing from one small mess to another, something is amiss with your process. Who is supposed to notice that the canary in the coal mine has stopped singing?

Beware a String of Pseudo-Crises

Tragically, some people (including some executives) actually enjoy gyrating from peaceful progress to periodic panic and back again. Having beaten down one or two crises successfully, they base their self-worth on fresh displays of heroics. Such people ignore small risks, dawdle over deadlines, and agree to impossible demands so they can feel alive while stamping out flareups that should never have ignited in the first place. At other times, even the most dedicated workers will put one last patch on a system or a machine even though they know that a complete overhaul is a must. All such behaviors set the stage for a series of pseudo-crises that can coalesce into a self-inflicted disaster.

Don't Make a Mountain . . .

More than a few senior managers have told us, sheepishly, that they have regretted asking a simple question of some department head who then propelled everyone into a blizzard of activity to get an answer. The VP asks for an estimate—a ballpark figure—an educated guess—and the overzealous department manager delivers a fifteen-page leather-bound analysis that kept some accountant up all night.

CONCLUSION: When responding to a senior request (especially a rare request), find out what is needed, at what level of detail. If you see that the options for servicing this demand might vary dramatically, then say so and establish the requester's real need.

Recognize a Killer Crisis

Let's define a real crisis as an unforeseeable event, often largely beyond your control, of such magnitude that immediate action is required. At least, with a real crisis you can justify the time, effort, and money you will spend to overcome the threat—and the delay and neglect of many other interests until the threat is overcome.

Tylenol famously accomplished this when their president pulled millions of dollars worth of product off drugstore shelves, nationwide, at the first sign of the biggest tampering scare in U.S. history. That unhesitating action cost them a fortune but it earned them massive public trust, which restored their financial health faster than anyone could have predicted.

Align Expectations and Actions in a Crisis

Let's look at a few typical crises, as they were handled by a variety of organizations. As in the Tylenol case, the executives in these cases—having planned against a broad range of eventualities—could act, calmly, rationally, and ethically when the crisis hit.

Crisis A: Conference Organizers Cover a Loss   Conference organizers discover that a delivery service has lost a shipment of expensively printed and bound manuals, right at the start of a prestigious international conference.

BUT—the organizers block any "drama" from marring the event. Because big-name speakers have prepared their presentations well, the large audience can understand and participate fully, assured that they'll receive their printed version later, on request. The shipper's insurance will pay for reprinting, if necessary. The post-event mailing will act as a powerful follow-up promotion.

Crisis B: Client Switches Loyalties   An ad agency's major client suddenly switches loyalties at contract renewal time.

BUT—because switching is always a risk in the advertising business, the firm moves directly to Plan B: working a measured plan to sell more services to both old and new customers. The owners can readily assess what the competing agency may have offered to tempt the account away. That momentum will be difficult to maintain, so the contest is likely to reopen.

Crisis C: Illness Sidelines Key Player   Illness sidelines a key manager, midway through a major project.

BUT—by dividing the work, and pitching in herself on crucial tasks, the VP sets the tone for sharing the load among fellow managers. They bring the project in on time, assured that the whole team will share in the triumph.

Crisis D: Strike Stops the Action   A wildcat transit strike is called in the middle of a business day, forcing suburban commuters to struggle home from the city, and not return until the crisis ends.

BUT—because a farsighted company has schooled teams in flexing their schedules, and has accustomed the majority to "virtual working" one or two days a week, workers can quickly adjust, keeping up production from home. (In fact, so many firms are prepared to cope, that the strikers—deprived of their full impact—will settle early.)

Crisis E: Fire Guts a Building, Not a Business   A block-wide fire jumps to a factory in the middle of the night, causing heavy damage and loss of all work in process.

BUT—because the factory has adequate insurance coverage and has built strong relationships with customers, suppliers, and even competitors, their recovery—though challenging and expensive—will succeed. To satisfy customers, they patch together shipments from their offsite warehouse and seek cooperation from both customers and contacts. To their surprise, some customers even share their inventories with others. Some competitors step up to help during the dramatic event, making favorable headlines for themselves.

Can a Crisis Be a Good Thing?

If you run your business credibly when times are good, the news of an unavoidable crisis can elicit empathy from people who had viewed your previous transactions as routine. In fact, a crisis can unearth a treasure of hidden goodwill that you never knew existed. A case in point:

A few years ago, when Pat Nickerson was a television producer at Boston's Public Broadcasting Station, WGBH-TV, a devastating electrical fire struck after hours.

When the late night news showed the blaze erupting, many off-duty employees threw on some work clothes, jumped into their vehicles, and raced to the scene.

While the fire department fought the blaze, long lines of off-duty employees and a few local citizens formed a reverse "bucket brigade" to rescue hundreds of cans of archived films and tapes as they were tossed out of a second-story window by the station's gutsy production manager, Bob Moscone. Timeless and irreplaceable, this hoard included historic Boston Symphony concerts, early Julia Child *French Chef* shows, rare operas, ballets, science shows, and children's programs—treasures that would have been lost forever except for the goodwill that had been building, unnoticed, for years. Dozens of sooty, sweaty citizens cheered when the gutted treasure house was emptied to the last precious film can. For many months until a new headquarters could be erected, live production continued unabated from an old, tin-roofed shed lent by MIT's sports department. Veteran workers remember that era for its rock-bottom creature comforts and its sky-high morale.

But the adrenaline rush of crisis-handling should be carefully reserved for unpredictable, unpreventable events, not squandered on minor mishaps that could have been foreseen and forestalled. So what you need as a time manager are plans—both team and solo—to prevent the stressful sacrifices that define management by crisis.

PLANNING FOR PREVENTION: SEVEN SMART OPTIONS

Though you can't say *when* a crisis will explode, you can uncover that trickle of leaks most likely to cripple your projects if left untreated. Try some of these moves:

I. Predict Possible Threats

If you are a project leader making a pitch for your next great project, invite your team to list any threats or issues they can foresee. You may resist doing this: "Awww, why poison the atmosphere?" you may think. "The project is valid enough to win them over!"

Sure, they may seem to be on board while you're delivering your rousing speech. But what will they be saying in the parking lot tonight? If you want your players to accept from conviction, you can finish your pitch, then invite them to list every threat they see, and then score each threat on two factors:

Threat	% Likely to Occur	% Impact on Operations
_____	_____ % of 100%	_____ % of 100%
_____	_____ % of 100%	_____ % of 100%
_____	_____ % of 100%	_____ % of 100%
_____	_____ % of 100%	_____ % of 100%

Once the team has agreed on the threats and their Impact/Likelihood scores, stop. Take a break. Give the team a day or two to mull things over. Then, let them propose steps or processes that will block the worst impacts, or prevent some threats from arising at all. Everyone will learn something, . . . especially you.

2. Protect Schedules

Recognize Murphy's Third Law: Everything takes longer than expected. Build a modest cushion into your project estimates. When requesting services from lateral groups, set your "drop-dead" date inside your team; then tighten it by 20 percent for the lateral group. If they deliver late, you can still recover. If they're on time, keep up your own momentum so you don't waste that time bonus; you may need it later.

3. Predict Standard Lead Times.

Keeping a record of time invested in new or unfamiliar parts of a project can help you build a standard lead time menu. Estimates on the distinct elements of a project can be reused on whole families of related projects. They'll easily yield realistic time estimates to help you negotiate scope and deadlines for upcoming projects.

4. Prepare Simple Reporting Tools

Structure your projects to include regular reporting templates or milestone charts, so you can spot potential delays, early. (Of course, if you are using Project Management software, you'll be setting automated flags to show the cascading effects of any hitch.)

5. Propel Action with "Insider" Graphics

If you know you are prone to procrastination, keep a visible, graphic reminder in front of you to keep you on track. Whether it's a purple sticker on your dashboard or doorway or a "beep" from your computer, let it signal: "This prod's for you!" (Outsiders need never know what it means.) Your whole team may devise some graphics to aid propulsion. Refresh these often.

6. Provide Key Player Support

In one of our earlier crisis cases, the big problem was the loss of a key player to illness. But sometimes, the departure of a key player is by choice—theirs. If you notice that a key player shows signs of restlessness, pay attention. What's the likelihood she's job hunting? As a supervisor you must talk with disengaged players in time to identify and solve any problems that may jeopardize the task. (At the same time, you'll want to cover your bases by grooming other team members in critical skills so you can all stay prepared, if a key player's commitment should waver.) Cross-training pays off by ensuring depth in your department, and providing some variety for fatigued specialists.

7. Preserve Postmortem Data

When you start working your way through a genuine crisis, you make a lot of ingenious moves, but you're so busy surviving, you fail to notice them. Start keeping a crisis diary—simple, quick notes on events as they occur. Include your first reactions, your guesses as to what was going on, your eventual discoveries, your interim decisions, time investments, outcomes, costs, surprises. Record what you notice: mistakes, betrayals, corrections, reconciliations, recoveries. Make these notes for your eyes only.

Your reward for bothering? Not so much a paper trail for defensive moves—though that could come in handy at some point. No, your notes will build a set of valuable lessons for reuse throughout your career, both as a manager and as a mentor. Review these lessons: pass them on. Events lived through and recorded accurately can teach more vividly than the best MBA case study.

This may sound like common sense—but, sadly, too many people fail to capture what they've learned from recent hassles. Often, they are so relieved that "it's over"—they just want to forget and move on. Diaries can pave the way to easier crisis management, and to possible crisis prevention, next time.

CRISIS RECOVERY:
A CONTINUUM FROM PAST TO PRESENT

Those who are ignorant of history are bound to repeat it. If you are a senior manager recovering from a string of crises, plan to unearth your company's published information, diaries, and benchmarking data from the past. It's all there. You may be able to mobilize a quicker recovery next time by installing a previously successful model.

- Review past crises. What did former teams learn? What eluded them?

- Solicit details about other companies' recovery efforts. Don't isolate yourself; join gatherings of professionals from other companies. At big conferences, people let their hair down after hours, they tell "war stories." Solicit their insights—and take them with a grain of salt.
- If you're in top management, talk history with some of your company's best executive assistants. They have memories long kept confidential, but with a new regime in place, they may help you interpret the records you unearth: the warning signs, the trends, the plans made and changed. If it's been a long time since company goofs made headlines, your corporate memory may have grown complacent. It's only human to deep-six our mistakes when the pain is still fresh. But with the passage of time, our old disasters and recoveries can teach us a lot. Capture those insights while you can.
- Read business books avidly. Learn prevention the inexpensive way—from other people's errors, writ large.

WHAT *NOT* TO DO IN A CRISIS: THREE CAUTIONS

I. Don't Panic

For a measured response to a new crisis, ask these questions:

- Before we lay our plans: do we really need to get involved here?
- Is this our business . . . our specialty?
- Could I humbly delegate the probe to specialists on my team, who are more able than I?
- Could I then protect those specialists politically while they do the work?

Once we decide it is our business, these new questions arise:

- Is this the time to spend some money on expert help rather than doing it ourselves?
- How much time do we have to refine our plans? Is there a lit fuse somewhere?

Panic is contagious. Great managers neither show it, nor spread it, even if they secretly feel it!

2. Don't Punish

Avoid the time-honored practice of "shooting the messenger." If you make this fatal mistake, your team will hesitate to warn you next time things start going wrong.

- Foster a climate in which mistakes are accepted as "experiments," which should be revealed when first noticed.
- Emphasize that early reporting of bad news allows early and inexpensive choices for recovery.
- Recognize and reward honorable behavior.

3. Don't Pave It Over

Don't protect last-minute requesters from the consequences of their own actions. Those who cause chronic emergencies should pay a premium for services rendered at the eleventh hour. This applies to customers as well as internal groups and even bosses.

If you are a mid-level manager facing repeat crises, don't let the guilty hide under the radar. Here, the old rule applies: "No consequence, no change." So don't muffle the consequences for repeat offenders.

EXAMPLE: You request data from a lateral group assigned to handle a set of issues. You agree on clear instructions and a specific deadline. But their response arrives late and incomplete . . . again! Under time pressure, you are tempted to correct their errors and say nothing. But, if you fix this quietly, you bear all the risks while reducing theirs.

QUESTION: Was that top management's intent? By overperforming for some people, you cheat yourself . . . and possibly others. Worse, you keep your senior managers blind to a dangerous pattern.

SOLUTION: At the very least, show the offenders their pattern of neglect in a graphic way so they "get it." Request a new commitment in writing. If they fail again, you can produce that graphic evidence when you escalate. It may take a management move to break your habit of irrational rescuing.

NOTE: In some bureaucracies, when another department repeatedly fails, the disadvantaged department can lay claim to whatever budget had been allocated for the work the other department failed to do. Laggard departments begin to see the light when their budgets are removed to "buy" the work elsewhere.

Finally, use your experience to work up standard lead time estimates on tasks done jointly with other departments. Use those time estimates to bargain with requesters and partners on future assignments.

On the subject of tending to one's own business to prevent a crisis, Process Manager Andrea Cifor made this thought-provoking comment:

> At work, I understand my responsibilities and set boundaries clearly when it comes to deliverables. I clearly state my dependencies—and the risks I see. I do not try to solve a problem that is not in my area of expertise. That way, I avoid what I term the 'expert-tax,' a high price to pay that leads to weak execution.
>
> If I keep the expert-tax low by referring work to the experts, then I will make the right contributions to the projects I work on overall.

So crisis management takes adherence to the three cautions:

1. Don't panic.
2. Don't punish.
3. Don't pave it over.

And, Andrea adds: "Don't pile on work that is not really your business."

CHECK YOURSELF

How do you score on escaping the crisis management trap? Rate yourself on the following questions; then repeat the process thirty days from now. Simple Yes/No answers will suffice.

Questions	Today	30 Days
1. When setting goals and objectives, we examine alternatives for achieving them, to choose the least crisis-prone option.	——	——
2. Our team anticipates possible problems and takes action to prevent them or limit their consequences.	——	——
3. We build contingency cushions into our schedules to allow response time for unplanned events.	——	——
4. We design in regular progress reports on all major tasks so that any slippage can be seen and repaired, early.	——	——
5. When managing crisis situations, we avoid overcommitting resources. We premap deployment of people and resources for a number of likely events.	——	——
6. After a crisis, we discuss lessons learned and steps needed to prevent a recurrence. We map and implement such steps, putting our energy into "what is still possible."	——	——
7. We don't allow adjoining departments to fail repeatedly on joint deliverables without graphic negotiating, and we escalate for a command decision, if necessary.	——	——
Total	——	——

CHAPTER

Inadequate Planning

How much of your day do you spend juggling the demands of bosses, team members, and customers? As your workload keeps expanding, do you find less and less time for planning? Do you reach many a day's end, drained by activity but with little to show for it?

HOW PLANNING PROTECTS PRIORITIES

When we ask these questions at our Multiple Priorities seminars (with nearly 200,000 managers responding so far), we see a startling contrast in the ways that managers budget their time, depending on the level they have reached in the hierarchy.

Senior managers (director level and higher) report their typical day this way:

Planning (proportion of the day)	30–40%
Organizing (strategic and tactical)	20–30%
Delegating	20–30%
Communicating	20–30%
Measuring (mostly handled by others)	5–15 %
Controlling (mostly automated now)	3–10%
Performing routines	2–5%

Mid-level managers (administrators and technicians) report this distribution:

Planning	5–10%
Organizing	10–20%
Delegating (varies with staff size)	10–30%
Measuring	10–15%
Controlling	10–15%
Communicating	40–50%
Performing routines	20–25%

Seen graphically below, the contrast is dramatic: the mid-level managers' pyramid reverses the senior managers' scores—with communicating, delegating, and routines swallowing up the lion's share of middle management time.

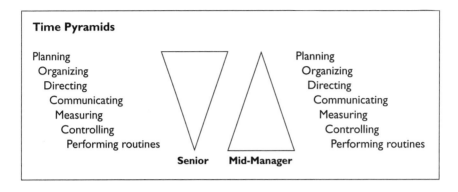

Time Pyramids

Planning
  Organizing
    Directing
      Communicating
        Measuring
          Controlling
            Performing routines

Planning
  Organizing
    Directing
      Communicating
        Measuring
          Controlling
            Performing routines

Senior   **Mid-Manager**

Overtime: Not Recommended for Critical Work

You may notice that totals for both groups ran to more than 100 percent. Certainly, most top managers and entrepreneurs work 80- to 90-hour weeks, with gusto. But heavy overtime is also the norm for mid-level managers in every business. People in service roles reach their day's end, glad to have helped many people, but bewildered by a blur of communication hits. Though demands can vary wildly in value, too many get labeled urgent by requesters.

On too many days, technicians and administrators incur overtime, because the work scheduled for the start of the day has yet to begin by day's end. Measuring and controlling are the province of middle management. Administrative help is so scarce that these managers handle their own communicating and routines, and they simply postpone planning—a solitary activity—"until things quiet down." Hence, planning time—the one investment that could prevent brushfires—goes up in smoke.

Consequences of the Inverted Pyramid

Lack of planning tends to bloat the lowest-ranking item, Performing Routine Tasks, because here you'll find all the repairs, redos, apologies, and explanations that follow a badly planned day.

In our seminars, it was heartbreaking for mid-managers to acknowledge the fact that failure to allot planning time would bloat communication and routine task time. Here's how dramatically it came home to mid-managers that the top of the chart represents managing your day while the bottom defines coping with consequences.

Planning	**5–10%**	
Organizing	**10–20%**	**Managing**
Delegating (Varies with staff size)	**10–30%**	
Measuring	10–15%	
Controlling	10–15%	
Communicating	40–50%	*Coping*
Performing routines	20–25%	
Total	100–155%	

You are invited to calculate your own typical use of time, just as those thousands of middle managers did. Are you any happier with your allotment? If not, read on.

Are You Planning or Coping?

How bloated is your communication load? Today all mid-level managers face expanded communication loads. Hundreds of messages clog your e-mail, voice mail, and smart phone, 24-7.

How choked off is your "organizing" time? Only a decade ago, when most of us reported to one boss, we knew whom to consult about conflicting priorities. Now, with multiple bosses, matrix management, and direct access by your clients across continents and cultures, you face blurred lines of authority and thinner senior support than ever. The message today sounds like "You're on your own, chum. Figure it out for yourself!"

Daily Plans Help You See What Matters

The following story is a classic, but so important, it merits retelling so that old and new readers alike can reap its benefits. As Alec reported it in earlier editions:

> When Charles Schwab was president of Bethlehem Steel, he confronted
> Ivy Lee, a management consultant, with an unusual challenge.

"Show me a way to get more things done," he demanded. "If it works, I'll pay you anything within reason."

Lee handed Schwab a piece of paper, saying,"Write down the things you have to do tomorrow." When Schwab had completed the list, Lee said, "Now number these items in the order of their real importance." Schwab did, and Lee went on:

"The first thing tomorrow morning, start working on number one and stay with it until it's completed. Then take number two, and don't go any further until it's finished or until you've done as much with it as you can. Then proceed to number three, and so on. If you can't complete everything on schedule, don't worry. At least you will have taken care of the most important things before getting distracted by items of less importance. The secret is to do this daily.

He went on to summarize:

- Evaluate the relative importance of the things you have to get done.
- Establish priorities.
- Record your plan of action and stick to it.

He finished by saying, "Do this every working day. After you have convinced yourself that this system has value, have your people try it. Test it as long as you like, and then send me a check for whatever you think the idea is worth."

In a few weeks, Schwab mailed Lee a check for $25,000. He later credited Lee with giving him the most profitable lesson he'd learned in his entire business career.

YOUR NUMBER ONE TAKE-AWAY ON PLANNING

If you take nothing else away from this chapter, remember to follow this highly important principle: Identify your number one priority and reserve your best time for it.

CAUTION: The classic advice that Ivy Lee gave—"start on number one and stay with it until you finish"—may no longer apply in today's multitasking milieu. Instead, we recommend the method laid out in Chapters 4 and 5 of Part I: Give your best task your best (not earliest) time of day.

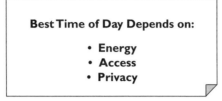

Best Time of Day Depends on:

- **Energy**
- **Access**
- **Privacy**

How to Plan Your Many Mid-Level Tasks

We've already talked about validating your top three tasks, estimating the time they'll need, then slotting them into safe Red Zone time slots where nothing can interrupt them. So far, so good.

But next, you'll need to plan the next groups of tasks—the more numerous mid-level jobs that also need timely delivery. The trick here is what we call "task-grouping." Check your to-do list or your Outlook task list. Then decide:

- Which tasks require calculations—several minutes or several hours of checking numbers and doing math? Do the math for several tasks—or all of them—at one time. Gain momentum by using only one warmup for several items.
- Which tasks require phone calls? List and make a whole roster of calls at times you are most likely to find people "in" and ready to help. Note the responses or agreements for plugging in later, to final decisions.
- Which tasks require combined reading and writing? Get some quiet time to take care of several. Note your decisions in the margins of incoming paperwork—or use the "Insert Comment" command to make your notations on electronic documents. Later you can wrap up responses to a lot of different items without needing to rethink or "warm up" again.

Variety Is Not the Spice of Working Life

If you get bored or tired from doing one type of task too long you'd do better to take a break: have a coffee, take a walk, get some R&R. You really will not save time by tackling jobs randomly, gyrating from math to calls to writing, for the sake of variety. Momentum is your goal in grouping tasks to take advantage of the "learning curve" effect.

MULTIPLE DEMANDS REQUIRE GREATER CLARITY

A decade ago, most of us reported to one boss: we knew whom to consult about conflicting priorities. Now, with multiple bosses, matrix management, and instant access between you and your clients, you face fuzzier lines of authority, and thinner support than ever. You're on your own, Manager!

You need three tools, used daily, as your twin anchors in your sea of change. These tools are:

1. A priority system based on Pareto's Law.
2. A written daily plan—first to protect Red Zone items, and then to assure momentum on mid-level items.
3. Finally, you need some sort of "limbo" or "holding area" on your plan to assure yourself that you will *not* allow unworthy tasks to keep competing for your time. This "limbo" should be seen as a kind of "trap door exit" for moving low-reward tasks off your desktop.

Your Written Daily Plan: A Must

In the previous edition of *The Time Trap*, Alec Mackenzie said:

> There's no more important activity for a serious time manager than a written daily plan. To be sure your plan will stick, you must commit it to writing. Only with your written or visual plan can you stay in control of your day.

Without a written plan, your friendly optimism can overrule your common sense. You take on too much; you put yourself in the middle of power struggles, you allow random interruptions, and you slow to a dead end.

Expect Multiple Gains

Your written plan will help you get your top 20 percent done; it will guide you in judging incoming priorities, and will bolster your visceral strength to resist drift.

Finally, for any interruptions you *must* allow, your written plan will help you get back on track quickly. Writing your plan is easier than ever. You can use the efficient tools on your computer, your hand-held PDA, or your smart phone. If you prefer paper, your "At a Glance" tools or a simple chart on the wall will help you stay on target.

Plan Team Priorities: Spot Threats Early

Because some incoming demands will actually outweigh your top 20 percent, you and your team may need to post priorities on a shared website or wall, so everyone can deal with changes that must be accommodated.

Certainly in large engineering organizations where competing long- and short-term projects coincide all the time, success would be impossible without a rigorous project management process—aided by PM software and collaborative tools.

Tasks must be graphically mapped with milestones visible across multiple disciplines. Possible threats must be forecast and flagged to show the ripple effect of any delay or surprise move.

In early planning talks, the best teams predetermine various fallback options and their likely outcomes so that alternatives, already agreed, can be pursued without further arguments.

MULTITASKING? WARNING YOUR BOSS EARLY

If you are a project manager, office manager, or administrator, you probably report to multiple bosses, so you need to take initiatives yourself. Build your own tracking chart to show your various competing projects, with potential calendar conflicts, and some recovery options.

If several requesters compete for your time, you should show your main boss the plans you have made to mediate disputes. Get your main boss on board early, with your plans and fallback options. Help your boss to forestall political "surprises" at senior levels by providing good data in advance. If you're a confident planner, you'll keep these charts on an accessible wall, ready for multiple requesters, your boss(es), and your staffers to study at will.

Why Updating Is a Must

If you are blessed with a photographic memory or high intelligence, you may blithely neglect writing things down. But if you face multiple bosses or competing priorities, you must be able to show conflicts quickly and convincingly. When fast-moving events upset your plans, written priorities will help you assess the effect of adjustments so you can renegotiate with bosses, customers, and lateral groups. With e-tools, you can adjust with a couple of keystrokes. Wall charts can be updated with a sticky note. It's so easy, we wonder why people still resist this notion at our seminars.

THREE BARRIERS TO MAINTAINING PRIORITIES

We've noticed three barriers shared by many managers and technologists who try priority setting for a brief period and then abandon it:

1. Confusion of priority-setting rules with time management rules. (They differ.)
2. Unclear criteria for setting priorities.
3. Fear of negotiating when priorities are threatened.

Let's get the definitions cleared up next.

Distinguish Time Management from Priority Management

Time Management Is Tactical   Time management determines *when* to do a task that has already been validated.

- Time managers slot validated tasks into the best time periods to assure delivery.

- But this tactic fails whenever tasks outnumber available time slots. Then, we make unsatisfying compromises, reduce task scope, and sacrifice quality to squeeze the tasks into scarce time.

Priority Management Is Strategic   Priority management determines *whether* to do a task at all.

- It validates incoming tasks against existing tasks, opting for those with maximum gains and minimum risks, while keeping ethical requirements in mind.
- Priority managers assess work on its merits, without considering timetables at first.
- In a separate calculation, they use urgency as a tiebreaker only between two items of equal magnitude or value.

TRIAGE: DEFINED ON SURVIVABILITY, NOT SCHEDULING

But for too many managers, the only clear piece of data in a demand is its deadline. This ghastly irony causes many otherwise sane people to service urgency before impact, as if urgency had some legitimacy of its own, separate from impact. Seminar attendees have a very hard time getting their minds around this problem. We remind them that in such serious endeavors as combat medicine, no such hesitancy could be tolerated.

The Field Hospital Model

In a battlefield scenario, the triage medic must judge incoming wounded, first, on their chance of surviving at all. Those needing surgery, with a high risk of recovery if they get quick help, *and* with a good chance of surviving the surgery, would be rated "A" and go into surgery ASAP. Those with serious injuries, but enough strength to wait, would go in later in the "A" queue. Those whose condition is stabilized, but who will need surgery, will be rated "B" and will be queued up after the "A's."

Those with no chance of survival (even with surgery) would not go into the surgery queue at all, but would be given palliative care. This set of realities can and must be thought through, courageously, in matters of life and death, when patients are many and surgeons are few. Once the rules are clear, decisions must come quickly enough to save life.

SET YOUR CRITERIA TO PLAN AND VALIDATE WORK

To reduce the number of times you must renegotiate work priorities, set up some basic Risk/Value Standards. Here's the question: what must a task be worth to let it bump tasks already scheduled? Once you have an answer, set up a chart like the one shown in Part I, Chapter 4, comparing risks like safety, cost, and compliance with government regulations, against values like income potential, position on a critical path, or service to a top-tier customer.

The criteria just listed are only examples. Yours may differ, depending on your business or industry, but they must still meet *objective, measurable standards or rules* for defining where in the queue a task will go.

Two Generic Rules for Validating

Consider your typical demands. Then, consider these rules:

Validation Rule #1:   To earn a top slot, a task must have both the highest risk and the highest value, compared with all other tasks facing you.

ACTION: Number your competing tasks in descending order of survival likelihood.)

Validation Rule #2:   Validity always trumps urgency. Urgency merely breaks a tie between two tasks of equal consequence. (Do not rate two tasks with the same deadline as comparable. Rank only two tasks with the same magnitude as comparable: then let urgency break the survivability tie.)

ACTION: Rank your current competing priorities in survival order: then use the chart to negotiate, clearly and calmly, with competing requesters.

Still Worried About Negotiating?

Once armed with objective standards, you, as the performer or SME, must use your data to highlight risks and negotiate priorities. Tough enough when dealing with in-house managers, the challenge really heats up when customers get involved. Lateral managers and their customers may hatch an attractive-looking plan that hides unacceptable risks for you or other performers.

Start the conversation with a graphic that helps insiders to focus objectively. Try a filled-in version of the Risk Criteria Chart proposed in Chapter 4. Use relevant, matched criteria to show threats to resources, or to compliance.

SAMPLE RISK/VALUE CRITERIA	Current Project A		Current Project B		Risks in Proposed Project C	
	Yes	No	Yes	No	Yes	No
Safety threat		x		x		x
Cost overrun		x		x	(x)	
High Income potential	x		x		x	
Compliance issue		x		x	(x)	
Top Tier Customer	x		x		x	
Critical path item on larger effort	x		x			x
Specialists needed					(x)	

Your data may help an eager customer-focused team to see risks they may have downplayed. They may rethink the deal they had hoped to seal with the customer.

CONCLUSION:

If a boss or client is not positioned to understand the volume of work required, the inadequate time available, or the possible technical or legal glitches—you are merely doing your duty to clarify these. Take three sober steps:

1. Show the risks that would affect them (lateral managers and customers) if you were to attempt the new task as proposed.
2. Show practical options, with roughly matched trade-offs (pain levels) for fixing one or another of the risks highlighted.
3. State your own preferred solution, and the reasons for it.

With a clear conscience, you can then accept a revised mandate and perform to your best. By electing to negotiate, you give all parties the chance to examine risks and options, and you encourage others to seek early advice from the one who must deliver the goods: That's you!

REAL VOICES

To illustrate the challenge of planning with lateral colleagues, we heard from Eric Hanson, production manager for a mid-sized manufacturing firm:

Sales and customer service have direct contact with our customers. When they sprang a surprise deadline on us for a big customer whose work wasn't on the schedule at all, this week, I pointed out the risks:

1. *We can't bump work currently on the line.*
2. *We can't understand, much less approve, the vague specs on this rush job.*

But both Sales and CS management insisted: Just make it happen!

Eric's Approach: Firm Diplomacy

With urgency and validity both jeopardized, Eric decided to escalate this decision. Because this request was part of a pattern with this big customer, senior management decided to accede, but not immediately, and not without some consequences to the requester.

Eric provided a standard lead-time menu—again—for Sales and Customer Service to present to the customer. Armed with these standards, which had been agreed jointly by Production, Sales, and Customer Service, the senior salespeople made direct contact with the customer. They were able to warn that adjustments could be made only by making some serious trade-offs. Further, the customer would have to bear the financial costs incurred by meeting this "late" request. The customer agreed.

PLANNING: THE KEY TO GOOD PARTNERING

To run a sane operation, each department must set clear, unequivocal standards in concert with their lateral groups. Options and penalties should be forecast and applied when customers (internal or external) exhibit chaotic or irrational demands, repeatedly.

If you and your company want to "partner" more effectively with your customers, then help both sides to plan jointly, acknowledging realities, and finding ways to avoid future crises. In any case, randomness is always harmful, but particularly so with last-minute, consequential demands. So debating crises, case-by-case, would drain your energy, and threaten quality and delivery. Setting standards in advance improves everyone's sanity.

Planning Enhances Decision Making

Finally, since decision making is the real work of senior management (Plan, Organize, Delegate), then mid-level managers like Eric must be congratulated when they summon the courage to insist on early warning when standards must be overturned. Get senior management support on this principle: the later the warning—the heavier the penalties. Your company is not "punishing" anyone. Instead, people are choosing their own path, with the natural consequences that are built in. If circumstances allow for the easing of penalties, that will be a gift, not a duty.

CHECK YOURSELF

How do you score on planning and priority setting? Rate yourself on the following questions; then repeat the process thirty days from now. Simple Yes/No answers will suffice.

Questions	Today	30 Days
1. Based on the goals and objectives of my organization, we set team objectives, and then prioritize our tasks.	———	———
2. We focus on our top 20% of tasks, gauged by risk and value.	———	———
3. We post team priorities where members and peers can see them, and we use them to guide negotiations.	———	———
4. Though we respect "political clout" and "favors owed," we still make validity the ruling factor in prioritizing.	———	———
5. When short-range tasks compete with long-range tasks, we break the larger tasks into short-range segments, before deciding which task or segment gets done now.	———	———
6. We consciously define "urgency" as a secondary element, then use it to tie-break between tasks of equal validity.	———	———
7. We may bow to last-minute demands, but we may also hold "repeat offenders" accountable for costs and consequences.	———	———
Total	———	———

CHAPTER

Inability to Say No

First, let's set some ground rules. Let's agree that 80 percent of the time you'll say a resounding yes to your obligations at work, at home, and in the community. Beyond that, you may also stretch on many occasions, going out of your way to perform "random acts of kindness."

But, what we're talking about here are those bottom 20 percent of requests that set an alarm bell ringing in your mind; you realize you ought to say no. Once you hesitate, all is lost.

There are dozens of reasons why we hate saying no. Most of them relate to wanting to be liked. But your time is too limited to allow this self-indulgence. Every yes, given to a trivial time waster, will cut available time and energy for Red Zone tasks. You will invariably end up overloaded and overstressed.

Let's stop here and draw a distinction between two time-devouring human drives:

- The urge to attempt too much.
- The urge to say yes to all our fellow humans.

Those who attempt too much may be suffering from overconfidence or ego inflation, convinced that they can do everything better and faster than others.

By contrast, those who say yes to everything may be driven by timidity, worry about offending, hunger for belonging, or yearning for gratitude. While the two drives differ, the result is the same: requesters learn they can get their expectations met, at no cost to them.

THE HARSH SOUND OF "NO"

As an astute professional, you've learned that the word "no" may insult the ear of a boss, colleague, or customer. A flat no can damage relationships and stunt your career, exposing you to labels like rude, uncooperative, egotistical, even insubordinate. Yet, you must set some limits, some boundaries, or be forced to accept tasks whose technical or ethical risks are plain as day.

A Five-Step "Softener"

Here's a five-part approach that should get no across, firmly but gently:

1. When—for whatever reason—you must decline a request, don't say "no" outright. The moment requesters feel denied or resisted, they stop listening and start building counter-arguments.
2. Open, instead, with a response like: "I see a risk to you." Or, possibly: "I see a risk to our customer/to the public," whatever is true. This way, you raise requesters' curiosity, not their defenses.
3. Let requesters see the risks, graphically. If you are in the same room together, start sketching the risks on a scratch pad. This puts their focus on the page, not on your face. Sometimes, the requester will want to retrieve that sketch if they must make the case, later, with their own higher-ups. (How nice that they can leave your office, armed for the next round!)
4. Avoid mentioning any problem or inconvenience to yourself or your team. Your requester will expect you to manage your risks—and muffle your pain—in private.
5. Finally, be prepared to illustrate workable options for every risk you list. In fact, the moment you hear an unreasonable demand, your mind's eye should envision a flashing two-column illustration:

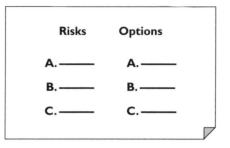

If you start sketching even before saying a word, you'll capture the requester's rapt attention.

Show Risks Diplomatically: Case in Point

A junior officer, attending one of our Priorities workshops at a U.S. Marine base, began to sweat, visibly, while we were wrapping up the morning session. When he was last to leave the room, I commented quietly on his sudden feverish look, and asked if he was feeling OK.

"I'm a community liaison officer," he replied. "I'm really sweating an order I've just been given. A local civic group wants to borrow our "ducking booth" for a fun fair this weekend. But I know the machine is damaged and can't be repaired in time. They should have asked sooner. The trouble is that my boss lives by the phrase: 'Make it happen!' so I'm sure he won't take no for an answer."

"I bet you're right," I agreed. "But people who won't or can't take no can often hear the word 'risk' more clearly, especially if you were to frame it like this: 'Sir, I see a risk to you . . .' or 'Sir, I see a risk to the public if we do that.'

After years of doing seminars for the Marines, I knew that some senior officers—like senior people in business—abhor debates with their juniors. But they hate hidden surprises even more! When the young officer still looked unconvinced I suggested that he try this: "Sir, let me point out a threat to public safety and also to our reputation. Then, let me come up with some other ways to help them out. I'll get back to you with options this afternoon. But at least, now, we're not taking a blind risk."

I had barely finished that thought, when the young officer bolted out the door with a grin. "Got it," he said, as he disappeared down the hall.

When he returned (a little late) for the afternoon session, he signaled a silent high-five, and gave his full and relaxed attention to the rest of our workshop.

KNOW WHEN TO DECLINE A REQUEST

Say no (or at least not yes) under the following five conditions:

1. Emergencies arising from another's neglect—especially after repeated warnings.
   REMEDY: Let natural consequences unfold. It's a fact of life that people continue bad behavior when there is no cost to them. If you don't feel empowered to allow natural consequences, then escalate the case to a higher authority. Don't take it on yourself to bury other people's negligence; they'll keep you busy shoveling forever.
2. Items of minor value but high urgency, placed in conflict with higher priorities.
   REMEDY: Even if you owe someone a favor—pay it another way, another day.
3. Demands, even from on high, that look technically infeasible, impractical, or too costly.
   REMEDY: Present the risks and offer better options.
4. Manipulation by a peer palming off tedious work, with no recip-rocal in view.
   REMEDY: Of course you help colleagues in need. Certainly, you forgive others, as you hope to be forgiven. But after a couple of lopsided bargains, you know a "dumping operation" when you see one. You need not define it aloud, but you cannot indulge it either. Find a civilized way to state your boundaries, using an "I statement." Sidestep sarcasm or sermonizing. Try: "I'm not able to do that." or "I usually say yes but this is one task I cannot take on." or "I am definitely not qualified in that area of expertise." Break off, pleasantly. No explanations required.
5. Demands that offend your moral or ethical sense.
   REMEDY: Don't feel obliged to justify your view. You simply say "I would feel uncomfortable doing that. Please find another way." Don't back down. Don't explain unless pressed. But, expect to lose popularity, for a while, with this person. Be willing to take your lumps at first. Possibly, after a requester gets a few more turndowns, you may get some thanks. Don't bank on it.

GIVE NO QUARTER ON ETHICAL ISSUES

Most people find it easiest to say no when a request clearly conflicts with their moral sense. While great books and films have dramatized courage in the face of ethical dilemmas, many managers have told me that it's harder to gain clarity than courage. Once they take a clear position, once they can draw clear boundaries of conscience around a hot-button issue, they can decline without hesitation. The more mature they get, the more choices they can tap for couching a refusal firmly, without tension or aggression.

As one manager put it: "When my mind is absolutely clear about an issue, I can be courteous and warm even while saying no. It's when I'm unsure or conflicted on an issue that I get tense and strident with people."

Another manager told us of a graceful exit she made (without repercussions) when her director level boss asked her to observe and report on the behavior of a fellow supervisor. She felt absolute certainty about her viewpoint so she was able to reply: "Usually, I like to say yes to any request of yours, and I usually do. But I feel uncomfortable with this. I would not act as an investigator this way, no matter who asked me. Please find another solution."

When her boss looked dismayed, she went on: "Perhaps you could ask HR to help you get this covered, but I must decline." "Hmmm," he said, with a frown, as he went back to his office.

She stayed perfectly unruffled. Nothing more came of it.

NONASSERTIVE RESPONSES TO AVOID

When you know you must decline a request, save time and stress by avoiding "victim vocabulary." Never let them hear you say:

- "I'm sorry but . . ."
- "I wish I could but . . ."
- "I'll try . . ."
- "I'm awfully busy but . . ."
- "I don't know. I've got many other things to do . . ."
- " If only . . ."

Or, worst of all:
- "Leave it with me. I'll let you know . . ."

Once you invite an experienced manipulator to "leave it" with you, the job is yours. As one victim admitted, "I went in there ready to say no, and soon found myself apologizing. Next thing I knew, I was out in the hall, with the files in my hand. I still don't know what happened in there!"

Determined requesters have heard and anticipated every likely excuse. They'll push back with responses like:

- "But we're counting on you. There's no one else . . ."
- "You're better at this than anyone—and the client asked for you, specifically . . ."
- "Yes, I know you're busy; that's why we chose you. You know how to get things done."
- "If I need something done, I give it to a busy person . . ."

Don't bother presenting specific excuses: they only draw counterarguments. Stay pleasant and positive while stating you are not available. Once you decide to say no to an inappropriate request, realize that requesters have no absolute right to know your reasons. Simply say, "I must say no this time." Keep moving, pleasantly, in the direction you were going when they interrupted you with this request. Will they love you less? Yes. Temporarily.

BUY TIME WHEN DEMANDS FLOOR YOU

When the demand comes without warning and you cannot quickly check your availability, don't make a semi-offer. Any response of yours that looks or sounds like "maybe" will be taken as "yes". In such traps, you can always buy yourself time. Count to ten. Allow the silence to get uncomfortable. Then say: "Phew! I'd have to negotiate several longstanding commitments to make room for this. That will take time. I could let you know by midweek. Meanwhile, if you're in a hurry for an answer, I'd suggest you pursue other avenues to save time and worry."

If the requester leaves, fine. If the pressure continues, study your schedule again. Then go on: "On second thought, don't wait. *I know* I can't back these projects off. You'll need to go ahead without me."

CURE YOURSELF OF PEOPLE PLEASING

The foregoing strategies presume that when you say no to something, you do it to say yes to something else—a more valid, pressing commitment. If you keep your valid tasks slated in front of you, in Outlook or on a white-board, you can quickly review the tasks competing for your time and con-firm your refusal with confidence.

Some busy people will sketch a quick pie chart every morning, show-ing the current workload with its standard operations and its projects. When bosses arrive with a new request, the two parties can do a joint "eye-ball" assessment. How big a slice will this new assignment represent? Then, they can examine possible trade-offs, together, amicably.

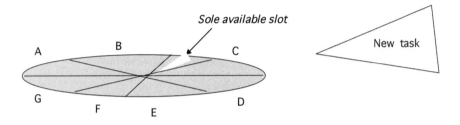

For example, if your boss has brought in the new task, but is also the requester of tasks E. F, and G, the boss may be able to provide relief, on the spot. On the contrary, if others—peers of the boss or more senior managers—have requested projects B and C, the boss may be able to help in escalating for relief.

The best practitioners of this process may be today's executive assis-tants. They tend to assist several top-level officers in addition to the CEO. So they face continual trade-off issues. Already skilled in diplomacy, they can use graphics, like the pie chart above, to lower the heat when negoti-ating task conflicts among their bosses.

REAL VOICES

Andrea Iadanza, Director of Seminar Operations for American Management Association, has made a specialty of running big nationwide conferences for administrative professionals. About saying no, she comments:

> Most firms no longer have enough administrative staffers to handle the load size. So the perennial issues of poor communication and "fly-by" requests have become even more critical. We suggest that beleaguered assistants opt for negotiating as a healthy instinct. That simply means:

- *Listen.*
- *Question.*
- *Clarify.*
- *Reach a new agreement.*

Negotiating can reduce risks and build respectful trust in Executive Suite relationships.

YOU CAN EVEN RESCIND AN ERRANT YES

On rare occasions, you may say yes, too quickly, and then realize your mistake. Right away, get in touch with the person and say something like this:

> Jeff: I must apologize to you. I didn't estimate the time needed for a job already committed for the boss (customer). There's just no way I can do both sets of tasks. So, I'm returning this assignment to you in time for you to find another option. I'll owe you one, but it can't be this; it can't be now.

If you know of a practical suggestion or referral, then make it now, to maintain the requester's good will. Otherwise, don't hang around for further commiseration.

WHEN SORELY TEMPTED TO SAY YES

When you're torn about accepting a task—for a friend, for your boss—or for a juicier-than-usual involvement, be especially careful:

1. Listen. Be sure you fully understand what is being asked of you.
2. Ask for a time estimate. If the assigner doesn't know how big this task is, don't just hope for the best. Take a few minutes to run an estimate. That, in itself, will constitute a favor for the requester. An accurate estimate may provide an escape for you, while arming the requester to make an honest deal with his next candidate.
3. Once you see that other commitments will trump a new task, you can say, "You'd be taking a risk leaving this with me: I'm

overloaded now, and I estimate this new work of yours at twelve hours, so you may need to get it into other hands right away."

Give Reasons, Not Excuses

Though you should never make excuses, you can show appropriate reasons that are both compelling and demonstrable. Better still, focus the requester on other alternatives. If you have good referral suggestions or fresh solutions for pursuit elsewhere, then offer these. They'll constitute your best effort at team play.

How to Offer a Rare "Conditional Yes"

Of course, you will sometimes take on a risky assignment beyond the scope of your job, as a stepping stone to promotion, or a chance at more exciting work. But speak up now. Insist on any preconditions to cut risk or assure timely delivery. Sometimes, you can take on a tough job if you can reduce unreasonable elements, shrink the scope, extend the time line, or improve the budget. Remember, your leverage is high before you say yes. It evaporates thereafter.

Here are some ways to express it:

- "I could do this only under the following conditions: . . ."
- "Before agreeing, let me point out something that would improve our chances: . . ."
- "To do this, I would need the following: . . . (specify technical, budget or other needs.)"
- "Before we go on, allow me to show you the track record. On previous attempts, customer delays have jeopardized both quality and delivery."
- "Let's run a test first. We'd need to assure XYZ before agreeing to this."

Not only will you increase your own credibility but you'll reduce your boss's risks, and enhance the company's bargaining power, later, with customers.

Roles Offers: Hardest to Turn Down

Some day you'll be offered a role—a chairmanship, a committee assignment, an extracurricular activity that really intrigues you. Great! But, when such offers arise at your busiest season, your ego can say yes too quickly. Before accepting a time-killing accolade, heed your instinct for self-preservation.

Smile and count to ten! Allow yourself time to check with loved ones. Be sure your extracurricular efforts will not push your family life, your intellectual pursuits, or any needed R&R further into the outer darkness. If, after sleeping on it, your answer is still *yes*—then accept or volunteer with gusto. If the answer must be *no*, then express your "regrets" with warmth and gratitude. You might try one of the following:

- "Thanks for asking me. Your offer kept me up late. Having discussed it with my (family, boss, team?), I do regret that I must decline, this time. Other commitments just won't allow me to take on a chairmanship (office, project) right now."
- "You know, Jim, on New Year's Day, I promised my family that I wouldn't take on anything more this year. It's crucial at this time in our lives that I keep that commitment."
- "Thanks for this compliment. I must decline for this year. I hope you won't write me off. In any other year I'd have said yes in a heartbeat."

Only you can preserve enough time for your life. As one company president confessed to Alec in a grateful letter:

Thanks for teaching me to say no after twenty years in business. I've just written letters of resignation from the boards of four organizations. In every one, I had held on too long, keeping younger people from taking over and contributing. I was under the illusion that they needed my services, since they kept reelecting me. Now I know they reelected me because they didn't want to hurt my feelings. I thank you, and my wife thanks you. We're looking forward to more time with the family, starting now.

LET YOUR TEAM TURN YOU DOWN

If you are a senior manager, it may seem odd, but you must teach your team to say no to you. Assure them they must do it early, while there's still time to seek alternatives. If they take on tasks when they shouldn't, the whole team pays the penalty with eleventh-hour struggles.

Encourage staffers to point out risks, expose overloads, and offer alternatives, all in total comfort. Let's face it: like most bosses, you may unwittingly overload your best performers. Sometimes you'll add tasks to someone's portfolio before any inroads have been made on tasks you assigned earlier. Because you trust them so much, you consider a task done the moment you entrust it to their care. Repeat that error too frequently, and you'll bury your best. Let your ace performers know that you respect their planning and estimating skills and that you'll listen attentively to any warnings they care to give you. You'll need to reinforce this message with consistent expressions of gratitude each time they save you from blind risks.

Use Graphics to Settle Project Conflicts

When you must say no, be sure to focus the requester's glance on an objective map or document, rather than on your face. Here's a "diplomatic" risk-reduction tool we've introduced into many organizations to help managers

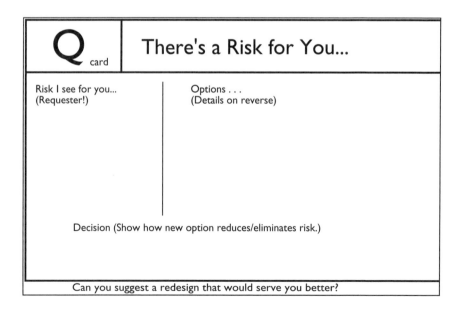

illustrate the risks in a request, without embarrassment to the requester or themselves. (We called these "Q-Cards" because the companies involved were deeply committed to Total Quality programs and needed to upgrade the feasibility of every request.)

The "doers" would state the main risk—whether time, cost, technical difficulty, or conflict with other priority tasks. Next, they would offer several bulleted options for the requester. The requester would be encouraged to collaborate on further ideas for getting the desired result at reduced risk.

SUPPORT YOUR TROOPS IN THE MATRIX

If you manage a project-driven team, especially in a matrix organization, you will face assignments coming at you from multiple sources. Let your team members know that you will support them, on the political front, when they must negotiate with your peers or seniors over competing demands. Assure them that you will not need to win every contest with your peers. Instead, you will sometimes back off, to give the team relief. Team members will simply need to give you early warning, and some options.

Distinguish yourself from those managers who would rather see a default than engage in an honest debate. Your whole team will thank you . . . and that's the brand of gratitude that generates *esprit*.

CHECK YURSELF

How do you score on saying no? Rank yourself on the following questions; then, repeat the process thirty days from now. Simple Yes/No answers will suffice.

Questions	Today	30 Days
1. When I am asked to do something inappropriate or perform a task that someone else should do, I am able to say no gracefully.	———	———
2. When I point out a risk, I point out possible options, using graphics so the requester stays focused on issues, not on me.	———	———
3. As a manager, I encourage team members to respond to my own unthinking requests by pointing out impacts on their other tasks.	———	———
4. I encourage them to suggest alternatives when "no" is the right answer.	———	———
5. I stay alert to other managers in the matrix, and support my team members when they must negotiate a trade-off.	———	———
6. If I agree to a request too hastily, I immediately back off with an apology, so the requester can pursue other avenues.	———	———
7. In general, I say no only to avoid neglect of more vital issues.	———	———
Total	———	———

CHAPTER

Poor Communication

My favorite adaptation of Pareto's Law is this: Spend 80 percent of your communication time on what is still possible. Remember: the present and future are all we have left. Unless you are a historian, keep no more than 20 percent of your focus on past events. You may even want to work toward an ultra-high 90/10 ratio, focusing your energies on *now* and *next!*

Here's one of the things Alec Mackenzie had to say about communication:

> Get a group of business people together, invite them to recall the biggest foul-up they ever witnessed, and you'll usually hear a story about somebody's failure to communicate. The punch line goes something like this: "When we finally figured out what was going on, the other guy said: '. . . But I thought you meant . . .'" The laughter is knowing and rueful.

Despite its challenges, we take for granted that communication is simply a natural activity, a skill or gift we are born with. It starts with our first wails in the delivery room—with parents and infant taking turns! Through a lifetime of encounters, we ascend to more and more convoluted conflicts in conference rooms, classrooms, or courtrooms—communicating every waking hour.

THE MOST NATURAL OF ACTIVITIES

Even if you are reading, studying, listening to the news, or watching the soaps, you are communicating—you just happen to be in "receiver mode."

Even when you meditate or pray, so theologians tell us, you are rotating between sending and receiving messages.

Can you agree that the only time you are *not* communicating is when you are asleep? Some spouses would swear that "snoring" actually communicates—and so does the gentle jab that makes the snoring sleeper find a less constricting position.

At Work, Technology Hikes Speed and Volume

When hundreds of e-messages stuff your inbox, you can't even delay or delegate without creating yet another communication, either responding to a request directly, or explaining the task when assigning it to a staffer. Despite convenient e-tools, each contact seems to drive several more.

Certainly, there are days when the overload is too much of a good thing:

- Ever-higher volumes of legitimate e-mail and voice mail traffic.
- Mandatory meetings with poor or no agendas, and only vague results.
- Walk-in visits—even from good buddies—that are emotionally welcome, but poorly-timed.

All this can make you feel powerless and overwhelmed. Only when you make a communication blooper do you realize how complex the process is, with its verbal, visual, and virtual impacts. It's a wonder we understand each other at all!

REAL VOICES

Andrea Cifor, the process manager whom you met earlier, noticed another communication hitch we face. As she put it:

> *Communication is declining in the workplace as multiple generations struggle to find a mutual sweet spot. We're losing finesse with the welter of text-message-y jargon that forces people to try translating what the sender might have meant. Simple rule of thumb:*

- *Say what you mean.*
- *Choose the right forum.*
- *Use right format for your message.*

Some Verbal Scenarios

Words mean different things to different people; we all know it—but sometimes that reality gets reinforced, the hard way.

Scenario #1   A draftsperson in an engineering firm is instructed to do something "ASAP." He takes the memo to mean "urgent." But the requester means "when you can get to it."

> REMEDY FOR REQUESTERS: Always state a specific deadline: give both the day and the time. Not only does it clarify, but it allows the "doer" to slot the request into an action calendar.
>
> REMEDY FOR RESPONDERS: Always ask for a specific deadline when accepting work. This allows you to negotiate as necessary.

Scenario #2   An executive traveling abroad sends a quick e-mail instructing the team to handle a particular problem. She lists a number of steps. Within minutes, instant messages are flying among the team members. "Does she mean Tuesday when she says 'tomorrow'? She's a day ahead of us." "Does paragraph six mean we've got the budget?"

Together they decide which steps in the message are unclear, even contradictory. But the boss is airborne, now, and unreachable for a few hours. So everything freezes until she lands.

> REMEDY FOR THE TEAM: Start collaborating to untangle the contradictory steps in the message. Then, lay out your questions in a simple Yes/No format so the boss can respond easily once on the ground, with less texting. This checklist can serve, later, as a template for assuring that all tasks were done.
>
> REMEDY FOR MANAGERS: Before leaving for a trip, cultivate the habit of "backgrounding" or briefing the team. Then if quick decisions come up in changing conditions, the team knows your intentions. Your instructions, if any, will be grounded in a clear context.

How to Give Feedback When Bosses Falter

Alec Mackenzie recounted at a seminar what his much-admired assistant, Shirley Wilson, taught him, early in his career, about too-hasty communication. While preparing to leave for the airport one day, he stood over her desk, and rattled off a dozen instructions, then grabbed his briefcase and dashed out the door.

Getting into his car, he realized she was trotting along behind him. Calmly, completely composed, she got into the passenger seat and said in her usual quiet way: "Now why don't we go over all this again, and I'll make complete notes this time. You drive; I'll write. I'll bring your car back from the airport, and I'll pick you up when you get back to town." With that, she pulled out her notepad, and started asking questions.

Never again did he attempt that "instruction fly-by" routine with Shirley.

Five Reasons Why Casual Communication Is Never Casual!

1. *The words we use* have different meanings in different contexts, on paper. And even more so in person. EXAMPLE: Someone asks for help, and the other person's one-word response, "Sure," can signal sincerity, or seethe with sarcasm, depending on tone of voice.
2. *The channels* we use can carry subliminal meanings: an e-mail of congratulations feels chillier than a greeting card or a handwritten note.
3. *The distance between cultures and continents* should oblige us to cultivate those nuances we'd sense so easily, if we were face to face. A silence on the phone can rattle our nerves, but a face-to-face silence can speak volumes when we can see and read the facial expressions and body language the other person is conveying.
4. *The timing and context*—ours and the other person's—may contrast greatly during an encounter. If either party feels distracted, tired, suspicious, or threatened—for reasons unrelated to the current message—those feelings can bleed into the exchange, distorting or blocking the message.
5. *The quantity or volume of data* may baffle us, too. How much detail should we include in a message? Will basic coverage

insult readers' intelligence? Will advanced coverage assume background that may be missing for too many receivers?

CONCLUSION: Communication is natural but not simple. It occurs in the human realm, in both sensory and extra-sensory channels; in the animal and insect world; in the plant world, even at the cellular and atomic level . . . every entity communicates.

At work, however, communication is the medium we must use to get things done. So it behooves us to learn and practice the best methods we can find, to inform and inspire great performance at work.

EIGHT SECRETS OF SKILLFUL SENDING

Invest time to plan vital messages. Carelessness, callousness, or discourtesy will cause misunderstanding, loss of trust, and the ruin of relationships. Then, efforts to rebuild trust will prove arduous, time-consuming—and sometimes, unsuccessful. To assure skillful sending:

1. Clarify your purpose. What do you want the other party to know or do?
2. Select the right channel: face-to-face, a two-way phone call, voice-mail, e-mail, conference, teaching video, demonstration, or entertainment.
3. Choose words carefully to compose your message. Plan one or two rewrites, as necessary.
4. Enhance written messages by choosing tone consciously.
5. Transmit clearly; avoid slang or acronyms that may puzzle receivers.
6. Don't assume reception: solicit feedback.
7. Facilitate feedback with a built-in tool that will save the other person's time.
8. Enhance any "live" message with vocal tone and body language that reinforces your meaning.

ROBUST RECEIVING: ELEVEN AVENUES FOR LISTENING

Most of the time, casual listening does the job for us. But when a message is important, or the sender's physical behavior triggers extra alertness, call on these listening skills:

1. Cut off distractions: no calls, visitors, or daydreaming just now.
2. Quiet your prejudices. Open your mind. But, listen only to understand, not to evaluate.
3. Buy time, especially if the matter seems too important to handle quickly.
4. Deal respectfully with any high emotions involved, but don't rush toward the solution.

EXAMPLE: Say your chief engineer, Ali, has come in red-hot and frustrated with some policy of the company: You might say:

> Wow, I can see this really matters to you, Ali. I'm glad you let me know what's on your mind. This sounds important, so I'd like us to wait just a couple of hours until we can both give this the attention it needs. Let's get together later today.
>
> In the meantime, will you do one thing? Take a piece of paper and head it up: "What I Want to See Happen." Get some absolutes down on paper in three clear bullet points, OK? Your needs will drive our meeting. The clearer you can make your objectives—what you really want—the faster we can get to a yes that we can both live with.
>
> Okay, when are you free this afternoon?

> With this invitation, you'll focus Ali on the "what next" potential—the near future—more than the current situation that's bothering him.

5. Once in the planned conversation, control your urge to react, even to red-flag words.
6. Avoid the temptation to interrupt.
7. Listen for main points; work hard to "defocus" the trivia.
8. Take notes (briefly) to capture main points, those that agree as well as conflict with your views. That is, focus on reception, not evaluation.
9. Ask questions only to confirm understanding. (This is not a conversation yet. The other person still owns the "air time.")
10. Observe body language with compassion.
11. Read between the lines for what is not said.

GOOD LISTENING ACTUALLY TAKES LESS TIME

Once you've had the experience of listening without a personal agenda (with no need to judge or decide anything) you'll never feel pressured again—no matter how painful or shocking the message someone wants to deliver.

Listening Exercises Prove It

In several years of conducting a well-received AMA seminar on Assertiveness for Managers, we asked audience members to prepare a heartfelt message on some topic of importance to them. They could report on something, complain, request, propose, or express a strong opinion. They would be presenting their views in various simulated pairings: boss to employee, employee to boss, peer to peer, boss to team, etc.

In the many repeat opportunities during the three days, we instructed the "listener" to refrain from commenting or suggesting anything, and to ask only essential clarifying questions. Their sole job as listener was to understand. Accompanying each twosome was a timekeeper. In all cases, no matter now passionate the speaker, no matter how episodic the events presented, not one single speaker was able to speak for more than four minutes. In fact, most were amazed how much information and passion they had conveyed in only two minutes. The "listeners" avoided interrupting, conversing, or decision making. Their only job was comprehension.

In all cases, when instructed to summarize, the listeners proved to have clearly grasped the main message.

CONCLUSION: One-way listening is quick. It's the two-way conversing that takes up time—and causes most of the trouble! The next time you feel like interrupting, recall this simple observation: here's how the letters in listen can be rearranged:

> **LISTEN**
> **SILENT**

VISUAL CUES HELP MANAGERS LISTEN:
CASE IN POINT

One day, when leaving her vice president's office after a chat,
Kumiko Matsui, marketing manager for a consumer goods company,
noticed a tiny scrap of blue painter's tape up in the farthest left-hand

corner of the wall, next to the ceiling. She had never noticed it before, but then—she spent most of her visits looking in her VP's direction, not looking at *his* view of the ceiling. She couldn't help asking:

"Has that little piece of blue tape been up there long, Stan? I've never noticed it before."

"No," her boss replied. "I put it there to remind me of something." But he declined to say what, and she was too discreet to ask.

Months later, when the whole office was being repainted, the tape came down. Kumiko said: "Ah, the patch of blue tape has gone."

Stan finally revealed his motive: "At one point, last year, I realized I wasn't really *listening* to people," he confessed. "I was racing ahead, preparing my reactions and hoping to wrap up quickly. So I put that little square of tape up there, where only I could see it. And I focused on it every time I felt impatient. It helped me to slow down . . . delay my response so I could react with more respect and empathy."

"Hmm-humm," she chuckled. "And I thought those long skyward glances of yours had been careful analyses of my proposals!"

"But they were!" he assured her. "I needed that visual cue to remind me that it was still your turn! Maybe it was something my father used to say years ago: 'What most people need is a good listening-to!'"

And he smiled as he said it. So did she.

BODY LANGUAGE: ANOTHER FACE-TO-FACE ADVANTAGE

By the set of your mouth, the expression in your eyes, your posture as you sit in a chair, you say as much about your state of readiness as any words could convey. Some experts say that as much as 70 percent more information comes through from our body language than from our words. So, we need to read the signals. Ironically, the people around you may know more about your actual state of mind than you do. In politically fraught situations, you may struggle to find words that will convey what you mean without getting into trouble. Meanwhile your body language is sending a powerful message, visible to others, if not to yourself. And unless you are a practiced "yogi," you won't be able to stall, stop, or mask your body language.

Gestures: Read and React Right

What does it mean when someone who is sitting with arms casually draped across the back of a sofa, suddenly folds their arms tightly across the chest. Unless an arctic wind is blowing, this sudden, tight arm-fold can signify self-protectiveness or resistance to a threat. Of course, people fold their arms many times a day, with no special meanings attached. But *sudden* gestures carry a message.

Some people learn to control and calibrate their body language, but for most of us, the changes are involuntary—we remain unaware of what is visible to others. A red blotch will suddenly appear on the neck of someone who is angry. They may feel the heat, without realizing how easily this "red flag" can be observed.

Let Subliminal Signals Speak

The boss may listen to your warning about an impending problem. If he leans far back in his chair, folding his hands behind his head and neck, he may be signaling that what you are saying is unimportant to him . . . he's not worried. (Or—he may be sending a deliberate put-down.) Whichever way you interpret the signal, take it as: "Don't try harder. Ask and listen."

A customer, invited to join you for dinner, gradually pushes all the condiments, her water glass, the flower vase, and other tableware into your half of the table. She is widening her own sphere of influence, and sending you a dominance message, consciously or not. You may think it offensive, at first, and then begin to see it as defensive, or passive-aggressive—depending on what is being said. You could ignore it, you could move them all back into place, or you could—as the host—ask the waiting staff person to remove the items so you can spread out your work. It's up to you: do you want to turn the tables or not?

How to React to Resistance

Ironically, you have choices when another person's gestures or words convey negative emotions. If you interpret the message as resistant, you may be tempted to try harder with your own position, repeating and reinforcing your points. But your intense efforts will likely increase fear. So, the real key to handling resistance is to reduce the voltage in whatever approach you use. Assume friendly silence for a moment. Retreat for a bit. Move to your listening stance: invite the other party to talk. Don't lead the witness, just hand them some air time. In short, resist your own natural impulse to win a resister to your viewpoint. It's likely to waste your time and energy.

HANDLING CONFLICTS:
THE BIGGEST CHALLENGE

When facing conflict, it may help to recall Friedrich Nietzsche's famous remark: "Nothing on earth consumes a man more completely than the passion of resentment."

In every decision and action you take during a conflict with others, strive to reduce resentments—both theirs and yours. Otherwise, long after the matter is resolved, resentments may linger, like a corrosive chemical in the gut.

Aggression, Assertion, Non-Assertion:
One Choice to Avoid

What's the most dangerous word in a conflict? The word "you." It's the most aggressive word you can use to open a sentence. Some people have been known to use it in such phrases as *"You are wrong . . ."* or *"You had better . . ."* or *"You people on the third floor . . ."*—at which point, any hope of collaboration is dashed. The other person has no option but to counterattack.

Even if you were to open a sentence with a conciliatory or complimentary remark such as "You're wonderful!" the other person can't help but wish you had been more specific!

Mutual Assertions Increase the
Comfort Levels of Both Parties

In a negotiation, even when you must take a strong stand, the most comfortable way to open is with a courteous *assertion* such as: "Here's what I need . . ." or "I need only this one thing—I'm open to suggestions on everything else . . ."

By expressing a legitimate need rather than a mere preference or selfish choice, you make it easier for the other person to see your viewpoint. Always assert with an "I" statement. When you link the word "I" with an actual goal or requirement rather than a mere preference, the other person can "hear" you. Then, you can follow quickly with a courteous invitation: "Thanks for hearing me out. Now, tell me what *you* need." The other party senses that they'll be getting "equal time." You'll hear them out, with respectful patience, and you will meet the requirements of *their* assertions. After that, it becomes easier for both of you to move toward to a closing element: "So—to take care of your needs and mine, can we both agree that . . . ?"

Non-Assertion Leads Nowhere

The most nonassertive statements involve openings such as:

"I wish I could . . ."

"If only those other people had . . ."

"Maybe if we . . ."

"I hope I'm not bothering you but . . ."

The most annoying non-assertions are scarcely statements at all. They are pseudo-statements framed in the form of questions.

For example, a manager asks a nonassertive subordinate, "What's today's interest rate?" The subordinate, who is supposed to know, answers, "Uhhh, 6 percent?"

The Passive/Aggressive Playbook

Perhaps the most frustrating communication habits involve those people who start an encounter nonassertively—passively—then attack when the other party comes within range. For example, a group from the department heads out to lunch. They invite Prue to come along. "We have a choice of Mexican or deli today," they tell her. "What's your preference?" Prue responds, "I don't care, I'm open."

But once they sit down at the Mexican place, she complains that the food is too spicy for her, and she'd have preferred a sandwich. Those tiny annoyances drive people crazy. Trivial, but memorable, they often lie dormant until a more serious issue arises at work. Then, a conflict erupts, seemingly out of the blue.

Why Inner Conflicts Scare Us Most

The toughest conflicts we face are those we rarely reveal at work, at least not at first. These are our internal/ethical conflicts. Something occurs at work that seriously offends our personal sense of ethics, rightness, or fairness. We usually brood over these, hoping to adjust the details in an order or an offer, until they come closer to meeting our ethical standards. Often, we're able to approach the goal or reach a compromise without breathing a word of our actual discomfort. Perhaps the other side is doing likewise, but they, too, keep the real issue hidden.

Interpersonal Conflicts: Thick on the Ground

By contrast, interpersonal conflicts surface easily, commonly. And they trigger people's lowest instincts.

Animal activists often brag that animals don't fight each other the way humans do. But just put two apes in a cage with only one banana: you'll see conflict! Put twenty conventioneers in a high-rise elevator and watch the jockeying for control of the buttons and access to the doors. Whenever you put two humans in a situation with apparent scarcity of goods, you'll see us revert to our lower natures, in living color—however much we try to hide our self-interest by couching the conflict in words that drip with civility or sarcasm.

One thing is certain: any hint of unfairness will set most people off. Perhaps that's why—at any of our Supervision seminars—we need only mention the word "fairness" and the audience groans in unison.

Of course, senior managers try to ensure that corporate decisions—policies, procedures, assignments, awards, and especially, division of the spoils—will appear fair to the majority. But even the wisest decisions will bring a disadvantage to a few—and will elicit conflict among groups. So decisions must be crafted carefully, and language must be chosen with deliberation.

Recall a recent conflict you had to manage. Which vocabulary did you hear being used—by others and by yourself?

Positive Vocabulary Reduces Aggression and Non-Assertion

AVOID SAYING:	INSTEAD, SAY
You have to ...	I can, I want to I'd be glad to ...
No, you can't do that ...	I see a risk for you ...
You'd have to ...	Together, we can fix this ...
You're wrong ...	I see a safer way ...
You'll have to calm down ...	I see how important this is ...
I don't have to listen to this ...	This sounds serious ...
But ... And ... (or Yet ...)	
You made me feel ... when you ...	Whenever I face this, I feel ...
You should ...	I need ...
Can't you ...?	Here's a possible option ...
You'd better ...	I'd suggest ... because ...
I can't ...	I'd prefer ...
Why don't you ...?	I see a possible advantage for you ...
I don't know ...	Let me research this ...
You'd have to wait until ...	Here's when I could start ...
You're always finding fault ...	Thanks for the heads up ...
I'm sorry ...	Please accept my apology ...

RELY ON THE POWER OF THE EYE

Regardless of how carefully you choose your words, the ear is a poor receptor compared with the eye. So notice body language when you are receiving a "live" message. And use graphic tools to keep your teams informed and inspired in live encounters. Millions of smart managers improve performance levels by posting milestone charts, Gantt charts, and progress charts to help teams stay on target and to celebrate team successes. Though you may live in an all-electronic world, remember that your people may skim from screen to screen just to get their work done—so they may miss the impact of your messages unless you post them on an actual wall.

Suggestions for Engaging the Eye

- *Keep news fresh*. Don't leave posted charts up too long, unchanged. People numb out.
- *Feature any upswing*. Use a big upward arrow and a congratulatory headline.
- *Highlight the winners*. Help your people to notice and enjoy their victories.
- *Signal with simple devices*. Code words known only to the team; colors, numbers, signals, flags, balloons—anything the team chooses—can signal progress, restoring energy during a long project.
- *Create heads-up message centers*. Designate a specific location to convey heads-up messages. Use kiosks, bulletin boards, wall signs, mannequins to draw attention to news. Urgent messages can get buried in e-mail glut.

Graphic Targets Motivate

One VP based in San Francisco would post the nightly production target right over the entry door of the night crew's secure data center. Crazy prizes were offered for reaching tough targets and these were eagerly pursued and displayed. The boss also bowed to joke penalties imposed on him by the team. If they managed to do the impossible, the boss complied with the penalty. Graphic devices, with the respect and symbolism they invoked, added verve to the workplace while boosting team unity. This VP never worried about his ego; great results rewarded his open communication style.

How One Smart Manager Helps People to Focus

Another of my most admired managers, a VP who handles production for a major international bank, keeps a whiteboard in his office. (I heard about it from his subordinates, long before I got to meet him myself.) Whenever an employee visits him with "a big problem" he listens intently for a sentence or two—then brings the person over to this whiteboard.

"Is this what you mean? "he asks. "Did you say that the process starts here?" and he diagrams his "take" on the issue being discussed. The visitor may alter the sketch, or confirm the view. Mutual understanding is reinforced.

Everyone on his team has been invited, at one time or another, to "make things clear" on that whiteboard. They testified to its power as a collaborative tool.

Eventually, I got to visit this VP in his office. Naturally, I looked for the fabled board, and noticed a powerful feature that no one had mentioned. The top and bottom rims of the board bore this message, hand-lettered in permanent ink by the VP:

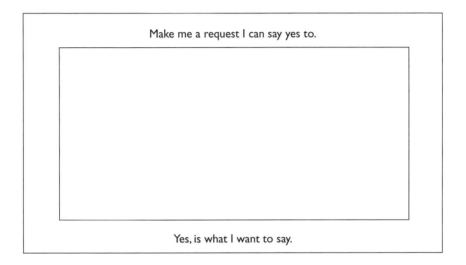

Make me a request I can say yes to.

Yes, is what I want to say.

He Keeps Your Eye on the Future

There's the message that reiterates his point: he helps his team to focus on what is still possible, to know what they want before they come to see him, with some clarity about what bank policy would allow him to say yes to. They tell me that their conversations end in a yes most of the time. What fabulous training for their own futures as managers!

SUMMARY: To recall the essentials of this chapter, simply bear in mind:

- *Your focus:* The future—"From this moment on" is all we have left.
- *Your mind-set:* Compassion for all human beings including yourself.
- *Your practice:* Clarity about what you need can help people say yes.

In the next chapter, we cover meetings, those gatherings that allow teams to think together, to express reactions before forming solutions. Being in the same room can help us gauge reactions, sense emotions, and detect needs that people might otherwise find impossible to express in words.

CHECK YOURSELF

How do you score on effective communication? Rate yourself on the following questions; then, repeat the process thirty days from now. Simple Yes/No answers will suffice.

Questions		Today	30 Days
1.	As a sender, I focus, then clarify my purpose before I begin.	———	———
2.	I compose the message, choose the medium and set the timing to minimize discomfort for the other party, so they can hear me.	———	———
3.	I provide feedback tools so people can respond or even resist, freely.	———	———
4.	As a listener, I focus on understanding, not responding.	———	———
5.	When providing feedback, I use assertive "I need" statements, avoid aggressive "you" openers, and check myself against using nonassertive or passive-aggressive stances.	———	———
6.	When I see resistant behavior, I avoid "trying harder" and give the other person "air time."	———	———
7.	I focus always on "what is still possible" and invite others to do the same.	———	———
	Total	———	———

CHAPTER 10

Poorly Run Meetings

In the previous edition, Alec Mackenzie reported that the average manager spends ten hours a week in meetings. (That's more than a day per week, times 40-50 weeks per year, 450-500 hours a year in meetings.) The majority complained that nearly half that time bled away through poor organization and execution.

Now, a decade later, you spend more of your workdays isolated with your computer screen, mesmerized by its tide of e-mails, projects, and calendar items, prodding you into action. But your computer is a robot: It must obey. You have control.

Not so with meetings! Whether live or virtual, meetings are the last live laboratory for observing rampant human behavior.

MEETINGS: WHICH TYPES DO YOU ATTEND?

We see four main meeting types, common to most workplaces.

1. Quick "stand-up" team meetings—where you cover emergency notices, good news, assignments, or reassignments due to sudden changes in conditions—are usually short, practical, collaborative, sometimes contentious, but usually effective.

2. By contrast, the obligatory "weekly staff meeting"—once it becomes routine, repetitive, predictable, and prosaic—simply interrupts real life for an hour. Everyone keeps sneaking a peek at their PDAs (under the table, of course) hoping to get something real done, or to ward off slumber.

3. The cross-disciplinary or problem-solving meeting is designed to unify groups around a common mission and motivate them to collective action. Some event—an opportunity or threat—usually drives these meetings. Something new and scary always stimulates human behavior—the best and the worst—so you can expect some raw reactions: unstructured, uncertain, uncontrolled, even unruly. These meetings can be unforgettable, too, depending on how well managed.

4. Finally, "all-hands" big-deal meetings with the C-level officers addressing thousands of employees—designed to foster motivation, celebration, stimulation, pride, and PR—are show-biz events, happily beyond the scope of this chapter.

In this chapter we'll work to improve where we can on meeting types 1, 2, and 3.

LET'S ADMIT IT: MEETINGS SATISFY OUR SOCIAL HUNGER

We must improve meetings, not abolish them. Human beings exhibit a built-in need to assemble, especially in times of trouble or triumph. So face it: meetings are here to stay. Virtual or actual—in times of trouble or opportunity, we can make meetings quick, constructive, comforting, and compelling.

We Meet to Share Our Strengths and Needs

When we assemble in a space, actual or virtual, with colleagues, bosses, or customers, we learn, through observation:

*   Whom we can trust.
*   How we and others respond to various conditions.
*   How quickly and brilliantly we can react, create, and commit to new or continuing efforts.

- Who can lead and inspire, whether by official appointment or by personal influence.

At meetings we learn about our own leadership capabilities. We learn how to offer input, how to take a role in team decisions, how to react gracefully when put on the spot. So, yes—"being there" will probably keep meetings essential whenever groups or teams must get work done together.

CONCLUSION: Let's not abolish meetings: Let's upgrade them!

Meetings Must Be Mutual

Whether your meetings are virtual or actual, you need to be there, in real time, to:

1. Coordinate action.
2. Exchange information when reactions are bound to differ.
3. Discuss and resolve problems requiring different areas of expertise.
4. Make joint decisions that work for the majority.

The common element among the four is mutuality, All four motives require multiple inputs, viewpoints, and agreements before buy-in can occur.

CAUTION: The fourth item, joint decision making, can hide a trap. We can easily convince ourselves that all decisions are better when shared. But remember, if deciding is in your job—your responsibility—you must control your urge to fragment your responsibilities among others.

Here's a typical misuse of meetings:

A manager or SME faces an uncomfortable decision. Too tired or scared to think it through, the manager sees an opportunity: the regular weekly staff meeting is coming up. So this item finds its way onto the agenda. Getting everybody's input raises the cost of the decision, while reducing the burden on the decision maker. In the end, the manager will still decide. But now, if the decision goes against the consensus, the team will have every right to be miffed. They'll certainly be less motivated to help, next time.

REAL VOICES

Program manager Andrea Cifor suspects "decision dumping" in some of the meetings she's witnessed in her business life. Here's her view:

> *Too much consensus-seeking in a large group can be a huge waste of time. Is it really necessary for everyone to feel all warm and fuzzy about a decision? I think it is time for managers to step to the forefront and just drive again in business. Democracy has its place, but so does the hierarchy that empowers the decision maker.*

Don't Call Meetings Just Because You Can!

Having witnessed the kind of cases outlined above, you may want to make yourself some rules about calling any meeting: Here are five ways to make meetings bearable:

1. Call a meeting only on topics requiring two-way communication.
2. Call a meeting only when the topic cannot be covered in a memo.
3. Hold team meetings on a reliable schedule—but without a set length. This gives every member a chance to suggest items of concern for your pre-agenda. Teams work better when they know they can rely on airing an issue of concern to several team members.
4. Keep meetings short. If you only need 20 minutes, that's all you take.
5. Prepare well. Today's teams are smart and easily bored.

There are some tasks done better by team than by solo operators. They include work planning and coordination, new policy development, settling issues involving fairness (like task allocation, coverage, duty rotations)—the kinds of decisions people want debated, not dumped on them. Meetings are also best for creative problem solving, giving recognition, and celebrating victories.

If you get it wrong, however, you'll elicit complaints from your "meeting hostages."

REAL VOICES

From Claire Chen, PhD, a medical researcher:

> *Unannounced meetings keep bumping other vital tasks and wrecking my work schedule. I spend hours per week calling or e-mailing team members, physicians, and clients to reschedule deliverables because these meetings chew up our time. They also run over their allotted time because no one is prepared with decent data.*

Claire readily admits that some unforeseen events or opportunities might require a meeting, but she insists that a *pattern* of ad hoc meetings must be exposed and either justified or corrected. With any emergency meeting, the first task must be setting an agenda, so people can see— at the start—whether they have sufficient data to discuss or decide, at all.

A Take-Your-Lumps Tool: Create a Critique Card

If you really want to justify your meetings (emergency or routine), then offer attendees a simple, easy, and anonymous tool for commenting. Keep it simple. A postcard or single-screen template is enough. Offer only three choices; attendees can check one.

> ❏ Glad I was here. My input was required; data offered was sufficient.
>
> ❏ Held prematurely. Data not adequate for decision or vote.
>
> ❏ Unsure why I was invited. Material not aligned with my responsibilities.

Some people will feel strongly enough to sign their card. If they do, invite them to say more and listen, intently. Then, sleep on it before you comment further.

Think about some of the meetings that you have to attend. Would they benefit by letting members score them?

HOW TO REORGANIZE YOUR THINKING ABOUT MEETINGS

Here are some ideas that may help you.

- *For senior managers: Try appointing stand-ins* for certain subject areas. Post a list of people authorized to vote in your place, on specific subjects. Many high-tech, hierarchical organizations do this routinely.
- *For regular meetings, prepare a timed agenda.* Specify time limits for each topic. Circulate the agenda in advance. Two groups benefit. First, presenters can prepare and time their remarks so they don't exceed the time limit. Second, each voting member can attend only the sections that apply to them. This approach, called "floating attendance," is common in many organizations where a costly two- or three-day event will drive a whole year's work for many different teams. In these meetings, an aide watches the clock and counts quorums to assure that a quorum of authorized voters can get a decision passed.
- *Invite members to validate frequency and duration.* While your staff meeting should be held on the same day and time each week (for reliability), it need not cover the same duration each time. Respect for people's time increases their willingness to attend. If they get the job done in 20 minutes, let them say so—and end the meeting. Do this for virtual as well as actual meetings.

When You Take the Chair

By following (and posting) a few simple rules, you can overcome most of the evils that make team members hate meetings. Imagine the following notice on the wall:

In this meeting room we:

- Start on time
- Liberate contributors
- Stick to the agenda
- End on time
- Thank you for your input

Let's take a look at these points in a little more depth.

Start Time   Don't hold up the meeting for latecomers, even high-ranking latecomers. Otherwise, you penalize those who made the effort to show up on time. Before long, more and more people will drift in late. Furthermore, resist the temptation to repeat or review data for latecomers.

Liberate Contributors No Longer Required   Organize the agenda around groups or teams involved in a topic. Invite them to prepare and present their views. (You should not be the main—much less the sole—presenter.) Then, release contributors (and participants) as soon as their topics have been dealt with. This "floating attendance" helps companies to get through a welter of work in a single day, whether assembled, "live" or in a Web-based setting. Liberated people are grateful to return to their own work.

Stick to the Agenda   Once allotted time is up, move on to the next item. When people see you are serious about this, they prepare more focused presentations, perfectly timed.

End on Time   Assign a timekeeper. Obey when time is called. When participants know that your meetings end on time, allowing them to meet other commitments, they'll gladly attend. Another chance for you to build trust and respect.

Thank Meeting Members for Specific Contributions   Not only does this advance sincerity, it also lets them know which good behaviors to repeat.

MANAGING HUMAN BEHAVIORS AT MEETINGS

Maybe meetings were simpler among the cave dwellers of prehistory. (They were probably too focused on fleeing from cave bears to do much politicking.)

But there's plenty of proof that people have been meeting and voting, and probably exhibiting the same human behaviors you see in your meeting rooms today since before Hammurabi's Code thirty-eight centuries ago. Even if the ancients chiseled their decisions into stone tablets while we display ours by hologram, we'd all recognize the issues—and welcome some of the solutions below:

How to Beach a Red Herring

If someone brings up a topic not on the agenda, make sure you have a whiteboard off to the side of your main board or screen where you can "park" odd items that arise. You might say:

"Interesting point, Jerry. But that would take us off the agenda, and most of us are not prepared with good data. So, I'll ask you to post that on the Future Issues Board, where it can compete for a spot on a later agenda."

If Jerry insists that the issue will only take a few minutes, then you may opt to put his motion to a vote.

"OK, Jerry: If we want to be democratic about this, let's put it to a vote. How many of us agree that this issue must be discussed right now, even though it will make us late?"

Now, both you and Jerry will bow to group opinion.

(Incidentally, some people call this side board a "parking lot," but we suggest finding a better term. Parking lots are usually located outside the building, either in the merciless sun, or in the cold and rain. There's an unwelcoming flavor to parking ideas out there.)

How to Break a Stalemate

When one faction tries to force acceptance of its position, and the other won't bow, you face a stalemate. If both sides carry equal weight, and if this is a one-topic meeting, you could adjourn and reconvene when people have slept on it. Often the matter can be resolved quickly once people have regained perspective.

If they cook up a good solution, take time to record it: the who, how, what, when and why of the resolution.

How to Combine Agendas and Minutes

Take an idea from Admiral Hyman Rickover, who was famous for running tight meetings. He developed a wonderfully concise format that served as both agenda and minutes.

Topics were listed with a starting time. As the meeting unfolded, the decisions on each item were recorded with Y, N, or H—yes, no, or hold. Initials on the board showed who was responsible for follow-up. Finally, the due date was established.

Some companies, having adopted this system, have added a column on the far right for comments designed to cut off further discussion by disgruntled meeting members who want to keep refuting the majority opinion.

Agenda/Minutes: Admiral Rickover-Style

Time	Item	Decision	Responsibility	Deadline	Comment
10:00	A	Yes	BJ	9/15	
10:20	B	No	—	—	
10:35	C	Hold	DD	10/21	
10:45	D	Yes	CB	10/01	
11:00	Adjourn				

HOW TO DECLINE ATTENDING A MEETING

Why are you invited or summoned to a meeting? If your senior role, your authority, and/or your subject matter expertise are required, you may feel obliged to go, without question. But think again. Is this meeting in the top 20 percent of what you must do at that hour? Always ascertain the true purpose and status of a meeting before you agree to attend. You may be able to provide the requested data or authority without being there yourself. Ask the host what is required from you—and whether you can provide it in any other form—perhaps with written data, a supportive statement, an authorized stand-in, or an endorsement via video.

Four Ideas to Get You Started

1. *Attend only a portion of a timed meeting,* either to contribute, or to protect your interests from bad decisions pushed through by others. If your boss (or another meeting host) will be offended by your cutting out, you can sometimes beg off because you are doing other work for the same host in the same contested hour.

You may need to remind them of that fact because many bosses will delegate time-consuming work—and then consider it magically done once off-loaded onto you. You can't meet new deadlines and attend the usual meetings at the same time. Demonstrate that in detached fashion.

2. *Use your boss as your excuse.* With other hosts, you can sometimes use your boss as your excuse, but this must be legitimate: it will probably be repeated to your boss. You might say: "Sorry, I have to meet a deadline given by my boss. I'd need to clear it—and frankly—I think her priorities will come ahead, this time."

3. *Avoid onerous one-on-one meetings.* If someone requests a one-on-one with you—especially if it would involve delay or travel—ask what it would take to make a joint decision without a meeting. Suggest: "Let's see if we can get it done on the phone, now? We're here now, and we have the data in front of us. Why don't we just decide?"

4. *Send a sealed opinion: one CEO's custom.* One smart CEO will sometimes send an opinion to a meeting she wants to influence, but cannot attend. She instructs the meeting moderator to hold her opinion until near the end. When all the members have finished their debate, the moderator can decide whether to use the CEO's message. For example, if the vote is going "our way"— the moderator can close with the CEO's written vote of confidence. It supports the majority vote. The CEO is then satisfied that she had been correct in not attending, but her influence can still help affirm the action.

On the other hand, if the vote goes contrary to the CEO's position— and if there is new data that she may need to hear, the moderator can adjourn the meeting without a final decision, promising the team to present their new data to the CEO, without delay.

The moderator keeps the CEO's message sealed. This avoids tipping the CEO's hand, and leaves the matter open. When we heard this story, we realized how much confidence this CEO placed in the good judgment of the moderator.

Embrace More Virtual Meetings—
Web and Video Conferencing

With today's double whammy of higher fuel costs and fleet cutbacks, airline problems are stimulating demand for group voice and video conferencing. With only voice conferencing, you miss body language, of course. And, instead of listening, a lot of energy is spent on hasty texting during the discussions. Half the people in your space are trying to clue the moderator and their colleagues on ways to respond to the distant voices—and no doubt half the people on the other end of the call are doing the same: working their thumbs to coach the spokesperson on their side.

And with voice conferencing, it's harder to interpret pauses and silences. These can hike anxiety, accelerating capitulation by whichever players "blink" first.

So even though high travel costs may reduce the number of trips you make this year, don't swear off travel, altogether. There are times when there's no substitute for being there to shake hands or bow, to meet the glance of the other person, to share a drink or a meal, and to get to know your counterparts.

POLITICAL SAVVY SAVES TIME

Consider two instances where your actions may enhance a meeting, if your authority is adequate to win support.

Instance 1: Meeting Slow to Start?

If you feel time slipping away but you're not in charge, there's something you can do—if you judge it wisely. Let's say the person who called the meeting arrives on time but doesn't start on time. People are standing around chatting, waiting, tapping their pencils while someone has collared the chairperson. Provided you're a regular contributor at this meeting, you could say—loudly but with a note of surprise—"Hey, it's ten o'clock." Some will stop and check their watches. The chairperson, probably chatting with someone up front will say: "Ok, let's get started, here."

Or, if the person who called the meeting fails to show on time, you could say something like, "Janice is probably tied up somewhere. What do you say? Let's get started, and when she gets here, we can catch her up. This first item, what do we all think about this?" (You'd need to be the next-lower ranking member to attempt this.)

Then, when Janice does arrive, you could say:

"We figured you got held up, so we went ahead and started on the Carson proposal. We haven't voted yet, of course. Let me summarize what's been said."

CAUTION: Do this only for a strong manager who prefers progress to protocol. Of course, if the meeting chair is famous for being late and ineffective, don't risk it. Just get some work done *on your own*, or engage in some useful politicking.

Instance 2: Tempted to Launch Unorthodox Ideas at Meetings?

A savvy mid-level manager recently commented:

> In my experience, VPs and top decision makers don't want new ideas sprung on them in a group. Yeah—they can handle it, but why should they? Meetings are held to cement a proposal that's already been exposed to some senior scrutiny in private. Usually, it has been further researched for feasibility, before being introduced to wider groups.

Bolstering this advice, a tech manager testified:

> In our company, if you want the CEO's support on something dramatic, you lay it out for him beforehand, as clearly and briefly as possible, giving him time to think it through, ask questions, and consult with others. By the time we're in a big meeting, he may listen as if he's never heard of it before. But he's got his ducks all in a row. The meeting is really held to convince the rest of the folks, so the boss's support, at that point, is the clincher.

SOME SUGGESTIONS FOR KEEPING GOOD ORDER

Once you and your team have established that you'll use timed agendas and that everyone will respect those times, there's a good chance that presenters will prepare their remarks and demos to fit the schedule as well. We've seen some further favorite rules in many a smart company, including the following:

- List agenda items in order of impact: if time runs out, damage is minimal.
- Members will not interrupt presenters: instead they reserve questions for a question period that can be slotted after each agenda item or held to a timed Q&A session at the end of the meeting.
- Members will not interrupt one another in mid-sentence, or will raise hands to be heard next.
- No "been there, done that" reactions, please. Don't criticize: offer a better idea.

Make your own etiquette rules to fit your company's culture. Years ago I spotted one memorable wall sign in a meeting room at an IBM meeting room in Vermont. I've never forgotten it: It said simply:

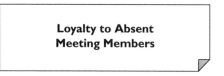

**Loyalty to Absent
Meeting Members**

I took that to mean: Don't lay any blame on people who aren't sitting here. (A really nice antidote, I thought, to the less-than-admirable human behaviors that meetings sometimes elicit.)

CHECK YOURSELF

How do you score on escaping the poorly-run meeting trap? Rate yourself on the following questions; then repeat the process thirty days from now. Simple Yes/No answers will suffice.

Questions	Today	30 Days
1. For any meeting I call, attendees get a timed agenda in advance.	_____	_____
2. For a rare emergency meeting, we open by creating the agenda.	_____	_____
3. My meetings start and end on time.	_____	_____
4. Our timed agendas, sent before large meetings, allow "floating attendance" so people stay only for the parts that apply to them.	_____	_____
5. When topics come up that aren't on the agenda, we put them on a "side-issues board" for treatment at later meetings, or for "off-line" solutions.	_____	_____
6. I present top management with new or unorthodox ideas in private, not in meetings.	_____	_____
7. We observe "meeting etiquette" to get things done without strife.	_____	_____
Total	_____	_____

CHAPTER

11

The World Gone Virtual

For centuries, the world and its maritime commerce ran on Greenwich Mean Time. Then came the atomic clock, to run the space race and endow the Internet with new precision. Today, millions of us inhabit a new phenomenon—*virtual time*—and are able to immerse ourselves every waking hour, in an electronic work-and-play space that can entice, amuse, inform, and enchant at blinding speed—on the good days—or entangle, enfeeble, and engulf us on the bad days when our network goes down, or our batteries bleed out.

Yet, thanks to the brilliance of electronics engineers, cybertechnology is amazingly reliable. Only a few bother to protest the industry's fondness for planned obsolescence that keeps us on a roller coaster of learning curves.

True, there are some famous holdouts. According to press accounts, some well-known CEOs have declined to digitize themselves: Donald Trump (who needs no introduction) and Colleen Barrett, CEO of Southwest Airlines, are numbered among the maverick few. In fact, many less illustrious top managers still prefer pen and paper. Some even use land-based phones on occasion, or—like Richard Branson of Virgin Airways—they keep the cell phone a cautious two feet away at all times. Some closet Luddites argue that trusty scratch pads and sticky notes need no electricity, no maintenance, no batteries; they rarely attract theft and can be employed during boring phone calls with no telltale tapping of the keyboard to tip one's hand.

Some of us may want to tread a practical middle path, sensibly blending high- and low-tech tools, but the sway of the cyberworld forces most people to conform. Some futurists predict that we'll soon have a discreet chip embedded in our foreheads for thought transference without bothersome tapping, typing, or swiping of screens and keyboards.

HOW'S YOUR E-LEARNING CURVE?

When your shiny new hardware or software arrives, you must break it in. You must invest time before you can reap the new momentum promised by the upgrade. It will save you time, eventually, but not at first.

If you run a small business, you could accelerate learning by taking some classes at your computer store or night school: that will save you endless searches through incomprehensible manuals. Or, get one of the excellent *Idiot's Guides* or *For Dummies* books, or learning videos: they speed up the process, too.

Once surfing the net becomes a fascinating activity for you, as it is for millions, then maintaining focus will become your next big challenge. We in the Internet generation are always trolling for the next big thing: flitting is our favored form of motion, and speed our driving demon.

Speed Drives Expectations

At work, with the ease and speed of e-mail and smart phones, your bosses and customers can solicit answers from you, day and night. While your rapid response may give you a competitive edge, your speedy service may also stoke customer hunger for even more service, even faster! Indeed, your contacts may already expect you to respond at the speed of inquiry.

Unless you indicate otherwise, people will assume that you need no time to:

1. Research.
2. Consult with others.
3. Make decisions.
4. Take actions.
5. Offer options.

So, if you do need time for any of those things—and you probably do—you'll want to say so, emphatically, early and often, to guide other people's expectations.

Use Technology to Your Advantage

Managed with some forethought, the tools of technology are helping millions to succeed in managing multiple priorities, at accelerated speeds. Here's some testimony to which you may easily relate:

REAL VOICES

From Kris Todisco, Director of Quality Assurance for a major East Coast investment firm:

> *My favorite time-saver tool? I'd have to say my BlackBerry. I can keep on top of my e-mail and my schedule whether I'm riding as a passenger in the car pool, commuting on a train, or waiting for a meeting to start. It allows me to use time that would otherwise be unproductive. I can also dial into a virtual meeting from almost anywhere.*
>
> *At work, I'd be lost without Outlook. I'm a great fan of the color-coded follow-up flags. I've assigned a color to each team member; then, during our one-on-one status meetings, it's a snap to review all their outstanding work items.*

YOUR UNAVOIDABLE E-REQUIREMENTS

With tools this helpful, it is incumbent on you to take good care of them. Whatever level of responsibility you hold, your organization will rely on you to:

- Secure the data and equipment assigned to you.
- Inhibit your own Internet addiction.

Let's detail some tools and tactics to support each of these requirements

Secure the Data and Equipment Entrusted to You

- If you work in a large company, their security system is already mandated. If you own a small company, however, you must install a security system of your choice. (Don't worry; your newly purchased screen will advertise relentlessly until you choose one.)

- Promptly heed your security provider's warnings when trolling the Internet or downloading attachments. Viruses and worms can put you out of business.
- Set up your Preferences to block unwanted traffic, then filter and file the data you need.
- Unless file backup is built in, set your computer to back up all work-in-progress. People still lose valuable work through carelessness. Recovery, if possible at all, can take hours or days.
- Delete old mail, attachments, and files, monthly or more often, to avoid stuffing your storage capacity. Store them by subject line, project, or client, whatever suits your needs the best.
- Autoarchive materials that might be needed in the future.

How Hard-Shelled Is Your Hardware?   When traveling, how often do you hear a loudspeaker calling someone to a checkpoint for a lost cell phone or laptop? You may shudder at this hapless exposure of data—so common at major airports. As a remedy, thousands of vendors offer security locks, tags, and cables; programs for encryption, detection, authentication, and distortion-prevention—along with data-erasing tools for the day when you must recycle your aging super-phone or laptop. Check these protections and choose one.

Some Equipment Essentials for All Who Travel   Your computer, hand-held devices, and cell phones must be password-protected and kept out of the wrong hands. Protect your company's data and your own: protect the hardware, too.

- Don't store vulnerable data on your devices.
- Keep your personal data elsewhere: your social security number, credit card numbers, and banking information can be tapped by determined thieves.
- As for physical security, apply a visual ID—a length of colored tape, a tag or decal to your laptop or notebook to distinguish it from same-brand others when you are traveling—especially when your own team travels in a group with same-brand equipment.

- Don't expose devices to damage or loss by letting cab or van drivers load them with the rest of your baggage.
- Don't leave your laptop sitting around in your hotel room, a favorite target for thieves. Secure it with a steel cable attached to something that can't be moved. Or put your laptop in the hotel safe if you cannot take it with you.

Remember, when your hardware is disabled or compromised, you lose time, money and composure before you get operational again.

Inhibit Your Own Internet Addiction

As with all good things—food and drink, work and play, self-care and service to others—we humans have a hard time striking a balance. Trolling the Internet, an activity unknown to prior generations, has addicted millions of us.

In the United States, the majority of households now have access to the Internet. That's the good news. Here's the bad: a well-publicized study by the Stanford University School of Medicine found that one in eight U.S. adults is internet-addicted. And worse, many youngsters, "baby-sat" by television and computers, get hooked early. Social networking sites draw millions of devotees, and make a tempting playground, not only for the good kids, but also for school bullies, and for predators aspiring to become "best friends" with people much younger than themselves. Households have installed parental controls to monitor Internet use by the children, but these are not foolproof: many children, far more computer-savvy than their parents, continue to wander at will.

Patchwork Controls in Communities

A few city councils and school districts across the United States have banned texting and cell-phone use by youngsters driving vehicles in the vicinity of the school, with fines up to $200 per offense. High auto accident rates among teens triggered these moves. (Apparently, some daredevil youngsters kept on texting while negotiating highway off-ramps and congested parking lots.) Daily, states are passing laws requiring hands-free phoning, but there are still dashboard buttons to push, and messages to read at speed . . . and new court cases pending to challenge each new restriction.

Asia: Internet Anxiety and Excitement

India, among the world's top five advanced Internet nations, rates nearly 40 percent of its cyberfans as heavy users. In one reaction, government-funded hostels run by the prestigious Indian Institute of Technology pulled the plug on Internet games after 11:00 P.M. (Access was curtailed when too many sleepy scholars failed to show up for morning classes.)

China's national legislators recently drafted an amendment to automate termination of on-line games after a fixed period of play. Authorities estimate that 10 percent of China's 210 million computer users show addictive behavior on the Internet. And at this writing, more than 1,500 young users have had their enthusiasms curbed at Internet addiction clinics or boot camps in various cities.

By contrast, in commerce-minded Japan, hip mobile phone users can "point and shoot" a bar code on a magazine page or billboard. In a wink, they are linked to a website for more information and "instant shopping." The ultimate in impulse buying, this capability will soon come to magazines and billboards near you!

You Don't Need a Computer to Play—or Learn

Most Internet activity no longer requires a computer. Instead, in the United States, cell phone subscribers now number 250 million, or 80+ percent of the population, with smarter phones emerging almost daily. Consumers trade up to phones with touch-screen simplicity, Internet access, unlimited music, GPS, social networking, and integral digital cameras.

Podcasts allow iPod owners to tune in, free, to current lectures by outstanding university professors. Fabulous opportunities abound to stay updated on the latest research and the best thinking available: a learning advantage open to all, undreamed of only a few years ago.

On This Amazing Internet, We Must Manage Ourselves!

Here's the reality. The Internet has outdistanced the dreams of its early advocates. Instant contact, worldwide, is now a reality, open to rich or poor, young or old, educated or ignorant, saint or villain, except in the remotest places. At schools and public libraries, at cafes and adult education centers, access is free and instruction, nearly free. There are no limits to the Internet's potential for good—yet there are few limits on its dangers, either.

Therefore, each of us must make conscious decisions about when and how to use this extraordinary facility.

COOL TOOLS NEED CAREFUL USERS

Because there is so much we can do and learn on the Internet, we must budget our time and summon our common sense to serve our best interests.

- Search engines can respond to any keyword we care to type, giving us instant access to hundreds of thousands—sometimes millions—of entries, complete with dated references and links to even more sources.

    But, while enormously helpful to disciplined users, at least for an initial pass, our searches can gobble up hours or days as curiosity keeps driving us onward.

- We can socialize for hours on chat and blog sites, "twittering" on diverse topics with other stimulating thinkers.

    But, unlike print media writers, "netizens" are unhampered by editorial disciplines or rules about libel or plagiarism. So the "facts" you find may be unchecked and the original authors may remain uncredited.

- We can "shop 'til we drop" both day and night, buying and selling everything from pottery to platinum, bikinis to beachfront estates. Indeed, for nearly two million small business owners, eBay and other providers have opened a wildly successful global marketplace.

    But both buyers and sellers must take care to use the safety offered by escrow until delivery is secured, and the product is found to match its description.

- We can program our cell phones to permit keyless entry to our car or home, using radio frequency identification. We can manage our bank accounts and invest our money, also from the phone.

    Just don't lose your phone. And remember to change your password often.

- Without leaving home, we can use the Internet or smart phone to summon up every service we may need. What a boon to shut-ins! We can even text-message for a pizza!

Perhaps ordering a pizza was obsessing the young woman who roller-bladed right up my back on a busy San Francisco sidewalk, recently. After a quick mumbled apology, she went right on thumb-typing as she sped to the next corner.

- On social sites, we can set up a date or search for a mate, by answering multiple-choice questions on dimensions of compatibility—intellectual, economic, emotional, or erotic.
  But, to paraphrase poet Robert Burns, humans rarely see themselves as others see them. So, better to view those words and pictures on the screen as a preview, not an objective image of the person who sent it.

- If finding a parking space is tougher for you than finding a mate, here's more good news. You may now ace a parking space, instantly, in a congested downtown area. Some cities are embedding sensors in the curbside pavement to detect spaces as they become available. New electronic street signs will map available spots as motorists round the next corner. Great time saver for drivers.
  Pedestrians beware! Motorists may be looking at overhead maps, not at you, as you negotiate the crossing on foot!

The Thin Line Between Freedom and License

There is no democracy on earth more free than the Internet. And freedom always comes at a price. So each of us must drive defensively on the "Internet Superhighway," to avoid colliding with small-time crooks and big-time predators. Some examples, in ascending order of seriousness, follow:

- Students can submit perfectly polished term-papers purchased for mere dollars per page on the many sites that sell them. Then, professors must burn the midnight oil, checking the text on the many sites designed to catch students cheating. Only then can the professors evaluate the student's actual work.
  Talk about new ways for serious people to waste each other's time! Worse, think about the "catch-me-if-you-can" attitude being set.

- People can and do troll for kiddie-porn; they can also practice identity theft, or download bomb-building instructions.

  Lucky for us all, their efforts are likely to rouse the attention of the local police, Homeland Security, or Europol . . . eventually. Meanwhile, the lethal coupling of accessibility and anonymity makes the Internet a paradise for villains, and it requires that we ordinary users protect our personal data, vigorously.

- Strangers invite us to become home-based entrepreneurs, for a modest cash investment, up front. "We need only a phone and Internet access," we are told, "to earn thousands in our spare time."

  Sadly, when jobless numbers spike in a poor economy, common sense seems to desert the hopeful. They apply; they send the upfront cash; they get burned.

- Finally, for a modest "handling fee," we are asked to enter our credit card data and Social Security number in order to claim a fabulous fortune, bequeathed, inexplicably, by a deceased millionaire who happened to share our surname.

  As a parting shot, we are instructed to enter our bank data to enable direct deposit of our inheritance check. Hope springs eternal!

The Workplace: A More Serious Space

Yes, we can face exposure to all of the pleasures and perils of the Internet, but probably *not* from work, with its well-monitored firewall, its serious mission, and sensible policies. For the most part, our own diligence and our company's security systems will block the worst excesses of the 'net—to protect the company's information, and to focus our attention on work, at least part of each day.

HOW TECHNOLOGY LEVERAGES TIME

Perhaps you are one of the many fans of combined techno-tools who use them to enhance time management, a constant theme of respondents' survey replies:

REAL VOICES

Lindsay Geyer, VP Human Resources at Port Blakely Companies, the forestry and real estate development company based in Seattle, had this to say:

> I use Outlook and BlackBerry to manage my to-do lists, but I use a low-tech whiteboard, too, for collaboration. If interrupted, I keep my work "up" on the computer so I can quickly regroup, where I left off.
>
> Every time we grow our business, we need to reshuffle work. So, we'll always revisit our use of technology to handle expanding workloads.

Software Remembers What We May Forget

Many processes that once required attention each time we used them can now be handled reliably through preprogrammed software. What we get too tired or frazzled to remember, our software will easily remember and perform. Here's one IT engineer's experience:

REAL VOICES

Richard Shirley, an IT manager for the military, relies heavily on the calendar function in Outlook to maintain alerts for dealing with upcoming issues. And, he adds, referencing the rigorous approval process required in defense logistics:

> At work, I use purpose-built software (not available to the public) to create and track projects. This software allows me (and upper management) to view the progress of the work assignments for my team. It also features a workflow function that places the assignment in an electronic in-basket.
>
> Once I complete my part of the task I'm able to click the advance feature that sends it to the next person in the chain for either input or approval.

Deb Smith-Hemphill is founder of DSH Enterprises, specializing in management productivity. In her practice, she helps companies develop more rational uses for technology.

REAL VOICES

Here's what Dr. Smith-Hemphill says about the life cycle and future of the Internet:

The Internet started as a place for work—evolved into a place to play—and now has morphed into an expanded and seamless space for both. With our global economy, active 24-7, we are enhancing electronic collaboration and communication to improve business processes and productivity. With more automated activities and "smart agents"—we can soar into a common electronic orbit that breaks the boundaries of space and time.

The Internet is poised to help us create massive efficiencies no matter where we are located, no matter the hour. The old 9-5 work day in one location is a paradigm of the past. Instead, wherever we can collaborate, we can cooperate—to reduce cycle time, condense our supply chain, speed our time to market, and share our solutions for creating or managing change.

So think, gratefully, about all the milestones you have met with the help of the Internet and your favorite software programs. Then begin working, deliberately and creatively, to set up criteria for time-efficient use of these marvels.

REAL VOICES

Here's Dr. Smith-Hemphill's advice on today's information "hide and seek".

The old rationale was to plan and execute good cross-filing systems so we could easily store and retrieve information.

But information now proliferates as never before, from so many sources, that the name of the game is no longer storage, nor even retrieval, but instead—the design of search criteria, so you retrieve precisely the result you need . . . no more, no less. This applies not only to searching the net but to tapping your own hard drives for e-mails sent and received, for plans, project trackers, schedules, research documents, presentations—the whole gamut.

Note: To continue this discussion, you can reach Dr. Smith-Hemphill at dshconsult@compuserve.com.

Apparently, we're just getting started. There's more work ahead. Of this, you can be sure: while I am writing this—and while you are reading it—brilliant engineers and marketers are rendering obsolete every conclusion on this printed page.

In the next chapter, we deal with the one aspect of our electronic lives that seems to have slipped past all our defenses: today's e-mail overload!

CHECK YOURSELF

How do you score on escaping "virtual" traps? Rate yourself on the following questions; then repeat the process thirty days from now. Simple Yes/No answers will suffice.

Questions	Today	30 Days
1. I log my Internet activity, just for a day or two, to track time spent: this helps to check possible addiction.	———	———
2. I protect my e-devices with security codes, IDs, and cables when traveling and especially when staying in hotels.	———	———
3. I have taken steps to protect my identity, as well as my professional and financial privacy, when using Internet services.	———	———
4. I promptly adhere to my company's security directives regarding Internet and software use.	———	———
5. If my company does not provide classes, I study the literature on applications that interest me, or join classes at the local retailer or night school to maintain proficiency.	———	———
6. I take advantage of tools that integrate my e-mail, calendar, and project schedules to give me a complete "at a glance" picture of my deliverables.	———	———
7. Thanks to e-tools, I can use commuting and waiting time to make progress on work, when appropriate.	———	———
Total:	———	———

C H A P T E R

E-Mail Mania

E-mail! What a rock star! It's technically sound, fast, and convenient; it's so affordable, so easy to send, receive, scan, copy, forward, file and retrieve that, once we are in its thrall, we can't imagine life without it. We use it for everything—even tasks it was never designed to do. Then, we complain about the glut of messages clogging our incoming files—and our recipients complain about the quantity we send in return. What to do?

Let's get realistic about e-mail's virtues and its real risks. To begin:

- E-mail has "tone" issues. Some receivers take offense at our brevity and our well-meant informality.
- E-mail lacks privacy. We might as well plaster our messages on outdoor billboards: sensitive subject matters don't belong on e-mail.
- E-mail is undoubtedly overused and abused by otherwise sane businesspeople. Does that include us?

OUR PROBLEMS WITH E-MAIL

Let's look at the above list of problems in some detail.

Chilly Tone

Early e-mail mimicked the telegram—a prior invention that sped emergency messages across the world faster than airmail but at a high cost-per-word. Even briefer than telegrams, early e-mail could afford only a few characters per message.

Though designers have beefed up capacity and reduced costs, e-writers have maintained that terse style out of habit. As senders, we are asked to "get to the point" immediately and to condense the details onto a single screen, if possible. Receivers are grateful.

But terseness can be chilly. The next e-generations—instant messaging and "Twittering"—tend to exaggerate the speed model, with even tighter, more mechanistic acronyms and abbreviations. Often witty, but not warm, e-mail and IM are poor choices for sending complex messages, and should never be used for harsh, negative, or argumentative correspondence.

Ah, but we're so hooked on the easy technology, we use it for everything. Only later, do we realize that we ought to have picked up the phone or visited the person we wanted to influence. Or perhaps we should have let our opinions mellow overnight. The time we hoped to save by using e-mail must now be spent repairing damaged feelings and rebuilding trust.

Lack of Privacy

While e-mail creates a convenient data trail with easy storage to help reconstruct events, our e-mail mistakes can't easily be expunged. Instead, they can be revived, restored, and revealed—in court—for or against us. Some of the "evidence eliminator" products on the market tend to leave a trail of their own, exposing users to even greater scrutiny by their opponents in any legal battle. Newer releases offer "private browsing," claiming to leave no trace of the sites you visit in your Web history, once you close a session. Is this a good thing?

Apart from the legal issues, our e-mail messages can and will be seen by our IT departments when the organization exercises its right to monitor e-mail randomly. Therefore, humor, teasing, indiscretions of various kinds—along with more serious errors like leaking of proprietary data—can leave us open to changes of careless, if not malicious, behavior.

In addition, most companies are checking on the time and keystrokes being spent trolling the Internet on sites that offer no business benefit. Our companies want our working time, and their e-mail address and corporate identity, to be used on company business.

Overuse and Abuse

Warts and all, e-mail is here to stay. We all want it . . . need it . . . love it . . . and actively overuse it, often without conscious thought. Eager senders readily click "Reply All" when only a single receiver should get a message. People forward third-party mail without permission. Thoughtlessly, senders escalate first-time complaints that embarrass errant colleagues.

On the receiving end, we do our best to filter unwanted mail by subject or sender name, but our natural curiosity often overrides our common sense. People complain: "I get about 150 e-mails per day, and there's nothing I can do about it."

Nothing? Remember those CEOs in Part I who tended to see interruptions as beyond their control? Like them, we aren't likely to own up, at first, to our own role in a problem.

WHY DOESN'T VOLUME SHOCK US MORE?

To grasp how passively we view e-mail overload, let's check history once again. Any mature worker, doing business in the days before e-mail, would have hooted at the sight of 150 envelopes piled onto a desk at the start of a day. Mailrooms simply could not have distributed such volume to hundreds or thousands of headquarters workers daily. (In fact, only companies in the direct mail business—having soliciting responses in a mass mailing—would have welcomed that kind of massive volume: it simply didn't happen, otherwise.)

Now, because e-mail is so fast and facile, because everyone has learned to "keyboard," and because people are so tempted to click Reply All, you end up getting volumes of mail of no possible interest to you. Unless you are vigilant, you may even feel obliged to react, reply, or retain this friendly junk, "just in case."

Overload: Perceived Political Necessity

If you get mail from a colleague or boss, you hesitate to get yourself off their recipient list on this topic for fear you'll be deleted from everything, that you'll end up a hermit, living in a desert cave on a diet of locusts. Hesitate no more: send a polite response stating: "While I need to keep seeing mail on most subjects, please drop me from the recipient list for Topic A . . ."

Find Safe Ways to Stem the Flow

An international CFO reported, at one of our seminars, that his three administrative assistants, based on three continents, had handled a total of 980 messages by mid-week, none of it junk. This was a new and frightening record for him. So we launched an exercise with that audience, to solicit current, practical controls. He liked the results.

Since then, we've repeated this exercise worldwide, with an eye to helping managers and specialists gain control of e-mail. Here are a few of their ideas:

TEN WORST E-MAIL ISSUES AND SOME BETTER IDEAS

Issue #1: High Volume

I can't control constant interruptions from e-mails and instant messages.

Suggestions   As we stated in Part I, Chapter 1, it's not the interruptions that stall you; it's the randomness of the interruptions, so, unless you operate the help desk—or cover emergencies—you can afford to stem randomness in several ways:

- Start your day with your priorities set, in writing, in front of you. Only then should you check your e-mail.
- Turn off your incoming e-mail signal.
- Set regular times for checking your mail.
- Set your "check mail" intervals wider apart. Unless you're in charge of treating heart attacks, or running a city hot line, most things can wait, certainly up to an hour. In that hour, you can think, plan, and make useful inroads in your work. If you can't envision this, you may need to join an Internet addiction support group. We're not kidding
- Sign out of IM, too, for increasingly longer intervals.
- Finally, some morning soon, prepare this outgoing message: "I'm on a deadline: will not be opening e-mail again until __ o'clock. If your issue is a true emergency, please phone."

One company went one better: Recently, Chicago-based US Cellular inaugurated "E-Mail Free Fridays." And they're in the communications business. Another nationwide company we met recently has launched a Six Sigma study on e-mail efficiency.

Issue #2: Oversized Load

Huge attachments fill my inbox. I can't download these to my handheld.

Suggestions

- Post large documents to a shared site or server. Then, send an e-mail announcing this post and include a link in your e-mail notice.
- Your transmission or "cover e-mail" should always outline main points and conclusions for team members too busy or otherwise unable to open attachments.

Issue #3: Long Threads

Too many "conversations" extend back in time with multiple players, diverse arguments, no conclusions. Who's in charge here?

Suggestions

- Start by "templating" your requests so people can check a box or fill in only a word or number. If you're the one seeking their input, do them a favor: make it easy to reply.
- When you need several experts to check your text, number the items or paragraphs in your original; then invite comments "only on those numbered lines or paragraphs in question." Tightly restrict the portions of text offered, and request comments only in areas corresponding to each person's expertise.
- When sending lengthy text for approvals, exercise control from the very beginning by choosing fewer recipients. Limit the right to edit your text to a select few. This reduces long threads, and helps people to budget their remarks.
- As your conversations move on, and the focus of your argument changes, be sure to update to a new subject line that reflects the current "state of play."

Here's what Deb Smith-Hemphill, whom we met in the previous chapter, advises her clients regarding "thread" control.

> *Long threads circulating around and around your organization are a waste of time and a clear indication that e-mail is the wrong tool for this conversation. Instead, use a common posting location through Microsoft Sharepoint or Webex Connect. Place the document or project on its own page to host comments, and then distribute the link only to those whose input you require. Set a time limit for input, and use the space to meet virtually for discussion of your issue. No long e-mail trails and everybody wins.*

More on Thread-Heavy E-Mail   Until you adopt the sensible suggestion made by Dr. Smith-Hemphill, you may still have some preexisting threads to clear up. Here are further suggestions:

- Decide, at some point, to consolidate thread data to "high points only."
- Establish ownership of any long e-mail conversation. Make the owner responsible for periodic thread cleanup.
- Establish policy. Some companies publish this rule: "If you are the fifth (or even the third) recipient of an e-mail with threads appended, delete all comments below yours."
- If your software is fairly updated, you may try using a "thread compressor" application in your toolbox. It can find and merge divergent threads by topic.

TIME SAVER HINT: If you must edit long conversations, transfer the e-mail text to your Word program. Then use the AutoSummarize feature in the Tools menu to edit and tighten the text to the length you want, automatically—to 25 percent, 50 percent, whatever you say. Most people are ignorant about this amazing capability. It can save you hours of work on any lengthy text.

Issue #4: Junk Mail—Their Treasure, Your Trash

Despite policy reminders, we can't control internally-generated junk touting the sender's enthusiasms, hobbies, charities, humor, etc.

Suggestions

- Most companies forbid junk and monitor it frequently. Does yours?
- Use presort rules in Outlook to ward off unwanted topics and senders.
- Your company may offer classes in effective filtering: sign up for a session.
- Organize team-level "e-mail reviews" to agree on acceptable practices.

Issue #5: Indiscretions

Third parties are mentioned unfavorably by sender. Invariably, the comments are reported to the criticized party, causing internal strife.

Suggestions

- When circulated among insiders, indiscreet comments will arouse ill-will. Indiscretions can trigger litigation about "hostile atmosphere." Exercise due diligence and coach staffers, formally, on e-mail use.
- When vendors or customers are the target, indiscreet e-mail can trigger more serious litigation, with loss of contracts and damage to your reputation.
- Teach staff to avoid third-party comments about any named individual or company without first consulting higher management.
- To complain or request improvements from peers and lateral groups, teach staffers to write "I need" rather than "they should" or "you should." Any sentence that sounds like an accusation or criticism can cause discord.

- When you are annoyed, keep fingers off the keyboard. Switch to plain paper to work off your negative energy. Most of the time, you'll shred that message, having thought of a better approach within hours.

NOTE: For simple errors, not so much indiscreet as just inaccurate or untidy, you can expunge your error if you act fast to recall your errant e-mail. In Outlook, simply open your sent e-mail: Using the drop-down "ACTION" menu, choose "Recall this message." Time zones can help you here. If your recipient isn't awake yet, you can make your error vanish before the other guy can open it. If that fails (because your recipient is on a different server or system) send a new e-mail, cued to the subject line, correcting your error, and apologizing for the nuisance.

Issue #6: Vague or Outdated Subject Lines

Current content deviates widely from original topic. On a huge project that will generate hundreds of e-mails, the subject line offers only a project name with no indication of focus, so I have to open them all.

Suggestions   The easiest fix is to settle this at the start of any project. Set rules to control e-mail flow. Here's how some project managers do it:

- Set your communication protocols when you are structuring other rules for the project: What subject lines will you set for financial, technical, marketing or other aspects of the project?
- Establish very few files: Specify, under a relevant topic, for example:
    Project X: Financial: 2009 Budget.
    Project X: Technical: Interface Issues.
    Project X: Staffing: Outsourcing Production.
    Next, to your subject line you may add AR (Action Required), RR (Response Requested), or NAR (No Action Required).
- Appoint a clearinghouse person as the SME to manage mail distribution on those specific files.

- Determine some "need to know" criteria. Then, SMEs will forward mail only to those people who need to know. They will post information of general interest to a shared project site, using Webex, Sharepoint, or the like.
- Agree on rare uses for "Reply All." Establish rules—and enforce them.
- Concur that you will delete mail with nonconforming subject lines.

Issue #7: "Reply All" Annoyances

○ *Intending to respond only to a sender, I inadvertently replied to all on her mailing. Embarrassment followed.*

○ *Despite my requests to be deleted from certain internal lists, I continue to get mail as new people move onto a project and add me to their lists.*

Suggestions

- As a sender, disable "Reply All." You need it so seldom, you're safer making its use deliberate. One embarrassing event is enough.
- You still have control. Use presort rules to filter unwanted mail by subject line, sender, or key word.
- For mail that still gets through, delete without reading. Then, update filtering instructions by topic and/or sender.

Issue #8: Messages Misinterpreted

My innocent message was misunderstood by a senior recipient. I've lost career points.

Suggestions

- Invest time to create e-mail templates for complex issues that may repeat.
- Ask someone with judgment and discretion to read mail you will send to this person in the future. You can mask the name of the recipient: it's your own tone you are trying to correct.

- Avoid using e-mail for any negative or argumentative message. When dealing with a sensitive issue or party, go for a personal chat or phone call. With tone of voice—even silences—each party can modify tone and approach as the other person reacts.
- Set your spell-check function to flag "flamers and blamers" you might use by accident. These include words like: "wrong," "neglect," "mistake," "ignore," and "you" in any negative context.
- Take an effective e-mail writing class or read some good books on the topic: take notes.
- Write templates when you're at your best, never when angry or tired. You'll create proper structure and logic. Later, fill in current details as needed.
- When you see that you've crafted a good e-mail on a complex topic, file it in a special folder of your "best writing." Keep it where you can easily retrieve, reuse, or adapt text on your less-than-brilliant days.

Issue #9: E-Mail Isolation

People on our team isolate themselves, using e-mail to substitute for interpersonal communication, even with the person in the next cube.

Suggestions

- E-mail was invented for speed and brevity, not as a relationship builder. Unless you're on a different continent, rely more on personal contact.
- Phone conversations—not as good as a face-to-face interaction but a close second—work because the other party can hear/sense tone, humor, and hesitation.

COMMENT: Relationships are built on a consistent record of promises kept. To this end, e-mail can help by providing a record of requests made, responses given, and satisfaction confirmed. E-mail is a reinforcement, not an initiator of trust.

Further, many successful, long-lasting relationships are built by people, continents apart, who meet rarely, if ever. Such success takes a combination of strong motivation, willing empathy, deliberate message-crafting, and a lot of pleasant phone conversations. The time you save by not traveling, you must pay back in careful and caring communications.

Issue #10: E-Mail Procrastination

I confess a tendency to reread e-mails repeatedly, without taking action.

Suggestions   Just as the victims of personal disorganization confessed to keeping heaps of useless paper on which they have been slow to act, now victims of e-mail procrastination must bite the bullet and put a corrective plan in place. Try a simple efficiency system on incoming mail:

- Not sure it's your business?
  —Read or Refer.
  —Reject or Delete.
- Yes, your business: Looks quick, easy, and valid?
  —Read, Respond, Act, then File.
- Yes, your business, but not a quick-fix item. There are six steps:
  —Read.
  —Acknowledge receipt. State response-time needed.
  —Determine what latitude you need (scope, cost, staff help).
  —Research, consult, calculate, decide.
  —Respond or take action.
  —File.

SET E-MAIL ETIQUETTE TEAMWIDE

Although you may need to invest time to carefully draft some e-mail etiquette rules, you and your colleagues will spare yourselves the agonizing effort of mending trust so easily broken by a thoughtless sentence, an outdated thread sequence, a tap of the "Reply All" key, or a suspect download. Your team agreement can also set periodic boundaries on material to be tossed, filed, or archived.

In Daily Practice

Once your team has posted its e-mail policy, consider refreshers, reminders and rewards to motivate upkeep of good practices. If you can't imagine doing business without e-mail, ensure its continued effectiveness by using this time-saving tool with awareness, courtesy, and commonsense.

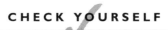

CHECK YOURSELF

How do you rate on escaping the e-mail excesses? Rate yourself on the following; then repeat the process thirty days from now. Simple Yes/No answers will suffice.

Questions	Today	30 Days
1. I have taught myself to focus on priorities, opening e-mail only at specified times of day, unless we're in emergency mode.	———	———
2. Rather than burden others with long attachments, I provide a link, and store these documents on a shared web space.	———	———
3. My team reduces those months-long threads by soliciting opinions on templates instead of stimulating more text. We limit the number of commentators. An SME tidies up, periodically.	———	———
4. As for internal junk mail, we ask people to use our internal social web page for this. Policy bars it from e-mail.	———	———
5. To avoid indiscretion, I never write e-mail when angry. If time presses, I get an objective person to check it before I send.	———	———
6. We have banned "Reply All." Each member of my team uses presort rules to filter mail that is legitimate but unwanted here.	———	———
7. If we find ourselves sweating over wording, we realize this matter may be better handled with a visit or phone call.	———	———
Total	———	———

CHAPTER

The Untamed Telephone

A decade ago, business people ranked phone interruptions at number two among the top five time wasters. Today's new technology puts us owners in charge, with caller ID and voice mail ever-present, so our complaints about phone interruptions have dipped to eighth place among irritants. We admit it's not so much that callers "bug" us any more than they ever did; it's our own knee-jerk response to the custom ringtone, and our fondness for all the "time-saver apps" that keep our telephones untamed. Technology is innocent: we're the culprits.

Dozens more "apps" appear daily at pennies apiece. We can load our contacts, project lists, schedules, family photos, favorite tunes. We can shop-direct, or watch movies, news, and sports events on our tiny, eye-straining screens. We can free our hands for dining or driving, and still take calls through that "swat-team" earpiece hugging our cheekbones. At least we should go hands-free on the road. But do we?

HUMAN COMEDY

The California state law barring the use of hand-held phones while driving came into effect just in time for July 4th weekend. The highway patrol—out in force for the holiday—easily picked off offenders. Troopers reported that one woman tossed her cell phone out the window of her SUV when she saw the patrol car in pursuit. But she was going at such a clip that the phone blew back into her lap as the officer caught up. The same day, a man—stopped for the same offense—swore he was just scratching his head with his sleek, slim phone. . . . Right.

THE B2B QUEST FOR LIVE SERVICE

As business people (or as parents) we feel guilty any time we "unplug." As customers, we resent that harsh reality of the automated customer service response: "Your call is important to us. Due to heavy traffic you can expect a wait time of . . ."

Savvy companies strive to handle calls live. After all, in service professions, handling interruptions *is* the job. And in today's competitive marketplace, "live help" is so valued that customers actually transfer loyalty to get it.

It Takes a System to Excel at Phone Coverage

While doing some training at a major accounting firm, we noted their mastery at handling peak season calls. You may face similar challenges at whichever high season occurs in your business. But this company took some trouble to build a better system. Here's how it worked:

At corporate year-end, all their CFO clients wanted premium treatment, simultaneously.

Financial officers, calling about details on their annual reports, would expect live service as if they—and only they—were showing up on the accounting firm's radar. The account executives would do everything possible to maintain this pleasant fiction. While talking with any client, they'd have at least one other on hold. "Not good enough," they thought.

The first line of defense—the executive assistant—would take the waiting caller, find out the problem, often handling it quite expertly.

The assistant would promise to get an answer shortly, with minimum inconvenience to the caller.

"Leave it with me," the assistant would assure the CFO. "You'll have your answer before lunch."

But they did even more. Once the executive assistant's line got tied up, too—the call would automatically bounce to the firm's "Intelligent Message Center," set up especially for this yearly crunch time.

Here, a trained accountant (sometimes, a retiree hired only for this period) would speak to the caller, gain clarity about the issue, provide a solution, and report it, via e-mail, to the appropriate account executive. If no solution could be found, the Message Center accountant would assure the caller that there would be no need to call back or repeat the message, later. Instead, the Intelligent Message Center would brief the account executive on the problem, and the caller would receive a final answer by a specified time.

In this way, the firm handled larger volumes of calls with quality professional treatment for all. Clients never needed to repeat a request or await a vague promised callback.

Planning was the difference maker and time saver here.

CONFERENCE CALLS SAVE MONEY AND TIME

Today, companies use phone and web conferencing to save travel time and cost. Many service providers host these events, providing multiparty discussions at low cost with utter simplicity for the callers. At mere cents per minute for the call, you can seal a deal and cement relationships, without asking multiple parties to travel.

Computer and video support can enhance clarity when conferences involve a lot of detailed product specifications, images, drawings, or calculations. With good preplanning, you can help your virtual attendees to fathom and settle details that once would have required their physical presence.

The key: good facilitation. As a skilled moderator, you need to assure that all parties have heard and been heard, and that your summaries accurately reflect any agreements or debates. For parties who already know and trust each other, phone conferencing can accomplish your goals even better than a face-to-face meeting because there are no jet-lagged travelers at the table.

CONCLUSION: Technology supports us brilliantly. But success, the human element, depends on good preparation. And that is up to us.

PLANNING IS KEY, EVEN ON SIMPLE CALLS

Why is the telephone still among our top ten irritants? Humanity, not technology.

REAL VOICES

From Roger Nys, Regional Manager, Howard Hughes Medical Institute, we hear:

What irritates me? E-mails that fly back and forth with too many follow-up questions. What bothers me even more? Voice mails that ask you to call back without mentioning what it's about. How can you think ahead or provide useful answers? Either you don't know the caller at all ... or you do know the caller, along with a host of topics that might be involved. In either case, you must take another step before you can even begin.

One Minute Prep: Four Minutes Saved

Roger is right. Too many of us pick up the phone and start talking, with only the barest idea where we need to go. This wastes time if the other party has to "interview us" toward clarity. If they're crafty enough to bump us to voice mail, we may leave a harebrained message that fails to do us proud. Most of us have had this experience: a caller leaves a puzzling message, then calls back in a minute saying: "It's me again . . . What I meant was . . ." We try to laugh.

Allow No Phone in Your Red Zone

The phone time trap is easier to escape, if you are willing to open up segments of your day for live coverage, and drive the traffic toward those times.

First, you safely reserve Red Zones for your priority work. You keep this time absolutely clear of phone calls, using voice mail to cover. Then, during contact cushions (see Part 1, Chapter 5), you'll gladly take calls—and you'll shepherd callers toward those times.

Now let's look at some systematic methods used by smart communicators to tame telephone randomness while giving great service.

Reduce Random Incoming Calls

We've found the following tips very helpful for keeping others from eating up your valuable time.

- *Introduce clinics.* If you introduce a change in your operation, don't force users to phone, randomly, for help. As word gets out, people seek information—even if they're on the periphery of the change. Handle change proactively. Set up "clinic sessions" in meeting rooms or chat rooms where users can get coherent help without needing to call. Start with the parties most concerned: then open up to others.
- *Establish specific callback times.* If customers or colleagues contact you (leaving voice mail or e-mail requests), you can respond with a stopgap acknowledgment. (That saves them from repeating and duplicating their messages.) Specify a time when you will call them back. Let them know they will get your full attention at those times—with research done and useful answers ready. Try something like: "Hi Jim, I got your call and I understand the issue. It requires some work at this end. I'll get back to you with some answers around 4:00." Don't handle complex issues with a series of fragmented, piecemeal calls.
- *Publicize your contact cushions for colleagues.* Once you've protected Red Zone times and bracketed them with contact cushions, illustrate that on your shared calendar so that insiders can see blocks of time reserved for them. They can feel comfortable about phoning you, knowing they'll get your full attention. This helps them prepare their own queries so the call is more productive for both parties.
- *Ensure a "privileged time" for premium callers.* Here's how it worked for one company:

  An account manager noticed that an important client was calling frequently, at the heaviest traffic times each day. Sometimes, despite his best efforts, he could not get to her quickly enough, against the tide of phone traffic. So, during a regularly scheduled one-on-one, the account manager illustrated the problem on a scatter chart and showed it to her, saying, "Of course, I jump off as quickly as I can when I see it's you calling, but your account deserves an edge, some dedicated time of your own, when we can discuss your more complex requirements. I hate to see you idling in traffic, despite my best efforts. Could we find a better time slot, at your convenience, but away from our heavy traffic?"

They made the deal. She still calls whenever she wants—especially when "hot news" draws a lot of traffic—but she places most calls in her new "privileged time."

UPGRADE SOME COURTESIES AT YOUR END

Following the suggestions below will sharpen your own phone behavior and increase your telephone efficiency.

- *Prepare and batch your outgoing calls.* Don't "wing" your own calls, either. Jot down your needs so that you and your target can handle several things at once. Even if you only reach the party's voice mail, your request will be logical and complete.
- *Use a time-savvy greeting on your voice mail.* Help callers save time by adapting this practical greeting: "This is Mike. Please leave your name and number. Then, please say what you *need*, so I can get back to you with an answer."
- *Manage expectations about a callback.* You can enhance your service image by making your promises clear. Tell callers what to expect: say how soon you'll reply or how much you can get done for callers, today (especially in cases when a publicized emergency may make people anxious). Here's a good example: "You've reached Glenna Brent: I'm out of the office (or working on the hurricane crew) and will get back to you today, but not earlier than 2:00 P.M."
- *Hide but provide!* If you know that callers will face a delay, say so on your outgoing greeting and include a referral to another party who can assist: "I'll return calls not later than 2:00 P.M. For emergencies, call Jerry Evans, at Field Service Extension 6500."

SENIOR EXECUTIVES NEED SKILLED SCREENING

If you are a C-level officer, your main involvements are strategic: the decisions you make will bind your organization to major commitments over years or decades. So random calls must be screened, at least some of the time.

At your level, you probably work with an executive assistant. What percent of the time do you want screening of your calls and mail? A trained assistant, committed, competent, and courteous, can take care of callers' needs in up to 80 percent of cases, leaving only the most important, urgent or personal calls for the senior manager to handle, at sensible intervals.

Here's an example of how the screening process, performed by a professional, might go.

In the office of Laura Jackson, CFO, the phone rings and the unknown caller asks for Laura. The assistant starts the screen: "This is her personal assistant. She's not available now, but she has asked me help you so you won't be delayed."

At this, many callers start working with the assistant right away. If the assistant can help now, this caller will readily accept help on future calls, too, saving time, again and again.

Conversely, the caller may say: "No, I'd like to speak with her directly."

The assistant now offers: "Certainly. She will call back after 3:00 P.M." The caller has little choice but to leave "callback" information.

The assistant then asks: "May I take a brief note on what you need, so she can give you an answer when she does call you back?"

The reply to this last question is the key time-saver for both parties. The caller may say something like: "I'm preparing the budget draft for tomorrow's meeting and I need the numbers on raw materials. Laura has that report. I'll need less than five minutes but I need it today."

Once the astute assistant knows what the caller requires, she has some choices:

- *Handle it.* "I think I know the report you mean. Would you like to hold while I retrieve it? I think I can help you now."
- *Refer it.* "Actually, Purchasing is working on that now. Would you like me to transfer you there? I'll clue them in on what you need."
- *Postpone it.* "I believe she'll want to talk with you. How about 3:45 today?"
- *Expedite it if crucial.* "Let me try to locate her (interrupt her). Please hold."

Why Should You Care About Screening?

You may be thinking: "I'm not a C-level officer. I can't expect screening service." As a specialist or mid-manager, it's true; you're less likely to have regular access to a trained assistant. But consider this: you may need a colleague to cover you on some occasions, using the same kind of diplomacy that administrative professionals deliver so well.

Good Service Saves Time

Executive assistants have years of practice evaluating call priorities without missing a beat. Note how Vicki Farnsworth and her colleagues handle things for teams of senior executives and physicians. Technology is the servant, not the master here.

REAL VOICES

Vicki Farnsworth, Executive Assistant at HealthAlliance Hospitals, Inc., in Leominster, Massachusetts, tells us:

> On calls, I use both voice mail and caller ID, so I have the luxury of seeing who's calling and knowing whether it can wait. I return the calls in time to be helpful, of course, but not necessarily immediately. Since physician-executives work heavy schedules, we exec assistants use conference calls to set up meetings. Once connected with our fellow assistants on campus or off-site—we can all scan our bosses' calendars simultaneously, for available time slots. This saves streams of time-wasting e-mails flying back and forth. We achieve immediate accord.

IMPROVING LIVE SERVICE, DAY BY DAY

These days, executive assistants are as rare as snow leopards, working mostly for top-echelon executives, but you could arrange with a colleague to cover one another, routinely, if you face opposite traffic peaks. Maybe you are frantic at the start of each month, while his or her pressures come at the end. If an unusual event occurs (a project recall or a new service introduction) you may need some "live cover."

CAUTION: If you rely on callback devices or voice mail during peak traffic, your frustrated customers will tend to redouble their efforts, using both phone and e-mail repetitively, until you "surrender"—or your system breaks down. Plan some better approaches. Many small improvements, taken together, can help you ace the response game.

Time-Saving for Both Parties

When you do set up a chunk of time to handle calls in person, be sure to link brevity with courtesy. The average call takes six minutes, yet most people realize that they could have handled an incoming call in two minutes if they'd been more efficient, by setting the tone at the start of the call. (Some busy day soon, set your computer to time calls—or use a low-tech egg timer—to help you notice your typical call duration.)

The most critical point in a call is the opening sentence. This sets the tone, either for business or chitchat. Since most people tend to answer questions, you can use this tendency to save time. First—if you are placing the call—open with the right question. Don't open with: "Hello Louise, how's the weather out there in Seattle?"

Instead, open more directly with: "Hello Louise. This is Jeff. I know you're busy but I have one quick question about the Rialto contract, Okay?"

This way, even if Louise is in a chatty mood, she will focus on the contract first. If you decide to schmooze, later, about the weather or the family, let it be mutual.

Similarly, if you receive a call from a business contact, respond first about business. Don't say: "Nice to hear from you, Chuck. How was your vacation?"

Instead say: "Nice to hear from you, Chuck, what can I do for you?"

Use Powerful Voice Mail Greetings

When we did a series of Priorities Workshops at NASA Houston, we needed to phone the Quality and Reliability Manager (an admirable leader who knew how to focus his team.).

I had never phoned him before; his phone greeting surprised me: "Good morning," he opened in a pleasant voice. He identified himself and went on: "Please leave a message. You have thirty seconds."

Startled, I hung up. I'm usually prepared, but that thirty-second limit threw me. I jotted down my message, timed it, called back and left it for him. And he replied, with equal brevity. How right he had been! After all, another manned flight was imminent. His team was busy.

Help the Long-Winded Caller Wrap Up

Alec Mackenzie used and recommended the following strategy, with some cautions. When a caller should wrap up, but doesn't, you can interrupt *yourself* in mid-sentence.

". . . so I figured I could . . . Oh, Pete, excuse me just one moment. Looks like we've got a minor emergency here. Do you want me to call back, or would you rather hold on?"

If Pete is a nonstop talker, he may hold on, so you can go off and do some quick task of yours; then come back on the line with: "Sorry about that, Pete. I'm going to have to go in just a minute. Was there anything more we need to cover?"

ONE CAUTION: Know whom you're dealing with: don't try this on a first-time encounter or with people who take themselves very seriously.

SIGN OFF SMOOTHLY

Many people tell us they have trouble, themselves, bringing a call to a close. You might try one of these approaches:

- *Cue the close:* "Kim, before we hang up, I want to be sure we agreed on . . ."
- *Mention a time limit:* "There's only a minute before a meeting starts. Was there anything else you needed?"
- *Use candor:* "Joe, I'm gonna have to jump off now. Can we pick this up when I see you . . . ?"

Don't worry; you'll still win friends and influence people.

Stay Vigilant on Addictive Behaviors

Despite the caller ID option on your phone, you may be among the majority of business people who cannot sit by a ringing phone and ignore it. As we've seen, taking random calls can stall your top priority tasks until the day runs out. Caller ID helps you derandomize calls by showing who is calling—but the subject matter remains hidden. Even if you choose, correctly, to give live attention to a high-profile caller, you may find that the request itself was trivial but is now binding.

Away from work, resisting the response-urge is even tougher. You've seen them: people who respond to that custom ringtone, no matter where they are. Mid-sermon, mid-concert, mid-wedding, mid-funeral, mid-romantic moment—some people never turn off that phone.

HUMAN COMEDY

Recently, a nurse told me that she had to wrench the cell phone out of an injured woman's hand while wheeling her from the ER to surgery. The family chats had already taken place: her boss had been informed.

She was calling customers!

You can't control other people's behavior, but you can control your own!

CHECK YOURSELF

How do you score on escaping telephone abuse? Rate yourself on the following; then re-peat the process thirty days from now. Simple Yes/No answers will suffice.

Questions	Today	30 Days
1. I pay more attention to the length of my calls. (Easy to log.)	———	———
2. I use caller ID and divert low-priority calls to voice mail.	———	———
3. My outgoing voice mail greeting asks callers to leave name, number, and say what they need, for better callback servicing.	———	———
4. When I must be absent, I specify when I will be returning calls to reduce call repeats.	———	———
5. In high traffic emergencies, I leave callers a referral person to contact or have calls diverted automatically.	———	———
6. I prepare my outgoing calls so my requests are clear. Then, whether I speak in person or not, my request is clear enough to service.	———	———
7. Though I don't have an assistant, I have made a deal with a colleague: we screen and service calls for each other in opposite peak times.	———	———
Total	———	———

CHAPTER

Information Overload
and the Paper Chase

Information fuels your enterprise. In a typical year, you may scan industrial and market research, news outlets, learned journals, and your corporate intranet—to scan millions, indeed billions of words in dozens of languages. Access is easy: selection is tougher, validation and deployment of the data, even more challenging. So, to gain control, you face two tasks:

1. You must tap information sources efficiently, for precisely the information you need, and no more. (See Part II, Chapter 11 for discussion on today's e-storage and retrieval issues.)
2. You must control the paper chase that still rages around you, twenty years after the pundits predicted you'd be paperless.

FIRST CHALLENGE: HOW TO GAIN THE INFORMATION YOU NEED

Despite your access to Internet sources, your most heavily tapped information sources are likely to be right next door, in adjoining departments where specialists develop the data you will need for joint projects. When you part-

ner with insider teams, you improve your chances for good collaboration by
assuring that:

1. Your internal information partners know what you need
   and why.
2. They assess urgency the same way you do.
3. Your own spadework is finished early, so you can "plug-and-play"
   their newly arrived data, at speed.

You can do a lot to assure items 1 and 3, but you're up against their
competing interests on item 2.

So here are some suggestions on winning cooperation from insider
teams.

Anticipate Needs Early

For a systematic assessment of what you'll need for any task, your team
must think through your data requirements early. You could ask yourselves:

- What information will we need? At what stages of a project?
- Where will the information originate? Which department?
  Person?
- Who is empowered to gather it? How many players are
  involved?
- What deadlines are critical?
- What cushions must we build in to our request? (The other guy
  can't be answerable for any lateness of ours.)
- What could go wrong?
- What steps could we take to buffer errors or delays?
- What alternative sources could we tap? When? At what cost?

Do these questions indicate paranoia? No, they represent planning.

Request Data with Tact and Diplomacy

Requesting data from people outside your team will require good planning,
good timing, and good manners.

- Start by choosing the right medium: phone call, informal note, formal letter, or request for permission to quote. What will make it easier for them to say yes?
- Outline the aims of your project, considering your relationship (if any) with the other party.
- List what you need, by when.
- State why you need their data (unless there's a good countervailing reason to omit the motive, such as protecting third-party privacy).

Communicate with honesty and clarity so you don't waste the time of those who help you.

How to Send Reminders

If the information fails to arrive in timely fashion, speak candidly with the person involved. Explain how the delay will harm the project. Never ask, "Why the delay?" Questions that open with "why" tend to trigger defensiveness. Instead, ask, "What would it take now to expedite the request?" Questions that open with "what next?" tend to elicit a response about the other person's competing priorities. Then you can empathize with each other, without resentment or excuses.

Offer Response Options to Enhance Cooperation

Once you see that the other party's priorities may deep-six your project, you have some options to offer:

- If the collaboration is in house, could you or your team offer help with some task of theirs within your capabilities—something administrative, not technical?
- Could either of you negotiate with higher-ups for a delay, a scope reduction, or acceptance of ballpark estimates rather than detailed numbers?
- Could the other party recommend another source, inside or outside the organization, to provide the information?
- If all else fails, could you jointly escalate—laying out for both your bosses the remedies you've jointly applied and the dead end you've reached at your level of authority?

Lateral teams' priorities are bound to "bump" a priority of yours on oc-casion. Then, you need the kind of honorable and sensible approach just outlined.

Get Confirmation from Your Lateral Teams

When we deal with contractors, we get everything in writing, up front. Strangely, when we deal with insiders, we sometimes leave too many ele-ments unspecified. In so doing, we expose both sides to disappointment. Often, we focus only on the *when* (deadlines) while remaining perilously vague on the *what* (standards and requirements).

When requesting vital information (the fuel for your project), do at least the following two things up front, to make it easy:

1. Provide a checklist of requested items on a cover sheet, so partners can confirm that your request is both understood and feasible. Keep in mind that the first deadline is the "feasibility" deadline, not the delivery deadline. You might include this note: "If you doubt the feasibility of providing anything on this list, please notify us before starting the work."
2. Once assured that your target person understands your request, make their data entry job easier. Prepare a checklist format so partners can fill in the data you need in the sequence or format you prefer. Why should they have to compose sentences and paragraphs (creative work) when they could simply enter data into slots (factual work)?

Make It Easy to Say Yes

In the same way, when requesting an opinion or approval from a senior man-ager, avoid writing paragraphs or asking that they write paragraphs. Instead, to make approvals easy:

- Briefly list the items you want approved. Be sure to provide an electronic link to the details so decision makers can access the details at will.
- Provide Yes/No boxes to simplify their response to listed items.
- Attach one of the following "unless I hear" notations, reading as follows:

"Here are details of a decision on which your approval is
required, along with those of the other five executives listed.
The deadline for action is _____ [supply date]."
"Unless I hear to the contrary by _____ [supply date],
I will assume that you approve this outline. Work will
begin accordingly."

For either of these approaches, you must allow adequate lead-time
so the "approver" can consult with the other decision makers listed.
Even then, this approach may cause political trouble the first time you
use it. But many hierarchical organizations use this technique successfully. For a first-time use, you might poll managers involved for their
early reaction.

Do Unto Others: Simple Courtesies

Remember that cooperation is a two-way street.

When others ask for your decision or for information, respond promptly
with a feasibility confirmation; then, meet the deadline on the actual sub-
mission of data, or give the earliest possible warning if the schedule starts
slipping. Two-stage confirmations can save disappointments.

THE SECOND BIG CHALLENGE: MANAGE THE INFORMATION YOU GATHER

Your ability to apply the information you gather will depend on building a logical storage and retrieval system (probably electronic) and on
improving your personal organization skills to avoid drowning in paper.
We are hoping that you do not recognize the following setting as one of
your own:

- Fat file folders clutter the top of your credenza.
- Several tasks are flagged on your electronic organizer, still
  untouched since yesterday.
- Scribbled scraps of paper—reminders of hallway conversations—
  lie half buried in clutter.
- Two reference books with pencils sticking out indicate facts still
  to be checked.

- Last month's professional journals lie unopened as this month's issues arrive.
- Your coffee goes cold while you dig through your briefcase for a missing flash drive.
- People kid you, kindly or otherwise, about your rumpled desk until an important task, buried in clutter, slips past your notice. Then it ceases to be a joking matter.

If too many elements of that scene point straight at you, then we hope your trouble is temporary. If losing data means you're losing ground, even the sincerest apologies will sound hollow when repeated. You may try working later or coming in earlier each day, but chaos simply won't diminish by putting in more hours. You need a better system for managing paper.

Remember, administration requires a specific skill set. Don't be too hard on yourself if your administrative skills are thin. Contrary to common wisdom, administration skills are not inborn. Indeed, since universities offer doctoral programs in administration, it's no wonder our amateur attempts often prove unimpressive.

Seek Administrative Solutions

If you are a small business owner with a dedicated personal assistant, assign administration to him or her and be scrupulous in adhering to the systems your assistant sets up. If you are a CEO, CFO, or CIO with shared access to a professional executive assistant, ask seriously for help; then, respect and follow it.

If you're a mid-level manager with no access to such administrative help, you might try recruiting a retired administrative assistant to take a one-time consulting job, dig you out of your hole, establish order—then set you up with a system for filing and retrieving data, both electronic and paper-based. Finally, such a person could give you checklists and instructions to preserve your newfound order. Once you've seen what a real administrative pro can do, you'll want to maintain that contact.

Recently, at one of our seminars, a sales VP said he was considering hiring more salespeople to handle their current overload. As I listened to his description of the disarray they were creating, I recommended they recruit an administrative assistant instead. In their disorderly situation, with no administrative capability, the hiring of more salespeople would only produce more customer contacts and commitments that would go unfulfilled. Bam! He saw, as if struck by lightning, that sales follow-through is about administration, not persuasion.

Sweep Your Desktop

But like most middle managers today, you'll have to develop your own administrative skill without paid help. To begin, get rid of the notion that a loaded desktop signals busyness or importance. No doubt, you've met those disciplined managers who cheerfully ignore teasing about their pristine desk tops with only one item at a time in view. Once they've listed pending items in their scheduler/planner, these organized managers keep their immediate area clear, so they can focus on priority tasks right now. They produce results on time and complete, in an atmosphere of relative calm.

Don't Defend the Heap

Start the day by sweeping non-urgent files and paperwork off your desktop. You'll still face enough live walk-in and phone interruptions without toggling back and forth visually between a current task and all the other tasks you've put on hold.

Give up defending a heaped desktop with this common rationale: "I keep everything in view so I won't forget it." You *may* not forget, but since you'll have Projects B and C vying for your attention while you're still trying to finish Project A (most errors occur near the end of one project when our attention starts shifting to the next), just make it a rule for yourself—clear your work area of all distractions until you get current tasks done.

Abandon the Dreaded "In" Tray

With determination, you may be able to move some paperwork along quickly. But the paper you retain usually requires thought, consultation, or decisions of consequence. So, you may be right to keep such paperwork "pending" for a while; just don't keep the paper in your in tray, or any other flat pile.

Picture it: most in trays keep paper in a horizontal pile—not a file. When paper sits in a pile, the items nearest the bottom get buried. To reach them, you must riffle through all the sheets and clusters of paper on top. As you riffle, you tend to notice some of the topics and consider what to do about them. Each single act of noticing will drain off the focus and energy you need for the item you're actually looking for.

Take Paper Vertical

Get rid of those flat in-trays and take your pending paperwork vertical. Keep this week's paper in subject folders, in a standing box-file on your desktop. When you want to access some items, you'll riffle from front to back, not top to bottom. Since you can't really see or read the paperwork that's now standing on edge in folders, you won't waste time en route to the item you need. If you use alpha or numerical filing, you'll head straight for the item you need.

Prove It with a Few Dots

As a matter of fact, one manager, Jillian Sandys—unable to give up her fancy in-tray—cured herself of the "pile-scanning" habit with a quick experiment. Here's how it went:

Each time she searched through a pile en route to a paper she needed, she would jot a dot on any document that caught her notice. Going through that same pile, repeatedly, searching for data placed lower in the pile, she soon amassed a lot of pages with penciled dots, indicating she had expended some thought on them.

The inefficiency of pile-scanning came home to her. But the exercise raised an entirely new question. She stopped to ask herself: "I am known as a decisive manager. Why can't I get this stuff off my desk?"

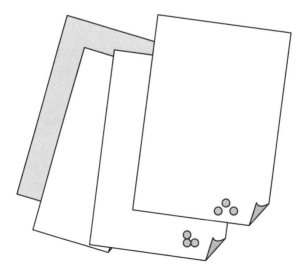

Analyzing those dotted sheets, she saw that she had made preliminary notes and taken some decisions on issues within her power, but her doubts had involved many other issues outside her key responsibility areas. Further, she noted questionable items that were incomplete, inaccurate, or unconvincing. The people who had originated the documents were all in other departments or companies. This paperwork, now delayed in her in tray, was only partly hers to complete. She would have done better to commit only to those actions she could authorize, while bumping the paper back to the originators for corrections.

At this point, she knew that fixing the "paper pile" problem would require negotiating a complex process improvement, and she resolved to do it. But her insight was instantaneous: namely, that horizontal in trays tend to bury the important with the trivial in a common grave.

Convert Paper to Data

A few advanced companies take the paperless pledge seriously. Some convert every bit of paper into electronic data within an hour of receiving it. You could do much the same thing on your own, saving time and upgrading personal productivity. Whether you are running a project, planning an event, or collecting data for a decision, you can create a spreadsheet with columns for recording the data you'll need. Then, as confirming paperwork comes in, transfer the relevant data to your spreadsheet—and discard the paper or file it out of sight. After all, paper in itself is useful only for handling lawsuits. Just plug the data into the context where you will need it. Rely on the originator to keep a copy.

CONCLUSION: Clearing your clutter will certainly help you focus on the work at hand. Using dots to record your many passes through the in-tray may cure you, as it did Jillian. Best of all, you may prove that some pending matters are barely your business at all.

What to Keep at Arm's Length

Keep your written daily plan at eye level, on your screen or on the wall. Focus your attention on what you must handle now. Keep support files for current work dead-center. Map, off to the side, those projects due later and keep their materials out of sight.

Create convenient "drop zones." With no administrative assistant to run interference or accept deliveries, you can still protect your time by providing a "drop station" just outside your cube (or barely inside), Then, people who want to offload things, legitimately, can do so without interrupting you.

Equip your drop zone with a vertical sorting file, labeled with what goes where—so that visitors don't amass a miscellaneous pile. The visitors know what they are bringing. Let them file it in the proper slot for you.

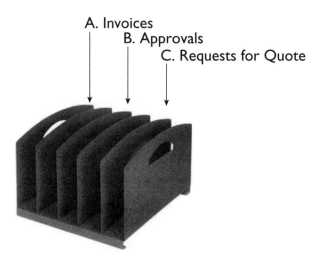

A. Invoices
B. Approvals
C. Requests for Quote

HOW ADMINISTRATIVE SKILLS CAN BUILD A BUSINESS

A Florida-based insurance company struck gold, almost by accident, when it found itself with four administrative assistants returning from maternity leave at one time. The company had been transitioning to a new computer system, and faced a lot of backed-up work in several groups where paperwork was kept in place as a fail-safe.

The four returning administrative assistants asked to be deployed, as a team, to handle paperwork overloads that were amassing in those departments. Once there, they noticed that the procedure manuals were totally outdated. Not only did they thin out the paper, they updated the manuals to reflect the transition to the new electronic system. Soon, the "Flying Squad", as they called themselves, was in demand everywhere in the company. Within a year, they saw a chance to bring back a "secure" credit card printing job that had been outsourced for several months.

With further economies, they made a huge saving. By the following year, they were ready to launch a spin-off business, handling administrative work and secured credit card printing for other organizations in the insurance field, even for competitors. They earned big bonuses for their innovative work, built a new profit center for their company, and had the fun of building a business from the ground up.

CLEAN UP CORPORATE PAPER

We now know that computers don't create less paperwork: instead, they produce vast volumes of better-looking paperwork, at speeds faster than ever before! Even orderly managers can feel overwhelmed.

In the third edition of *The Time Trap*, Alec Mackenzie reported that a single division of a large company ran a clean-up campaign, removing ten tons of paper during that single exercise.

A California association surveyed more than 900 personnel directors about the portion of their time that was devoted to routine paperwork. More than half the respondents estimated between one and three hours per day. Now, they'd be handling most of the data by computer.

Even so, you may be able to judge whether the work of your organization would generate even more data, on paper or on-line. Copies of reports, memos, and lengthy attachments tend to circulate widely with no one questioning whether they are necessary. All that data must be backed up—archived onto storage devices—drives, disks, off-site caches, all convenient, but none free.

Look at your own office right now. You may have the latest and greatest hardware and software, but unless you have made a company pact to go paperless, you may be further burdened, hemmed in by filing cabinets. Most investigators estimate that only between 5 and 15 percent of files will ever be referred to after the first year. How far back do your files go? And how much expensive floor space do they occupy?

Screen Incoming Paper, File Frugally

There's a legend that William Randolph Hearst never answered his mail; he claimed that after two weeks, people either came to see him, phoned him, or wrote a second letter. Then he would wait another two weeks before replying. (But his was a uniquely independent personality.)

We also know one chief executive of a Fortune 500 company who uses what he calls "the ninety-day drawer." All his mail goes into that drawer to ripen. It's not a tickler file . . . indeed, he says it's surprising how little of it has any importance after ninety days.

Some Simple Standards

We don't insist on either technique above, but there are ways to handle incoming information more efficiently than most people currently do.

Direct Incoming Data to Specialists   Of course, you can delegate whole swaths of incoming matters to specialists on your staff. In that case, you'll need to instruct the originators that their inquiries should now go directly to your appointee. Expect to repeat that message once or twice. People cling to their habits, but you need to liberate yourself, to focus on documents that really demand your attention.

Handle Incoming Documents Only Once?

HUMAN COMEDY

An old boss of mine really distrusted the "handle paper once" rule. He always said: "The paper you should handle only once? That's *toilet* paper!"

For simple paperwork, we agree with "handle a paper only once!" But not all paper is simple. Some documents must be analyzed, discussed, negotiated, and rehashed many times before the deal is sealed. It may be perfectly sane to keep the paper at hand for quite a while. But it need not become a burden. Here's how another of Pat's early bosses, the president of a Boston training company, handled incoming documents. He would pencil his reactions into the margins of incoming letters and proposals. His time-saving theory was:

> Never read a memo or proposal twice. Capture its meaning and your
> own reactions at once. Then—even if you must incubate your decisions
> for hours or days, you need not read the original again. You've already
> moved past that.

The added benefit? His staff members could always follow his thought process, laid bare. They learned a lot about executive decision making by example. With his penciled reactions, he was teaching his team how to think about problems and proposals with the company's best interests in mind.

Save Reading Time on Routine Reports

A few years ago, Alec Mackenzie visited the managing director of a large European consulting firm. The company had dozens of branches and associated companies, so the number of projects on deck at any moment was staggering. In fact, this executive's side table was groaning under a load of computer-generated reports and bound studies, inches thick.

"Do you actually read all that?" Alec asked.

"Heavens no," the managing director replied. "Most of it is just an update of last week's report. Do you notice where those reports are sitting? Right over the wastepaper basket!"

While this executive was joking, he was also covering his "due diligence" requirements by having the full report on hand, if needed. Meanwhile, he insisted that an accompanying note on each report must meet two requirements:

- Flag significant variances.
- Highlight any recommendations needing his approval.

If you must approve reports arriving from in-house sources, insist on an executive summary as the opening page of all proposals and studies. For many senior people, this summary is the only page they read. So instruct your own staffers to make it good.

REAL VOICES

Here's how Roger Nys, Regional Manager for Howard Hughes Medical Institute, sets standards for managing his own paper chase:

I read batches of incoming e-mail or paperwork—and do something with it, right away. Here's my routine:

- *Discard—if not of interest.*
- *Respond—if it's straightforward.*
- *File—both the request and my response.*
- *Refer—to the party that should handle it.*

I try to use the "touch it once" rule, whenever practical, reading and processing the paper so it doesn't linger.

Keeping Up with Business and Professional Journals ·

Here are some favorite reading practices shared by senior managers at our Time Management seminars:

1. Ask a staff member to skim, highlight, or summarize key points for you.
2. Assign different publications to different team members according to their expertise and interests.
3. Subscribe to a print or electronic digest service specializing in your field. You can delegate some of that data-hunt, too.
4. Circulate print journals around the staff, with a reasonable deadline. Attach a routing slip with your name at the bottom.
5. Encourage readers to add marginal notes on useful applications, for the edification of colleagues, not just senior readers.
6. Credit staff members when their comments add value. If in-house readers can't find anything worth commenting on, consider dropping the subscription. Your team may be ahead of the pack.
7. Take a speed-reading course or practice on your own, so you can scan paperwork faster. Most speed-reading courses suggest skimming vertically down the center two inches of any text. If you see anything of special interest, you can slow down for the details.
8. If you're the lone reader, be selective with those thick journals. Check the Table of Contents in each new issue, rip out the articles that might prove helpful, file them unread, but easily retrievable, for later. Discard the shell of the journal.
9. Many journals now publish in electronic form. Consider changing your subscription so your computer can weed out your reading for you.

TECH HINT: When voluminous data comes in as an attachment, try moving it to your Word program; then, use your AutoSummarize tool to show only the highlights. A drop-down menu will give you choices. You can select a 25 percent, 50 percent, or 75 percent scan. What a time saver! One caution: The AutoSummarize tool warns you that it doesn't thin out your lists. Its mission is to highlight the essentials from those big, boring paragraphs. That's enough!

CURTAIL OUTGOING CORRESPONDENCE: FIVE SUGGESTIONS

1. *"Prewriting" is a must.* Before writing a word, jot down two or three bullets (your main ideas) onto a sticky note. You'll eliminate the "blank screen" panic that hits most memo writers. Then, type your memo around these key points. As one of my old writing teachers says: "Never put the fingers in motion until the brain is ready." So don't "warm up" on the keyboard; doing so can generate 1000 meaningless words which you'll hate editing—or your reader will hate wading through.
2. *Avoid memos or e-mails* altogether when diplomacy is at stake. Opt for a conversation. You don't need to memorialize every transaction.
3. *Be brief.* Aim for simple, adequate memos, clear and polite, but not over-worked.
4. *Ban tired endings* like "Don't hesitate to call with any questions." Today's business people are anything but hesitant.
5. *Retrieve reusable phrases.* On occasion, you'll surprise yourself by writing a really superb piece. Keep a file of your best samples. Call on them and tailor them as needed when you're too harried or too tired to write a decent sentence.

Reuse Regular Report Formats

Build standard templates for regular reports. Then, stabilize them. Readers are grateful to find the same coverage in the same places on regular reports.

Ultimately, you'll want to reduce the team's reading and writing burdens by replacing those clunky paragraphs with charts, spreadsheets or checklists that readers can grasp instantly.

Finally, to discover whether you have been wasting your hard work on routine, repetitive reports, prepare a weekly report as usual—but delay sending it. See how much time elapses before anyone requests it—if ever!

CHECK YURSELF

How do you score on escaping the information and paperwork trap? Rate yourself on the following questions; then repeat the process thirty days from now. Simple Yes/No answers will suffice.

Questions	Today	30 Days
1. When we need data from adjoining teams, we create checklists to save them writing time. They simply fill in what we need.	————	————
2. We seek paperwork advice from administrative assistants, and implement what they suggest.	————	————
3. Personally, if I need to handle a piece of paper more than once, I summarize the data and my reactions so I need not *reread* originals.	————	————
4. We rotate "journal reading duty" to spread the burden among us.	————	————
5. We're frugal with filing: Unless we foresee legal issues, we dump the original paper and build relevant data into our own tools.	————	————
6. We provide convenient paperwork drop zones to avoid interruptions.	————	————
7. We keep a file of best letters and memos, and reuse when needed.	————	————
Total	————	————

CHAPTER

Confused Responsibility and Authority

Sudden change—the one constant in business—brings with it an immediate and dangerous condition: confused responsibility and authority. First, let's distinguish these two entities on which companies and careers rely. At the most basic level they can be defined this way:

Responsibility: duty or obligation.

Authority: power to take action.

OBLIGATIONS FOR THE LEADER WHO CONFERS POWER

If you impose responsibility, you must also grant matching authority. Whenever you appoint, promote, or elevate candidates to take on a task or manage a risk, you must also specify their powers to deploy the information, materials, funding, and human resources needed to accomplish the assignment.

Further, you must announce this handover of duty and power to all whose cooperation will be needed.

If the power you hand over includes supervisory responsibilities, then the department or team must be informed that they now report to a new supervisor. The organization chart must illustrate this fact, graphically: all parties must be able to see a "straight line" reporting relationship between themselves and the new supervisor. Oh, would that everyone conformed to these dictates!

Sadly, in our haste to adjust to sudden changes of fortune, too many managers assign responsibilities hastily or temporarily—almost as an experiment—with only a vague explanation of the duties or powers involved. Further, they often fail to inform everyone, to spare themselves embarrassment if the assignment should fail. But this very reticence threatens the appointee's success from the outset.

Risks for the Newly Appointed

If you are the one appointed to a new position or task, you must press for clarity about your duties and powers. Hoping that time and patience will clarify a careless assignment is a mistake. It will produce confusion for you, rebellion among staffers, and costly delays among adjoining departments and outside contractors whose cooperation you'll need. Time lost can multiply exponentially if multiple parties are left in the dark about your new duties and powers.

Clarity is a mutual obligation. Just as those in power must clarify responsibility and authority when appointing candidates, so newly appointed candidates must press for clarity before accepting a position or assignment. No matter how urgent the setting, you must negotiate for clarity: be quick, but be firm.

Consequences Come in Four Varieties

What should constitute a joyful relief for the manager promoting a candidate—and a career enhancer for the new appointee—can morph into a disaster, if mishandled.

First, let's look at consequences for the appointee. If you misread the new responsibility and authority vested in you, four different scenarios can unfold, each different, each wasteful and frustrating.

1. Two specialists, both thinking they're assigned to do a task, perform and submit the work.
   RESULT: Wasted time and unintended competition.

2. Emerging from a meeting, two team members think they heard the *other* person being assigned a task. Both return to work as usual.
   RESULT: No delivery on the task.
3. One person is assigned a task but no announcement is made to those whose cooperation is essential.
   RESULT: The assignee runs into resistance and resentment.
4. Two people believe they are empowered to get something done, so—unaware of one another—they give conflicting instructions to a crew or contractor.
   RESULT: Wasted time and money, with possible liability later if outside partners are involved.

If only these instances were rare, we would not need to focus your attention on this chapter before moving to Chapter 16 on delegation. But in most businesses, confused authority and responsibility still rank among the top ten time wasters, with damaging effects in material, money, and morale. In high-stakes industries—health care, energy, aerospace, and the military—confused authority can actually endanger life. So, we'll keep this chapter short, but we'll ask you to pay watchful attention to correcting confused authority/responsibility in your workplace.

FEEDBACK: THE DELEGATE'S BURDEN

In our talks with engineers, developers and technical writers we hear a common plaint. In the words of one frustrated process engineer:

> When assigning work to me, my boss waves off my initial questions, expresses confidence that I'll do fine, and leaves me to "do my best." Later, when I turn in the work, the boss finally comes to life, criticizes what I've done, and clarifies his original intent. All my initial work is wasted!

At seminars, when we listen to bosses honestly admitting failure to clarify assignments, we hear feeble defenses of their "drag and drop" delegation, such as:

> I had good reason to trust my appointee. She's been with us for two years. When I asked if she understood, she said yes. It's true, I was racing for the airport when we discussed this, but catching on fast is required in our business.

At the same seminars, when we listen to the hapless appointees, they blame the boss for "failure to engage," but admit to hiding their own uncertainties out of pride and optimism.

Mutual Remedy: Map the Gap on the Spot

There are steps you can take, whether you are the boss or the appointee, to help prevent disaster.

Appointees   If your initial questions are evaded, don't accept the assignment at face value. Instead, impose one condition. Offer to come back shortly—in hours, not days—with a couple of vital, written questions. Then, back in your office, sketch a quick two-column chart showing what you *do* know and highlighting what you *don't*. Take this graphic with you when you go back to your boss for answers. This will help your boss to cross any gaps quickly. Once you and your boss have resolved the unknowns, you can start the work with confidence, saving untold hours of trial and error.

Don't complain that you—as the underdog—have to do this protective advance work. In business, all work must get done at the lowest possible cost per hour. That's your cost, compared with your boss's cost per hour.

Bosses   When appointing someone to a new task, don't pose any question to which the answer could be yes or no. Excited appointees will hide their ignorance to confirm your wisdom in appointing them. They will tend to say "yes" when asked if they understand, and then rush to consult others for help the minute you leave the area. Offer an immediate Q&A session when appointing the candidate. Then, offer a later follow-up session, asking the candidate to write up further questions for you to answer.

FIVE CLARIFYING PRACTICES

To clarify responsibility and authority on any job being assigned, the boss must provide and the appointee must insist on the following:

1. An accurate job title that clarifies the appointee's level of authority. (This is tougher than it looks, as you will see below.)

2. A written job description agreed to by boss and assignee.
    (Keep it in list format. Use active or command verbs to
    describe each duty.)
3. An organization chart that shows who reports to whom and
    how members and teams interact.
4. A written change announcement to all whose cooperation will
    be needed.
5. A set of simple metrics to drive regular performance evaluations,
    to be conducted at intervals frequent enough to allow continuous
    improvement. Certainly, agree on some numbers that indicate
    what a good job will look like.

Let's consider some vital details about these five steps.

THE RIGHT TITLE CAN MAKE ALL THE DIFFERENCE

If you work in a large or mid-size company or institution, your full panoply
of job titles may be carefully defined in a formal directory. You may know
exactly what task sets and time intervals will take each worker farther up
the hierarchy. Therefore, ambitious people know how to perform and negotiate accordingly.

But, if you work in a busy small company or you join a start-up, you
may pay little or no heed to your title. In fact, you may have chosen that
small company because you hate "bureaucracies." At our seminars, we invite attendees to enter their job titles or involvements on their "desk
nameplate" so other attendees can readily consult them about shared interests. Managers from smaller companies often joke that they need more
space to list all the hats they wear. Fair enough!

But if, as a small-company player, you must deal with suppliers,
bankers, service firms, or government entities—then getting the right title
on your business card or e-mail address can carry a lot of weight. Rethink-
ing your title can save you a lot of time and frustration.

Cases in Point

Early in her career, Pat Nickerson—yes, yours truly—was asked by a small
U.S. training company to run its British branch. When she asked the president to give her the VP title she would need to maintain influence with
their 600 European clients, the president balked.

"If I were to give that title to someone so new to the company," he said (not mentioning "young" and "female"), "there would be hard feelings among the long-serving VPs here," he finished, without embarrassment.

So Pat asked, instead, for a title that no one else had—so no one could be offended. The title was Managing Director. This was accepted without protest because the VPs judged that a "Director," title, at least in the United States, ranked below VP. (They didn't realize that in Britain, the title "Managing Director" was equivalent to "President.") Pat got the title and made it pay off. By the time she finished an eight-year stint, the British branch had outstripped the U.S. parent in profits.

In another case, the CEO of a huge hospital conglomerate was retiring after a long career. His executive assistant agreed to stay on, for continuity's sake. Before leaving, her boss asked if there was anything he could do for her.

"Yes," she replied. "Give me the title 'Manager of the President's Office.' That will help me manage many of our outside contacts, until the new president gains his footing." Because he knew she could relieve the new president of many standard managerial tasks, allowing a focus on long-term strategy, the departing President readily agreed. The executive assistant retains that title to this day.

Show the Powers Vested in You

In many instances, with their company's complete approval, managers and specialists use more than one title, more than one business card, depending on the localities where they must operate. Your job title does matter: Get this settled before you say yes to a new assignment, while you still have some leverage. (Study the U.S. government publication, *Dictionary of Occupational Titles,* for clarity on thousands of titles and their meaning and range of powers.)

GET JOB DESCRIPTIONS DONE RIGHT

When job descriptions are vague or outdated, confusion reigns and time dribbles away. But to keep your job description accurate, subordinates need not wait upon the pleasure of upper management.

Take the initiative. Write up as much as you can of the five documents above with special focus on describing the tasks involved. Submit this for your boss's approval. Draft a list of the responsibilities you will handle. Be sure it's a list; not a set of lawyerly paragraphs. Get your manager to sign off on that list early, so that your next performance review focuses on specific, measurable job requirements and goals.

It's important to remember that a job description is a living, organic document, always advancing. Update it frequently! Most job descriptions end with a phrase like "and other duties as assigned." Specify these other duties. Each quarter, attach a dated list titled "Other Duties as Assigned: Current Quarter."

Once you are performing "other duties" to the company's satisfaction, your official job description should reflect the change, so update it, formally. (In fact, notice an opportunity: if you are asked to cover other people's vacations or absences, be sure to get their written sign-offs when they return—that you demonstrated competency on the task. Especially if that task is seen as more valuable than tasks in your current mix, this may qualify you for promotion when they move on.)

For that matter, you might add any task you carry out, repetitively and successfully, to your running list of "other duties." Don't be too laid back about this. Good time management means accelerating your chances for promotion. The best career hikes often come up without warning because the candidate has bothered to publicize recently gained competencies.

USE THE ORGANIZATION CHART TO CLARIFY ROLES, REDUCE OVERLAPS

Whenever you are asked to "keep an eye on" another worker, be sure this assignment is official. Some bosses may ask you to take a new or weak performer "under your wing." Don't feel flattered: instead, get clarity.

The quickest way: pull out the "org chart" showing your current "box" and that of the employee, currently shown in a direct line under the boss's supervision. Pencil in a solid line between your box and the employee's— and inquire whether this is a straight-line official assignment. Ask: "Is this a mentoring slot (no line), an SME advisory slot (no line), or a supervisory slot (straight line)? Go for the latter. Why take on an ambiguous supervisory role? It's all risk and no reward. Recognize that here you have a chance to negotiate.

As for task overlaps with peers, those tidy boxes on our organization charts can't quite depict the web of practical but temporary assignments that float on the surface in most organizations. Good team coverage often requires overlaps that are far from formal. Take note of tasks you do that impinge on other people's jobs. Acknowledge that not all overlaps are wasteful. Indeed, your department may routinely cross-train workers to back each other up. Your boss may wisely equip multiple performers to handle seasonal peak loads, and then let them return to their usual tasks, or take a breather when the time-crunch ends. This cross-training policy increases the team's breadth and depth, acknowledged or not.

But it's up to you to notice and prevent wasteful duplication of requests. Beware of any self-serving customers or bosses who assign the very same task to two different performers in a surreptitious bid to get served, no matter what. This is their "fail-safe" maneuver, trying to assure getting their priorities met, even if one performer should fail or slow down. They then award themselves the better of the two outcomes. (Believe us, it's been tried.) If you and your colleague discover this ruse, don't let it slide by. Open this subject with your boss, and ask for a correction—unless your company is replete with human resources these days.

BOSSES: REPEAT AND REINFORCE CHANGE ANNOUNCEMENTS

Because habit is strong, your first official change announcement may not suffice to gain everyone's cooperation. The experience of one organization illustrates this clearly:

> A huge growers cooperative in California was administered by a man who understood very well the independent mind-set of the farmers and ranchers in the co-op. In fact, Steve enjoyed their claim to being "downright ornery" and he had a track record of gaining their willing buy-in on most requests.
>
> Getting them to report compliance with government regulations had become a stabilized routine, mostly handled by phone, at required intervals. It was going so well, he decided to delegate this task to his assistant, Ella. He handed over the tally sheets and asked her to start calling the members. Thinking this a simple enough change, Steve didn't bother with a formal notice to the members.
>
> Since these growers contacted him about many issues, a few would conveniently report their compliance data while covering other subjects on the same call. For the sake of speed, Steve accepted this, jotting down the data, and later handing it over to Ella. The

first couple of times this happened, she said nothing. But one morning, when Steve came out of his office to grab the tally sheet from Ella's desk, she balked. They were each tugging the sheet by a corner when Ella said, "Wait a minute! You know what we forgot to do, Steve? We forgot to tell everybody that this is my responsibility now. Let's get that done."

With a grin, Steve agreed, and set things straight, right then, with that grower who was waiting on the phone. Next, he asked Ella to draft a notice for all members, over his signature, making the handover official. Ella included the news that she had designed a reporting template on a shared website to save time for those growers who were computer savvy. She offered to continue the phone method for those who preferred the old way. But here's the fun part:

Within a week or two, most of the co-op members were reporting their data to Ella, and quite a few were delighted with the template. By the month's end, in the informal newssheet that went out to the members, Steve listed and thanked the cooperating growers by name.

The following week, he listed and thanked even more growers. Finally, a couple of weeks later, he inserted a gentle, joking squib, "threatening" that the following week he would list the names of those who had not yet gotten the point. In turn, he received (and published) a few good-natured jabs they took at his expense—but he was able to announce full compliance, shortly thereafter. Time had been lost up-front by not announcing the change and empowering his assistant. By investing just a little more patience, Steve and Ella were to reinforce the message and make compliance easy.

PERFORMANCE EVALUATIONS: MAKE METRICS MUTUAL

The responsibility for performance management begins the moment a job is created—well before any candidate is recruited—and continues, throughout the life of that job, in all its iterations, until that job is replaced or ended. The duties, responsibilities, and powers vested in the job attach to the new owner who accepts the assignment. From then on, both the boss and the job owner must keep each other informed as the job's duties and challenges keep morphing. From the moment the job is designed, determine a few simple numbers to define it. Only then can you assign it.

- Production: Quantity per hour or day? (Widgets, phone interviews, ad layouts?)
- Time: Duration for each activity? (Learner speed versus experienced performer speed?)
- Money: What's the budget? How much can we spend on each? (Lab test, plane ticket, car rental, survey, incentive prize?)
- Quality: How close must we come to perfection? (For a go/no-go decision versus a final production run?)

If you can't forecast and quantify job requirements, how can assignees hope to measure up?

With new assignments, frequent informal feedback is a must. Feedback sessions can be stepped down (but never out) as the performer gains competence in the job. "Live" feedback must also be timely, occurring quickly once a behavior—praiseworthy or problematic—is noticed. Management lore attests: Behavior that is noticed is repeated—whether the behavior is acceptable or not!

For Bosses: An Instant Appraisal Tool

Sometimes, your truly promising appointee slips up on an important skill or obligation. You don't want to dampen his or her enthusiasm, but you do want to correct any pattern of error before it gets ingrained. Here's a simple format for drawing a worker's attention to a needed correction, quickly and cleanly. In the example below, it's a lab worker with an accuracy problem.

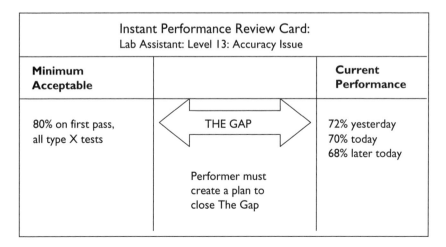

Instant Performance Review Card: Lab Assistant: Level 13: Accuracy Issue		
Minimum Acceptable		**Current Performance**
80% on first pass, all type X tests	THE GAP Performer must create a plan to close The Gap	72% yesterday 70% today 68% later today

Here are some suggestions on how to use this tool:

- Focus on a single behavior. Do not list a variety of items for upgrade.
- Do not place the person's name on the card: the requirements are standard for all performers at Level 13.
- Do not use the word "you" on the card or in conversation. It elicits defensiveness.
- Remember that standards are set for the job title. All "owners" of that job title have agreed to meet its minimum standards.
- If the job owner can suggest (and commit to) a plan to cross that wide gap between required and actual performance, then you are not seen as delivering a reprimand. Instead, the owner is committing to self-correction, once the gap is noted.

This simple, friendly, informal method helps appointees to correct their own behavior when the first signs appear. Many workers will self-correct, ask for your initials on their upgrade plan, and prove they can sustain it. Some people proudly include this card in their portfolio of accomplishments. For most, it relieves you of the need to do a formal write-up or start any disciplinary actions.

Of course, if this process fails, you would then begin whatever formal 1-2-3 process or performance plan that your organization requires.

Formal Feedback Sessions:
Once a Year Is Not Enough

While new assignees need frequent feedback, all employees should get, at least twice yearly, a formal feedback session—a performance evaluation written or scored by both parties (boss and performer) using the company's approved format. Why twice yearly? Because a decent performance program requires that the parties agree on needed upgrades or new commitments well before the year-end with its usual focus on raises and promotions. As so many managers report:

> If I tell them they've done a great job, but there's no money for a raise or bonus, they discount the praise. If, on the other hand, I coach them on poor performance, but they get the standard raise that "lifts all boats," they don't see a need to do better.

The once-a-year-only format comes too late to influence events. With the mid-year discussion, you can both give and get clarity about strengths and shortcomings; both parties agree on specific goals and timetables for getting to the next level, and they still have six months to make the grade.

The six-month session is also the best opportunity to tie performance to long-range ambitions.

Caution, Managers!

The most damning sign of mismanaged responsibility and authority? That the failing employee is the last to know. In any such instance, it is the boss who fails.

In the next chapter, we'll discuss the nuts and bolts of delegating specific tasks, but please pay heed to gaining clarity about responsibility and authority, no matter how pressed for time you may feel.

CHECK YOURSELF

How do you score on escaping responsibility and authority traps? Rate yourself on the following questions; then repeat the process thirty days from now. Simple Yes/No answers will suffice.

Questions	**Today**	**30 Days**
1. To avoid confused responsibility or authority (as a boss or a performer), I insist on a clear job title and description, with duties and responsibilities clearly detailed.	———	———
2. When assigning tasks or promoting employees to higher levels, I get them necessary tools and authority to perform.	———	———
3. I announce new assignments to all others who must cooperate.	———	———
4. I give (or request) frequent feedback on new assignments.	———	———
5. As a boss, I would use the Instant Performance Review Card to help a worker nip a bad habit in the bud.	———	———
6. When I assign a task, I avoid taking it back because of anxiety about performance. Instead, I retrain the assignee.	———	———
7. I give (or request) half-yearly or quarterly formal reviews so that agreed upgrades can be confirmed in the interval (3 to 6 months) before the next year-end review.	———	———
8. If an employee is failing in an assignment, I ensure that they are never "the last to know."	———	———
Total	———	———

CHAPTER

Poor Delegation and Training

Even when we are permitted to delegate, encouraged to delegate, *ordered* to delegate, something seems to stop us. Why do so many of us hesitate? Is it:

- The Super-Manager Syndrome? (*What? Me? Could I possibly need help?*)
- Pride? (*No newcomer could match my stellar performance.*)
- Fear the trainee may fail? (*It's quicker and safer to do it myself.*)
- Fear of losing touch? (*I need my face-time with my favorite requesters.*)

If delegation makes you nervous for these or other reasons, you're not alone. Here's an all-too true story shared by one of Alec Mackenzie's contacts.

Harry had been a highly competent and dedicated factory line manager until a sudden promotion forced him to question his delegation skills.

When his boss retired suddenly, Harry got promoted to plant supervisor, to manage three veteran line managers (his former peers), plus the new hire brought in to fill Harry's former slot. But the timing was bizarre. Not only was everyone busy with high-season orders, but the plant was preparing to retool. So Harry spent part of his first week completing as much as possible of his old job, and then he started to learn his new responsibilities. He waded through detailed design materials, visited benchmark installations at two other companies, and sat in on planning meetings where senior management consulted him and seemed to respect his ideas.

That first week, he put in seventy hours at the plant, and several more at home, just learning the job. With all this new work, his command of daily production details started to slip. Dreading that he might drop the ball, he insisted on heavier reporting from his subordinates.

The three line managers, resenting this micromanagement, quickly developed a form of "malicious obedience," not making a move without consulting him. Of course, the new hire kept showing up in his doorway, too, with random questions. By week three, his veterans started taking sick days. That caused current production to back up.

Fortunately, his boss, Vijay, kept an eye on things. On one of Harry's late nights, he stopped by for a chat. Harry readily admitted he felt swamped. With candor and genuine concern, Vijay pointed out that Harry needed to delegate more—not less—to the line managers: he needed to trust them.

Vijay assured him, "We promoted you, Harry, because we saw that you had the intelligence and planning skills to take us to the next level." Vijay fell quiet for a moment to let that sink in.

They went over the details for a few more minutes. Harry confessed he was worried, too, about his neglect of the new hire.

"Put your pride aside," Vijay advised. "You're not the only trainer—nor even the *best* trainer—for a new hire. You may be too close to the job you just left. Perhaps one of the line managers could take on some coaching—and you can offer a service award to whoever steps up."

Harry started to feel some hope, and his fatigue lifted.

"Let's just take a couple of minutes more to lay this out," Vijay suggested. He joined Harry at the whiteboard to map out all the tasks, current and upcoming, that faced the production team.

"Why not call the team in tomorrow, and let them loose on this map," Vijay suggested. "Let them study this, digest it, then refine their own plans to match. Coping with this much change, Harry—it's got to be a team effort. "

Harry got the message. The next day, he stopped for a private word with each of his line managers, to apologize for his anxiety about production. He let each one vent some feelings, and asked for a new start.

Later that day, all four people joined Harry at the whiteboard. He handed them some markers and freed them to illustrate the production kinks they anticipated. Together, they sketched out an efficient production process.

Their final checklist was posted on a board in the production area, so workers could see and agree to the process as it would play out. This board quickly became a gathering spot for the whole production team.

In the weeks that followed, everyone put in more overtime, but instead of emerging exhausted, they could see progress, trackable on the wall. At his mid-year review, Harry confided in his boss:

"Vijay, what I learned was this: whenever I'm doing work that could be delegated, I'm being overpaid!" They both laughed.

Can You Relate?

Harry's situation is common, especially for those who rise through the ranks. Why do we have so much trouble? Because of an all-too-human issue: our fragile egos. Many of us secretly believe that only we can get the task right, but we don't want to test that assumption. Others fear that our personal shortcomings may be exposed if the delegate outperforms us.

The solution in either case is simple: delegate anyway. If a staffer is able to outshine you, the entire organization gains. Your leadership skill, not your solo prowess, becomes the new focus of attention. As a manager, you must excel at leading others to top performance, not on protecting or outstripping your old performance records.

THE FIVE MYTHS THAT STALL DELEGATION

Myth #1: I must do it myself to shield the company from mistakes.

True. If your delegate makes mistakes, you will have to pick up the pieces. But, you can salvage the situation if you spot trouble early. So, build an atmosphere in which delegates can freely reveal their mistakes to you. All companies make mistakes; they just don't burden customers with them.

Q&A

Q: **Doesn't delegation mean I will have to train thoroughly, and then monitor closely?**

A: *Yes. Will that be a nuisance? Yes. But if you assign a stabilized task, your learner can acquire skills by repetition, gaining competence steadily, while earning career points. Will that save money and time for the company? Yes.*

Speaking of mistakes . . . there's a famous legend about Henry Ford's reaction to them. One of Ford's vice presidents made an error that cost the company $20 million. When he offered Henry his resignation, Ford held him off with this logic: "No way. We've just spent a fortune educating you."

Myth #2: It's quicker to do it myself.

True: It is quicker . . . once! But if your task is done daily or weekly, it cannot remain "quicker" for you repeat it the twentieth or fifthieth time. Even though your delegate will require watching, and corrective training, he or she will be handling the task competently by the fifth or tenth time. So, from then onward, all the repeats will be at a lower hourly rate than yours. From that point onward, you get time to take on more difficult, unstable tasks.

Q&A

Q: **I'm not sure how to begin. I'd be embarrassed to fail.**

A: *First—before you even recruit a candidate, sit down and start listing the steps in a routine job. What has become unconscious for you must become conscious again. Put each step onto an index card, one step per card: keep it simple. More on this later.*

Myth #3: I'd prefer to retain tasks I enjoy.

The design engineer who gets promoted to engineering manager, but still keeps doing circuit design, will be unavailable to train, manage team assignments and mediate with clients. By giving up tasks that once "made you famous," you free yourself to build the leadership skills that will matter in your next performance evaluation.

Q&A

Q: **Does this mean I'll have to give up all my regular work? Most of the team leaders in this company are also contributors as well as supervisors.**

A: *Of course, you'll still be a contributor: most supervisors are. But you must identify stabilized routines and delegate them as soon as possible. The more senior you become, the more you will be asked to handle unstable tasks—those with high risks, but also high potential.*

Myth #4: If I delegate, I'll lose touch with the details, and with my current contacts.

True, you'll need to install a simple monitoring system, to keep you and your delegate safely on track. And you'll have to make a concerted effort to stay in touch with your contacts without undermining your delegate's ownership of the particular task.

Q&A

Q: **What if my senior manager asks for a status report on work that I delegated and I don't have a ready answer?**

A: *You get comfortable with saying, "I've delegated that and we're not scheduled for a check-in just now, but I'll be glad to get you details. How soon do you need them?"*

Or, once you are confident in your delegate, you can have him or her report details directly to the senior manager.

Myth #5: Nothing less than my level of perfection will suffice.

Think again. If you retain a task to uphold your own exacting standards, be sure that your exalted level of perfection is still paying its way.

Q&A

Q: **Upper management demands perfect estimates, and full details, fast. Can I tolerate the risks while my subordinate gets good at this?**

A. *Just as in upgrading a computer system, you need double coverage until the transition is done, so you'll have to stay vigilant while your delegate learns. But this is the time, also, to revalidate the amount of detail/perfection needed on matured tasks. Sometimes the risks that were once monitored by your process are now controlled in several ways.*

Find out whether ballpark estimates will be enough at any stage. Determine whether a summary, without all the support detail, will do. After all, priorities change, and risks get reduced over time. See how much perfection is still needed.

TASK SELECTION MUST PRECEDE RECRUITING

Before you look for a new hire or recruit an internal candidate, take care of task selection. A task ready for delegation must be valuable, stable, and repetitive. Here's what we mean:

1. *Is the task valuable?* If you doubt the value of continuing a task, then negotiate it out of your workload. Don't dump it one level lower. Afraid you'll get an argument? Engage. Get agreement to redesign this task, to test alternatives, or to simply live without it for a set period.
2. *Is it stable?* Choose stable tasks with procedures proven reliable, so learners won't risk blundering, experimenting, or overhauling a task while trying to learn it.
3. *Is it repetitive?* Choose tasks that must be done daily or weekly so learners can gather speed, and garner skill and confidence as they go.

Construct Tasks for Ease of Supervision.

For safety, you may choose not to delegate a large task all at once. Instead, you may show the learner the overall goal, then divide the task into digestible, teachable parts. You retain the main burdens (decision making, for example) but delegate the stable underlying processes (data gathering, routine calculations, tests) so your delegate knows the value of the whole, and the coherence of the parts you are assigning.

Make some choices, as shown in the chart below.

Spend a few minutes looking at your own workload. Then chart the pieces you would retain and the pieces you'd delegate with reasonable comfort. Specify the overarching strategic tasks you would keep, so the learner knows you will still be providing support.

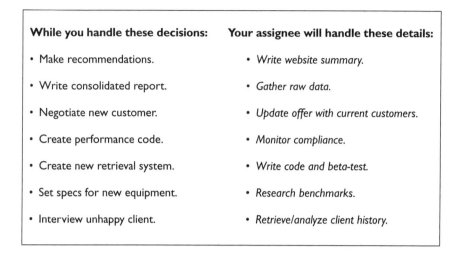

While you handle these decisions:	Your assignee will handle these details:
• Make recommendations.	• *Write website summary.*
• Write consolidated report.	• *Gather raw data.*
• Negotiate new customer.	• *Update offer with current customers.*
• Create performance code.	• *Monitor compliance.*
• Create new retrieval system.	• *Write code and beta-test.*
• Set specs for new equipment.	• *Research benchmarks.*
• Interview unhappy client.	• *Retrieve/analyze client history.*

Task Definition Precedes Transfer

Delegation offers two great benefits: freedom for you, and advancement for your trainee. So define the task on paper, not just in your head. Answer these critical questions in a written five-part prep to help you justify transferring a task:

1. Is this task both stable and repetitive? Demonstrate this.
2. What is the expected goal or outcome?
3. What specific skills are required? Statistical analysis, language, coding, drafting . . . spell them all out.
4. Quantify expected results—what outputs do you need, at what speed and cost?
5. List the actual steps involved in precise order. Highlight critical points.

Answer these five questions early, well before asking your boss to okay budget, or to authorize recruiting a candidate. The minute you recognize a task as valuable but stable and repetitive, you are ready to start preparing for hand-off.

UNEXPECTED BENEFIT: Sometimes you discover through careful preparation that the specific task can be done in only a few hours per week. This discovery can make it even easier for your boss to approve part-time, rather than full-time help.

Prepare Training Tools Early

Have you caught yourself soldiering on long past the point of pain, until a brutal workload balloons past the breaking point? When that happens, your problem may lie—not in waiting too long to ask but in getting such a quick response from your boss that help arrives before you have a work station in place, or training tools ready! In the worst case, your new recruit may sit idle, waiting for instructions, or else will tap busy coworkers for advice. Then, you risk embarrassment, resentment, and wasted time for everyone.

If you are new to delegation, first define and validate the tasks. Then, write up the major steps, then assure there is space for any helper who may arrive quickly. Show your plan to your boss. With so much spadework done, it's harder for bosses to say no.

"Here's the task, laid out," you say to your boss. "Here are the training steps. Here's the space and here are the tools. I'm ready to put someone to work now."

Your concrete plan makes it easier for your boss to assent.

TEN STEPS TO SUCCESSFUL TASK HAND-OFF

With your five-part prep done, and your boss's okay secured, you want to hand off the work quickly and smoothly. Here are ten steps to help you pass the torch successfully:

1. Recruit

Choose a person with relevant skills. Match talents to task. But keep in mind that a major purpose of delegation is employee development. Ideally, you would delegate tasks *related* to what a subordinate already knows or handles, but with some headroom built in. If the person's experience and education are already solid, then this assignment will motivate top performance.

2. Teach the Task

Once you have listed the steps in good order, write them onto separate cards, one step per card. Why do this? The learner can absorb the process, one step at a time. Show a map of the overview, yes. But if your task involves dozens of steps which could either overwhelm the learner, or tempt the learner to scan and skim, then you must simplify the learning tools to help the person master the steps at a reasonable pace. Let delegates carry the cards around for a few days, making their own special notations. In companies that follow this procedure, we often see people studying pocket cards while waiting for an elevator or standing in line for something.

3. Demonstrate the Steps Yourself

If the task is observable or sequential, perform a set of steps yourself, and then let the learner try. Be vigilant about modifying speed. Often, you tend to go at an "expert pace," not a learner's pace. Observe the learner's body language to assure that comprehension is occurring. Don't ask, "Do you understand?" Most learners feel bound to say yes.

4. Elicit Questions as You Go

Don't ask a learner, "Do you have any questions?" That would trigger a yes/no choice. Most learners are skittish about saying no for fear of appearing slow. Often, they'll respond, "Sure, I get it." Then, they wait for you to leave the room, so they can ask bystanders how to do things. Instead, frame your questions this way:

"Which steps look easy or familiar?"
"Which steps look harder, less familiar?"

This opens some meaningful responses. Then follow up with further encouragements like:

"Most learners find Step 9 a little difficult because of the math."
"I found this difficult at first. What about you?"

Make it easy for delegates to discuss their concerns. Then you can explain your company's reasons for setting up the process in this particular way.

5. Next, Let Learners Demo and Play Back

Ask learners to walk through and demonstrate the entire process themselves so you can both be sure they have grasped the steps correctly. Maintain an attentive, supportive, but neutral posture while they run through the demonstration. Listen without commenting or signaling approval or disapproval. This is not a two-way conversation, at least not yet.

6. Don't Interrupt to Correct Errors

As a learner tries a set of steps, you may notice an error. Don't interrupt. Let the learner finish all ten steps. If they've made only a single error, you'll be able to say, at the end, "Good, you got nine out of ten steps perfect! That's an "A" in my book. Now let's go back and have closer look at Step 7, so I can see how I should have laid it out better for you."

Perhaps you'll ask the person to demo that step again, or you'll add some helpful advice. But by not interrupting, en route, you preserve the learner's equilibrium. You also prevent another hazard: If you had interrupted the learner immediately to correct Step 7, the person may have censored other "radical" ideas at Steps 8 or 9. You'd never have learned of those changes, until they showed up later, on the job. Corrective interruptions can so break a learner's momentum that the learner may botch later steps out of sheer nervousness.

So wait. Sometimes, learners will correct themselves before you can—if you avoid breaking in. This would enable you to recognize and reward their self-correcting effort.

7. Set Mutual Checkpoints

When you turn trainees loose on a task, you need to reassure them that you'll help them stay on track and avoid errors later, especially on issues you know to be challenging. Learners, too, are often aware of their own strengths or weaknesses, and may ask you to provide extra check-back time at points you might not have chosen.

So, you should offer a chance to specify checkpoints at stages designed to protect both of you.

8. Create Standard Tracking Methods

Work out a simple progress reporting format or template, with quantifiable standards based on the criteria you set. This will ensure that if a task starts going off track, you will both see signals in time to correct errors. With Steps 7 and 8 in place, you will avoid micromanaging.

9. Provide Access as Needed

Even with checkpoints and reports, your learner may at first need extra access to you as questions arise. Set up checkpoints acceptable to you both. Never hover; it destroys confidence and momentum. As a time manager, you don't want to trigger undue randomness, so make your access times clear. Then the learner can list questions and come to you for cohesive advice.

10. Assign and Announce Authority

When you feel confident that the learner can handle the job, give the learner both the responsibility and authority to accomplish the task. Announce the appointment. Personally introduce learners to people whose cooperation they'll need, especially those of higher rank. Make sure your delegates can obtain whatever they need for a successful job—access, equipment, information, and cooperation from individuals and teams. Your announcement might say:

> Beginning April 7, I am delegating the Monthly Tools Audit to Jane Kemp. Fully trained and authorized, she will be coming to you for information on the same schedule that we've followed in the past.
>
> Please give her the same fine cooperation you've always given me. Thanks!

These ten steps may seem to require a lot of thought and work—simply to get a torch passed successfully. But heed the words of one successful delegator:

REAL VOICES

Lorraine Sergent, Systems Analyst for a major bank put it this way:

> How effective am I at delegating? At work, my delegation is exactly as effective as the instructions I give.

Two Responsibilities You Cannot Delegate

Delegation is difficult enough without setting yourself up for failure. You must retain two common responsibilities that callous managers sometimes try to offload:

1. Developmental work assigned you by your boss, to teach you a necessary skill. *This may be temporary.* Once you have learned and stabilized this process, you may get the boss's assent to delegate, so others in your team can broaden and deepen their knowledge.
2. Discipline. *This barrier is permanent.* If, as a manager, you neglect to discipline an unruly or malingering employee who reports to you, your team may feel forced to perform "rough justice" themselves—risking damage to morale, creating havoc with the operation, and exposing the company to legal consequences, later.

Discipline is your unshakeable duty, so get moving. Seek advice from your boss or Human Resources if you feel baffled, but don't ignore unacceptable behavior: it will not diminish or disappear by itself.

DELEGATION: NO EASY GUARANTEES

Sometimes, even with the best of intentions on both sides, delegation fails. Both parties may have papered over their reservations. Both may have been overoptimistic about the learner's ability to grasp new material at speed. Both may have ignored blanks in the learner's background—poor math or lack of writing skills or negotiating experience, for example. If, despite training and reinforcement, you must admit defeat, then accept your half (or more) of the responsibility, and withdraw this particular assignment, replacing it with a task more suited to the learner's capability.

CAUTION: Don't take the work back yourself. Remember this adage, practiced by smart managers since the days they built the hanging gardens of Babylon: "Work must be done at the lowest possible level where it can be done effectively."

So, whatever work you did a year ago—now stabilized and ready to delegate—you can no longer keep in your workload at your current rate of pay. If one candidate fails to work out, keep recruiting, keep training. Move on yourself, to tame those raw and risky tasks for which you are really being paid.

Kris Todisco, QA Director for an investment firm, told us:

I've been a people manager for a couple of decades now, and I think I delegate well. But it's still easy to get caught up in details and forget to delegate as much as possible, so I can focus on decision making.

Simple Signals that Your D-Day Has Arrived?

How can you tell that it's D-Day, Delegation Day?

- When you work more overtime, more often, without dramatic rewards.
- When you leave for vacations or weekends too frazzled to focus on fun.
- When you turn down exciting new work or miss out on new rewards because you're bogged down in stabilized routines.

When any of the above situations occurs, it's time to automate, relegate, or delegate!

BATTER DOWN CORPORATE BARRIERS

So far, we've discussed personal barriers based on all-too-human aspects of pride or fear. But let's acknowledge that tangible, corporate barriers can also impede your path to delegation.

Which of these are you facing?

1. *Short-staffed, or in a hiring freeze.* Current staff are so busy, there's no one who can help, and no money to hire.
   REMEDIES: Seek volunteers, or part-timers, retirees, or students. Tap any number of groups who seek temporary work without expecting benefits or high pay. Invest the time to recruit and

train some floaters. Stop hoping your overwork will ease by some miracle.

2. *Work that is complex and confidential.* Company rules—or my boss—require me to do it myself.

   REMEDIES: Dispute the confidentiality block. You may need to mask data on certain parts of the task, so you can delegate some processes, with numbers or identities hidden. As for complexity, you may poll local colleges or universities for star students, more adept at some specialties than you are. Probe that possibility. Don't cave in easily to the complexity barrier.

Look for Help in All the Right Places

Have you really tried everything? Consider the solutions others are using:

1. Volunteers

   We keep hearing from nonprofits and public services organizations about creative staffing solutions. To stand out from the crowd, offer:

   Flexible hours, or workdays of their choice. Then emphasize the value of the mission.

   Short hours. If you can get a regular, reliable helper for even as few as two hours per week, go for it. You'll pay less than you would with a temp agency and you'll get better continuity.

2. Students: For Credit and Continuity

   College and graduate students may come technically trained to do drafting, proofreading, or computer functions that would otherwise be costly to fill. Later, college students who have spent their summers with you may become full-time employees, with a track record you can both rely on. Stop doing your own library or Internet research. Research is what students do all day: they get good at it. Let them hit the library or surf some web sources while you stick to decision making or other tasks that require discernment.

   CAUTION: Of course, you will check their work for accuracy and ownership. People in school may take more liberties with other people's intellectual property than any corporation would venture to do.

High school students can often do typing, computing or simple research tasks for modest or no pay, to get added class credits. A written recommendation from your company may help them clinch a spot in the college they want.

3. Cross-Training for Job Swaps

    Trade some coverage with other departments whose production valleys may coincide with your production peaks. Too few companies explore this. We saw this done at a major East Coast insurance firm where six locations began cross-training teams to cover one another's peaks during coinciding valleys. The company was so delighted with the savings that they gave all participating teams a bonus for achieving the most orderly seasonal turnarounds in the company's history. That's creative time management.

Two More Gambits

Especially if you work for a small company with a small staff, here are a couple of ideas for you.

Try a Task Force   We've seen some companies form temporary alliances with noncompeting neighboring firms, even with their suppliers, their equally small law firm, or their accounting firm. They formed partnerships on a project basis, trading one kind of service for another—accounting for clerical coverage, artwork for text editing. Some firms form partnerships on a project basis.

Try Outsourcing or Spinning Off Daughter Companies   Outsource some work (bookkeeping, auditing) to someone who'll do it better than you can. Throughout history, companies have often rotated between vertical integration (doing all their own work) and spinning off work at which they find they cannot excel at an acceptable cost. Cut your losses. Get out of some businesses when you see you cannot bring them to your desired quality level quickly.

YOUR OVERARCHING ATTITUDE FOR SUCCESS

If you hope to succeed at delegating, you must act consistently to make each new assignment a reward, not a burden. Let people compete for the great assignments that they'll remember in later years as the projects that boosted their careers and gave them some fun, too. If the task you delegate is arduous and challenging, you might consider extending a "signing bonus" to someone strong enough and smart enough to take it on. Don't reject these ideas out of hand; they may propel your team or your company to outpace all competitors.

REAL VOICES

Richard Shirley, IT Systems Manager for the military, says:

> The key for me has been to delegate tasks properly and to cross-train the people I work with so they can interchange tasks as needed. It's vital to assign the right people to the task, and then provide them with all the tools they need. We are fortunate to work with very talented people who foster a synergistic approach to solving problems.

Like Harry and Vijay at the start of this chapter, you will win at delegation if you involve your team in joint graphic task-mapping that helps everyone tackle challenges creatively. Comfort with delegation is a sign of business maturity.

REAL VOICES

Roger Nys, Regional Manager at Howard Hughes Medical Institute, sees delegation as a lifelong learning project:

> When I was younger, I wanted to do everything myself, because I thought it took too long to explain what I wanted and how I wanted it. Now, I've become more willing to let others try. It took a long time, but I have learned to delegate effectively. I follow a rule of not taking work home. I tell my direct reports to follow the same rule.

Help your people get a good running start on delegated assignments. Then, make sure that all of you get home on time, more often. The boost in energy and morale can make all the difference when the next stressful period arises to test your mettle.

CHECK YOURSELF

How do you score on escaping delegating and training traps? Rate yourself on the following; then repeat the process thirty days from now. Simple Yes/No answers will suffice.

Questions	Today	30 Days
1. When delegating, I choose tasks that are stable and repetitive, but that offer a step up to the learner.	———	———
2. I assess the match between the task and the person's capabilities before delegating a task.	———	———
3. In training a delegate, I write up the task and demonstrate it myself. Then I have the learner demonstrate, and I invite open questions.	———	———
4. I delegate both responsibility and authority, and announce the change to all whose cooperation is needed.	———	———
5. I work with the delegate to ensure regular progress reports so any problems can be detected and corrected.	———	———
6. I regularly update job descriptions of all people who report to me so their responsibility and authority levels are clear.	———	———
7. We cross-train people for coverage, while building skills that enhance job security.	———	———
Total	———	———

CHAPTER

17

Procrastination and Leaving Tasks Unfinished

In previous chapters, we considered time traps common to all enterprises, with policies, practices, and people all contributing to the problems.

Now, we arrive at the final three traps, where the causes are all ours: we snare ourselves in our own unconscious habits. Our behaviors baffle our bosses and customers and they bother us, too, when we manage to notice them at all.

In this chapter we'll offer some practical remedies, but the initiative, the commitment, and the cure will depend upon us—on our willingness to change. These final chapters will raise the toughest challenges of all, but the rewards will be personal and permanent, with recoveries that can be deeply satisfying.

Let's begin with the perilous pair, "Can't get started—Can't get finished!" Two seemingly distinct traps—they occupied adjacent chapters in earlier editions. But, today, we see them as the same issue. Both are failures to engage, occurring at opposite ends of a task continuum.

Luckily, a single escape can spring us from both traps. The remedy—keeping intense focus from start to finish on any task worthy of our attention—will not be easy because we are surrounded by distractions and deceived by our own denial. To achieve the necessary change, the pro-crastinators among us will need three stimulants to willingness:

1. A *goal* clear and compelling enough to energize us at the start and sustain us to the finish.
2. A *priority system* to hold our focus on important/urgent matters, rather than on distracting smaller jobs, defined as "busy work."
3. A set of *alarm bells*—tools to help us notice and refocus when subtle habits drag us back toward delay.

CAREER CONSEQUENCES ACCRUE

Whether our "customers" are internal or external, we must beware: they'll impose stricter penalties for procrastination and delay than for honest er-rors or correctable quality lapses.

Why? Because bosses and customers acutely resent being taken hostage—being exposed to last-minute risk without warning. Bosses, customers, and teammates will strike back at any partner who denies them the power to choose options in time to recover.

And what will the eventual outcomes be? The procrastinator's boss may impose discipline outright (with commitments and timetables im-posed) or the procrastinator will be gradually edged out of important projects, quietly excluded from exciting team assignments—and finally, isolated with a set of routine tasks that are easy to quantify and self-supervise. ("Either you process 50 items per hour—the standard—or you're out!")

Eventually, such routine work gets automated, off-loaded, or elimi-nated in all companies. So the "demise of a chronic delayer" may be slow, but it's inexorable.

Denial Blurs Responsibility

Procrastinators do not notice the pattern: their behavior is not deliberate or calculated, or malicious. Procrastinators and "non-finishers" simply fail to connect their late deliveries to earlier missteps. They remain un-aware of repetitions that others easily notice. When a boss or customer complains, some procrastinators will actually blame the conflict on a "mood," a personality flaw, or "tantrum" on the part of the "unreasonable" complainant.

Sadly, the habits of denial and delay are mutually reinforcing. Here's a case in point.

> One morning, as a commuter train was pulling out of a suburban station, a regular patron was chatting, pleasantly, with the conductor. They both glanced out the window as the conductor said: "Oh-oh, here he comes again."
>
> A heavy-set man came pounding down the platform, briefcase in one hand, latte in the other, with a look of panic that increased as the train pulled away. A good hundred feet back, he made a try for it, running full tilt. But the train accelerated, and he pulled up in defeat. Exasperated, he shouted some epithets at the last departing car.
>
> The two men, inside the train, said, almost in unison: "Mister, you should have started sooner."

Can You Claim Immunity?

Perhaps, at some point in life, all of us have been like that tardy commuter. We have tackled a task too late, or let our energy fizzle out before the finish—foregoing a goal that really mattered to us. If this happens to you rarely, you can forgive yourself, reform, and move on. If it repeats too often, however, you may need to admit proneness to procrastinate, or failure to finish. Admit the reality and you become ready to apply remedies.

THE REMEDIES ARE REACHABLE

Once you get past denial, once you understand the consequences clearly, you have a good chance for recovery. Here are some minimum steps to liberate you:

1. Plan and estimate new tasks early, so you can see and negotiate load size. (We covered these issues in Part I, Chapters 3 and 4, and in Part II, Chapter 7.)
2. Map your plans and schedules on the wall where all can see them. Bosses and colleagues of good will can help you persevere.

3. Establish standard lead times for important repeat tasks. Use averages from a number of sources to validate your findings, so you can quote and negotiate realistic expectations with requesters.

If that three-part remedy seems like too much work, you may need to slow down a bit, study the root causes, and assess the career damage you risk by staying in this twin time trap.

Perspectives on Possible Causes

The first step to recovery—as with all human foibles—is to admit that you are acting in a particular way. If you procrastinate at work, consistently enough to draw negative notice, you must discover what underlying cause is driving these delays. Is it:

- *Fear of failure?* If a task is risky, if others' expectations seem too high, if you feel unsure of your skills, you may be loath to get started.
- *Lethargy?* Like a stubborn weed, low energy and indifference will send out roots in all directions, strangling motivation. Even simple tasks can fall by the wayside when there are plenty of distractions to run out the clock.
- *Anger or hostility* toward a requester? Even when justified, negativity can drive delays. Some procrastinators harbor resentment at an amorphous "them" or "they"—whoever is in power, wherever they may be. Blocked from expressing hostility directly at work, some people simply withhold effort, like an angry toddler holding his breath—as if doing so will asphyxiate the all-powerful parent!

Round Up the Usual Excuses

Of course none of us can easily admit to any of these motives. Instead, we rationalize our delaying tactics with excuses, some valid, some not:

- I don't have the necessary tools or materials.
- I'm forced to wait for other departments to deliver the details.
- There's no real rush: this demand is from someone pulling rank.

- I'll do it later: I work best under pressure.
- The last time I hurried for this person, I got no thanks.
- Others will take the credit for what I do, so why hurry?
- I never get clear instructions from on high; they're never available to clarify.
- Requesters change their minds every twenty minutes. I'll just wait.

There may have been times when you were correct to put off a task requested by someone famous for changing his mind. That's okay. But we may admit finding it hard to tackle a job with gusto when the requester has earned our hearty dislike.

At such times, we may have to summon up all our professionalism, and do the job anyway, because "it goes with the territory."

PROCRASTINATION TAKES A TOLL ON ALL

Unconscious or not, procrastination causes damage:

- Some people come late for meetings, and then noisily distract everyone else.
- Some put off answering e-mails and fail to return calls.
- Some delay delivery on their portion of a project, dampening progress for all.
- Some withhold information, believing that knowledge is power that need not be shared.

Ironically, some procrastinators see themselves as relaxed, easygoing, pleasant people who don't let anything rattle them. This delusion raises the hackles of colleagues who come to abhor the "whatever . . . whenever" attitude conveyed by the procrastinator's body language. As one programmer complained about a procrastinating teammate: "No, she doesn't *suffer* from stress: she's a *carrier!*"

Even for the clueless, overwhelmed procrastinator, delay isn't the worst price imposed on the team. Instead the greater risk arises during those frantic eleventh-hour rescue sessions as the team strives to avoid serious errors. In the last-minute rush to meet the deadline, the team may turn out inferior results at higher cost, with no chance of a calm review.

Hooked on Self-Deception or Self-Will?

People who fail to start or finish on time are not necessarily lazy. They don't simply loll about, blithely loafing while others work or wait. Instead, they busy themselves with the tasks they enjoy, while putting off tasks they consider taxing, unpleasant, or frightening. Many are skilled at looking busy.

Tasks requiring discipline or diplomacy are anathema—even if they could be dispatched quickly. True, most of us will steel ourselves before delivering a necessary reprimand, phoning a reluctant sales prospect, or responding to an irate customer. Tasks demanding extra effort, risk, or embarrassment are tough for all of us.

But, for procrastinators—the more repellent the task, the farther down in the pile it gets buried. The day wears on; the clock runs down. Then, it seems reasonable to just fold up and go home. Tomorrow is another day. Until the boss or customer gets hopping mad, the procrastinator avoids thinking about consequences.

Sometimes, a vigilant boss or requester does discover the delay—just in time for a rescue. If there's a showdown, the procrastinator feels genuinely shocked. Following is a case in point:

> Kazuko, a smart and compassionate manager, gave an important assignment to analyst, Doug, one Friday morning. To begin, she looked over his to-do list with him, and initialed the postponement of a couple of tasks to make room for the new one.
>
> "Don't worry about these," she assured him. "I'm clearing a trade-off with the department heads involved."
>
> When two days passed, with no visible signs of his having started, Kazuko asked Doug to stop in with a progress report. Walking into the room, he was already talking:

> DOUG: Yeah, I know, I know . . . I probably should have gotten going before now, but I've had all this other work to do. Don't worry though; I'm one of those people who works best under pressure. I know I can get it to you by Friday. That's your deadline, right?

> KAZUKO: Friday is the deadline, yes. But as I told you, Doug, my time estimate for this job is 8–10 hours, even if all goes well—and then, a couple of units have to weigh in on the results, so you can't wait until the due date to start.

DOUG: I still had a lot of other work to clear.

KAZUKO: What work? I relieved you of two big tasks when I assigned this one to you. That should have put the new project at Number One.

DOUG: Yes, but I was so far along in those other two jobs, it would have bugged me not to finish them . . .so I made a judgment call.

KAZUKO (*her face reddens but her voice is steady*): And you didn't think you should mention that intention of yours while we were still talking . . . or since . . .

DOUG: Not when I know I can get everything done. I do my best work under pressure.

KAZUKO (*after a few seconds pause*): You do seem to believe that, Doug. But frankly, I'm not persuaded. It's your natural ability under *any* circumstance that prevents outright disaster when you work under pressure. But when you tempt fate this way, you risk the level of precision we need on your "first pass." In the past, others have ended up correcting and refining your work after you submit it. That's not OK.

DOUG: I just know that in the past, when I've pushed a tight deadline, being near the edge has sort of stimulated me to do my best.

KAZUKO (*speaking more deliberately*): Like any manager here, when I relieve you of low-priority work to allow your full attention to higher priorities, I expect you to comply. No manager would allow you, secretly, to continue on unauthorized work at the expense of a priority. This is serious, Doug.

DOUG (*still not hearing her*): All right, Kazuko . . . but can I just finish those two? It would only take an hour or so more—and then I can start on your new task.

KAZUKO (*fixing him in her glance*): Let me be clear on this. In a company like ours no one can follow hidden agendas contrary to direct instructions. Not me, not you, not anyone. When I relieved you of those two tasks, I already had agreement, upstream, that those items would be delayed until next week. So your choosing to keep on with them will not advance the action at all. It will also dishonor the departments who've already accepted delay as a favor to us.

You're simply enforcing your self-will, Doug. None of us can afford that luxury here. Now—if you want to secure your job and overcome the serious problem you've made for yourself, you can do it by complying with direct orders from here on. Are you clear about this?

DOUG (*standing up, looking a bit shaken*): Yeah, I get it. And hey, I apologize. I didn't see how much trouble I was causing. Try not to hold it against me, will you?

Break the Spell

If the foregoing scenario seems painfully familiar to you (as requester or procrastinator) there are ways to take control before consequences harden. If the stakes are high enough, procrastinators can replace self-delusion with healthier behaviors.

If you can't seem to get started on an assignment, here are some ways to rev your engines and maintain momentum:

- Prove to yourself that change is necessary, now!
- Review some recent consequences suffered by you and others.
- Sketch out a plan showing current demands that are waiting for action.
- Break large jobs into parts, and set interim goals.
- Set deadlines for these shorter-term goals.
- Map your plans on the wall.
- Tick off finished goals, on a wall chart or whiteboard for visual encouragement.
- Celebrate segment completions.

KEEP A TASK DIARY AS A RESTART TOOL

On completing any project that you found hard to begin and harder to maintain, create a diary as a tool that returns your investment. If you must repeat this task quarterly or yearly, your journal will help you anticipate needs correctly. You might list, as an example:

Project X _____

- Task as originally assigned:
- Original deadline or timeline:
- Unforeseen problems that arose:
- Solutions found:
- Time actually required on key segments:

Segments	Estimated Hours	Actual
a. Initial task layout	_____	_____
b. Research	_____	_____
c. Findings	_____	_____
d. Validation steps	_____	_____
e. Approval issues	_____	_____
f. Final steps	_____	_____

Costs	Estimates	Actual
	_____	_____

By all means, design your own format. Include whatever data will help you tackle the job next time for fast and confident execution. These notes will also help you negotiate changes. (Down the road, they may also help you train a future subordinate.)

Especially if you are a self-employed solo operator, there will be no one else to remind you about lessons learned on completed projects: you must record them for yourself, set your objectives, and revisit your priorities daily.

REAL VOICES

Mel Northey, Owner and President of an architectural metals firm, writes from his Houston base:

To plot our strategy for a productive and profitable business, I specified both long- and short-term goals; then set company objectives based on those goals. In the construction boom of the past decade, we excelled at meeting tough production and delivery schedules. But I've learned to keep objectives flexible. Now, my challenge is to retain profit margins and protect my employees despite the chaos in financial markets that is choking off new building.

From my flexed list of objectives I categorize my priorities, keeping
them in front of me, to hold my focus, despite temporary turbulence.

MAKING TIME FOR TOP PRIORITIES

Ask yourself what percentage of your typical day requires hard choices and possible negotiation with requesters? As we demonstrated in earlier chapters, Pareto's Law posits that the top 20 percent of your daily tasks will drive 80 percent of your results.

Decide which of your current and incoming tasks comprise your top 20 percent. Then focus your best attention there during the best slots in your day when you can depend on energy, access and privacy to get work done. You may not cure procrastination altogether, but your top 20 percent of priorities *must* start and finish without fail.

No matter how rushed you are, short-list those tasks onto a humble sticky note. Post it where you can see it, and perform accordingly. Let nothing interfere that has lower importance.

Your New Ideal Day

You may complain that your day is so jammed with small jobs and interruptions that you have no time for priorities. Your plans evaporate so why make them? Yet, all of us handle specific tasks that occur more or less regularly. Teachers have to make up lesson plans for the week. Department managers must confer with section heads on vital production issues. PR consultants develop new campaigns for clients. Finance officers prepare quarterly reports for shareholders. Attorneys draw up proxy statements for SEC compliance. These tasks are not escapable, not optional.

What elements must you protect in your ideal day at the time of year where those prime events occur? You must be clear about which tasks really matter.

REAL VOICES

Lindsay Geyer, VP of Human Resources at Port Blakely Companies, puts it this way:

There's a fine line between being an effective multitasker and attempting
too many things ineffectively. If I have a lot of plates in the air, I try to

identify which ones are Melmac and which are "bone china." If I have to
let something drop, I make sure it's the Melmac!

For Lindsay, the "bone china" items are her top 20 percent. No matter who you are, your ideal day should start with your top 20 percent of tasks made visible in reserved Red Zone slots on your calendar, so nothing of less importance can trump them.

What About Mid- and Low-Priority Tasks?

In earlier chapters, we outlined exactly how to protect your top 20 percent of tasks. What we have *not* talked about until now, is the fate of tasks that don't qualify for Red Zone treatment. These are the tasks that procrastinators allow to crowd out their higher priorities. The procrastinator's rationale goes like this:

"Why not get a lot of small things out of the way early? Then I can tackle the big things with a clear conscience"

Sounds reasonable, but it's a delusion, a recipe for starting slow on priorities, failing to finish the high-impact tasks, and inviting demotion, if not career demolition. Still, some people find it hard to fathom: a weary seminar participant made this statement:

I have plenty of priorities. I'm swimming in them. And each of my bosses insists: "Here's your new number one: Drop everything and take care of this." Well, they can't *all* be number one for me. I usually jot down the demand while they stand there—and then go for coffee. More often than not, I do a lot of small things to get people off my back, but then I'm too tired to do the big things.

DISTINGUISH IMPORTANT FROM URGENT, ONCE AND FOR ALL.

Though we've discussed this dilemma in our earlier chapters on triage, distinguishing between important and urgent still puzzles most people. The distinction bears repeating:

- *Important tasks* are those jobs you'll look back on at the end of a year (or a career) and realize how right you were to invest your time, effort, and heart into getting them right. Important tasks usually link directly to important goals embraced by your company, your team, and yourself.

- *Urgent tasks*, by contrast, are emergencies or tight deadline tasks of importance to some—but not all—parties involved.
  - If an emergency can threaten life and limb, or corporate survival, it matters to all—so you will respond—and fast! But it's the importance, not the urgency of the task that validates your quick response.
  - Contrarily, if the only vivid feature in a task is its tight deadline, you must queue it up behind all the other more valid tasks competing for that time slot. You must protect priorities, no matter how much a requester yells, hoping to cover his own lack of foresight.
- *Important* and *urgent tasks* qualify for Red Zone treatment, but these two features rarely occur at the same time. Requesters must dedicate both planning and vigilance to important tasks so they cannot become urgent too late in a work cycle. If valid important tasks keep getting done on an urgent basis, negligence should be suspected. Responsible managers keep important (valid) tasks "in process" continuously, so time cannot run out on them.

When pressed for a decision that is merely urgent to the requester, many a wise and powerful senior executive has ruled: "If the answer must be *now*—the answer must be *no*."

It's amazing how effectively that works to tame the demanding party's insistence, allowing a more reasoned debate and a clear decision, without irrational appeals to urgency. Unless someone is bleeding from the aorta, you can make the time to judge matters on importance, keeping urgency in its place to "tie-break" between tasks of equal validity.

Graphics Help Everyone Get the Point

Don't attempt to validate tasks "in your head," as each new challenge arises. Instead, sketch your whole week's work graphically, so that you, your boss, and your team can see how you prioritize work. On a sketch like the one below, lay in your actual tasks alongside the three zones.

Show which tasks qualify for Red Zone. Those will occupy the top of the chart. Next, list the tasks that can claim a spot near the upper portion of the Mid-Zone.

Once you teach yourself to think this way, you will see that you have enough Red Zone and Mid-Zone tasks to keep you busy, permanently.

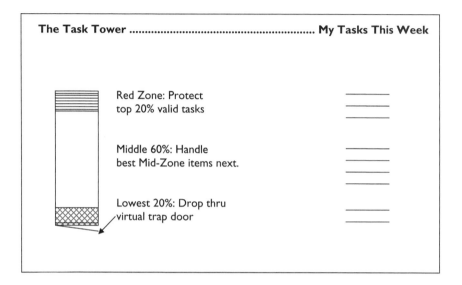

The Task Tower .... **My Tasks This Week**

Red Zone: Protect
top 20% valid tasks

Middle 60%: Handle
best Mid-Zone items next.

Lowest 20%: Drop thru
virtual trap door

Here's How to Validate Your Actual Tasks

1. Define and move to the top of your Red Zone list the worthiest 20 percent of current tasks (those with both the highest risk and the highest value). Also, note in your Red Zone any foreseeable but not preventable crises that could arise in a given season or circumstance (world events, shortages) to which you might have to react.

2. By contrast, at the bottom of the tower, specify the lowest or "dumbest" 20 percent of tasks, tasks you have accepted until now but which cannot pay their way. If you let them languish long enough at the foot of your tower, their visible persistence may irritate you long enough to help you delegate or outsource them at the lowest possible hourly rate. Mentally release them through a virtual trap door you envision at the base of the tower. Compared to your top 20 percent they should not stand

a chance with you. Don't fear this as a radical move. Every company has ceased making products or offering services that no longer pay their way. Do your company a favor and be the first to notice unworthy jobs in your own workload.

PUZZLED BY TIME ALLOTMENT QUESTIONS?

Here are some FAQs about how to plan your day:

1. *How much time should I allow for my Red Zone tasks?* For your Red Zone tasks, allot at least two hours per day (not necessarily full or consecutive hours, but segments of time you hold sacred). Let nothing interrupt or interfere with this modest daily allotment of time. Other concerns (in the middle 60 percent of your day) can claim up to six hours of your time, but they cannot usurp Red Zone time.

2. *Which two hours?* For your top tasks, reserve your *best*—not earliest—time segments in any day. Bear in mind that your days vary—Tuesdays differ from Fridays—in terms of incoming traffic flow, time-driven deliverables, formal meetings, travel, etc. So set aside time deliberately, consciously, into slots with the best chance of remaining whole.

3. *What factors define "best time"?* Choose the times, each day, when you can bank on:

   - Your highest energy level.
   - Fewest interruptions.
   - Best access to relevant data or contacts.
   - Lowest volume of routine traffic.

4. *What about the "Mid-Zone" 60 percent of tasks?* Once you have protected your top 20 percent and relegated your bottom 20 percent, you've removed 40 percent of your work from the field of contention. When your Red Zone tasks are safely in protected slots, you can start on the best of the middle 60 percent—often legitimate support routines. Do these in your average (not best) working hours.

This approach will take you a lot farther than the high-stress option used by most procrastinators: juggling 100 percent of the workload on instinct!

One More Important Insight

Only "major impact items" (or new "Reds") may bump an existing Red Zone task. Mark such a "bump" with a special color or icon on your schedule. For the rest of your career, that color or icon will mean only one thing: you bumped a major risk/opportunity for something that mattered *even more*. You bumped a Red with a bigger, incoming Red. If, over a few weeks' time, you collect enough of these new Reds then you must ask yourself:

- Has my job changed?
- Are these new risks and opportunities my "new" job?
- What are they worth?
- Are they temporary or permanent?
- By what percentage have they expanded my work volume and risk load?
- Do I need to hire help for this larger volume?
- Do I merit a raise for handling higher-value work?

SIMPLEST CURE FOR "SLOW TO START; FAIL TO FINISH"

As Alec Mackenzie stated repeatedly in his books and seminars, "A daily plan, in writing, is the single most effective time management strategy." Yet, he rued the fact that only one person in ten does the daily plan. The other nine go home at night muttering: "Where did the day go?"

Keep the Daily Plan Visible

Follow a simple, consistent daily routine to accomplish your priorities. The following seven steps will make it easy.

1. Use your calendar, appointment book, or electronic planner, not your wits and quick reactions.
2. List your top three tasks for the day, those with high risks and payoffs aligned with your goals.
3. Schedule those three tasks into the best, not earliest slots in your day.
4. Determine your best times: the times you know you can work well with energy, accuracy, access to data, and enough quiet for

sustained focus. You may also need privacy for conversations on sensitive performance issues.

5. Slot your top three tasks in the Red Zone before allotting time to any other demands.

6. Except for protecting the top 20 percent of your tasks, leave most of your schedule loose for unexpected as well as Mid-Zone jobs. But let nothing come between you and achievement of the top 20 percent.

7. Realize that your top three tasks may sometimes exhaust most of your day and at other times use only a couple of hours.
Whatever the duration, protect these Red Zone time slots. Start and finish tasks on time to conquer the procrastination habit in ways that pay off handsomely.

Credit Yourself for Work Done

If you have read this chapter thoughtfully, and honestly, then, congratulate yourself, with our thanks. Rooting out unconscious habits, overcoming denial—these are difficult tasks for all of us.

If, on the other hand, you were able to say, "Luckily, I neither procrastinate nor fail to finish tasks," then congratulations on that! In the next two chapters, you may see whether you can absolve yourself of the remaining human behaviors that constitute the final time traps of this series: socializing, entertaining drop-ins, and attempting too much.

The oddity with these final traps is that most people consider these behaviors virtuous, proofs of warm friendliness or intense dedication. They're not virtues. And they're next.

CHECK YOURSELF

How do you score on escaping the procrastination trap? Rate yourself on the following; then repeat the process thirty days from now. Simple Yes/No answers will suffice.

Questions	Today	30 Days
1. When tempted to put off tasks, I segment the task, set deadlines for all portions, and then focus on part one.	———	———
2. I watch for procrastination on my team and help them overcome it by pointing out consequences to the enterprise.	———	———
3. I run early estimates on new tasks, and negotiate deadlines.	———	———
4. I'm intrigued with a chance to list tasks at high, mid, and low impact. I focus on Red Zone first, then high Mid-Zone.	———	———
5. If I see any threat to finishing a project, I inform the requester, negotiating for clarity or extra time.	———	———
6. To sustain pace, I celebrate reaching interim goals.	———	———
7. Because some of my tasks repeat months apart, I will start keeping a Task Diary so I don't have to start from scratch the next time that task comes up.	———	———
Total	———	———

CHAPTER

Socializing and Drop-In Visitors

"Hey, got a minute?"

You've probably heard this innocent-sounding question several times a day, all your life. Sometimes, you welcome it gladly, because anything's better than what you're doing now!

But when your fondness for fellowship overrules your common sense, your schedule runs over.

Of course, most corporations list "ability to get along with others" as a sought-after trait in employees. So, people make the effort to be sociable—the majority coming to it quite easily, because they enjoy face time with their fellows, and they like staying in the loop.

Once you set a pattern of welcoming random interruptions, however, you give away control of your day. People who do a time log on just this one topic—socializing—are often astounded by the aggregate time drained away by walk-in visitors. They also notice that those "got-a-minute" guys seem to get home on time, while the "willing host" gets to exchange sympathies with the night maintenance crew far too often.

Two things you know for sure:

1. Drop-in visits always take longer than a minute. In fact, the average drop-in lasted ten minutes when Alec researched the previous edition of *The Time Trap*, and it's probably no better now.

2. For every one minute you allow the interrupter, you'll need four minutes to regain your original focus. When you accept a two-minute drop-in you can expect an eight-minute expedition getting back to your work—even if you kept a marker in place.

DEFEND YOUR RIGHT TO FOCUS

To minimize lost momentum, try this. If someone interrupts you in mid-task, take a moment to prepare the task for your return. Say to your interrupter: "Give me a second and then I'll be right with you."

Then do what is necessary. Finish your sentence, add that column of figures, wrap up the phone call, or stick a placeholder in your notes. Then, welcome the visitor with a smile.

REAL VOICES

Bart Denison, Operations Lead for a major software manufacturer, controls socializing this way:

> I love using the Outlook tasks list and calendar view together to block out time to work on specific tasks. This allows others to see that I am working on something and shouldn't be disturbed. It also helps me stay focused on getting results.
>
> If I am interrupted, I try to get to the end of the thought or sentence before acknowledging the interruption. I may make a quick note of next steps to help me pick up where I left off.

So, Whose Time Is More Important?

A drop-in visitor is a living, breathing conflict with your priorities. Let's look at a typical example:

It's 2:45 P.M. You are gathering up the presentation you'll conduct in fifteen minutes. A peer manager pokes his head in and asks, "Got a minute?"

Though your body language says "not now," he looks right past you because he needs a decision on something by four o'clock, and he knows you won't be back by then. You feel a slight flicker of annoyance because you judge that this guy waits until the last minute to ask for most things. But you soften up and say: "Well, OK, shoot, but be quick. I can't be late for this meeting."

As he runs his problem past you, several things become clear:

- This is a lower-priority matter.
- It's not urgent.
- He could have asked for input days ago.
- He could have made this decision himself.

But now, trying not to appear miffed, you start laying out some quick options as you gather up your materials, your phone, your remote control, and your PowerPoint–loaded laptop. You tell him he must decide for himself, or wait until you have time for a rational discussion. You hurry to your meeting, trying to steady your focus on the group waiting in the conference room.

Five Ways to Manage Drop-Ins

1. If someone asks for "just a minute" learn to say:
   "I can give you *five* minutes if we can get it done in five. Otherwise, we must leave it to later, unless you can fix it yourself."
2. If they opt to try it now, you must be ready to cut off at five minutes. Say:
   "That's it. Time's up. I must leave right now."
3. Before entertaining any talk at all, you may need to say a clear no:
   "If I'd have known about this yesterday, I could have planned time to talk. There's just no time right now. Sorry, I've gotta go!"
4. You could say: "I need to finish up a priority task. Can you come back later?" Then, name a time.
5. To a chronically tardy subordinate or peer, you could say:
   "We can talk when I get back at 4:30. Arrange a delay with the contractor. Take responsibility for it; don't lay the delay at my door."

Worried About Losing Friends?

Habitual caving in will not gain friends nor enhance respect, especially not self-respect.

HUMAN COMEDY

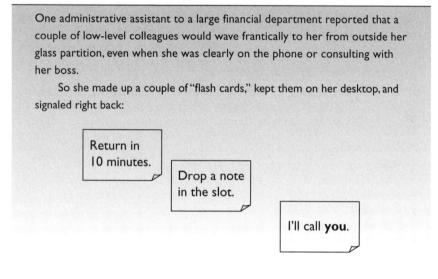

One administrative assistant to a large financial department reported that a couple of low-level colleagues would wave frantically to her from outside her glass partition, even when she was clearly on the phone or consulting with her boss.

So she made up a couple of "flash cards," kept them on her desktop, and signaled right back:

> Return in 10 minutes.

> Drop a note in the slot.

> I'll call **you**.

But if you dare not leave drop-ins to their own devices because you foresee risks to the project or company, you may have to get involved, even when pressed for time.

WARNING: Once you inquire about what's on the interrupter's mind—you've already entered the trap. Depending on what you discover, you can now take one of four possible routes, all involving some bother for you:

1. *Deal* with the issue. If it's "quick fix" or a real emergency, you're right to deal with it now. Often, you can use quick-fix interruptions to coach a direct-report toward self-help next time.
2. *Refer* the visitor to the correct source.
3. *Postpone* the problem by setting up another time to meet. Then, you may do some teaching/coaching.

4. *Assign* the interrupter to work out a solution and then check back with you.

In all four cases, your decisions are firm: your self-respect remains intact.

Scripts for Setting Boundaries

Now, let's consider the wording that can protect your boundaries without costing you friends. Consider these scenarios:

Scenario #1: Deal with a quick fix issue (and teach a skill, too).

DROP-IN DIRECT REPORT: "Oops, Boss, I just noticed the deadline on this discount option is this afternoon. Sorry; I had to put it aside because I wasn't sure how to . . ."

YOU: "Quick, sit down and we'll run the numbers. We need to go for the discount. Let me show you." (You point out the items to be tallied.)

DROP-IN DIRECT REPORT: "Oh, I get it. We should calculate current scrap rates as well as inventory to get that subtotal . . . then, take the discount."

YOU: "Yeah. Make a note of it so you'll have the formula straight for next time. Meanwhile, send this right out; you'll make the deadline.

Scenario #2: Use a Brief Referral.

DROP-IN PEER: "Hi! Did we get a final cost on that equipment?"

YOU: "Yup. If you bring up the project website, you'll see the new totals."

VISITOR: "OK, I'll take a look. Thanks."

You return to your work.

Scenario #3: Postpone.

DROP-IN TEAMMATE: "Got a minute?"

YOU: "Hi, What's up?"

VISITOR: "Well, it's that Petro-D case. I can't quite get a handle on it. Didn't you have something like this about a year ago?"

YOU: "Yeah. Judge Winston, Ninth Circuit."

VISITOR: "Can you tell me about it?"

YOU: "Sure. I think I have a few ideas for you. But right now, I've gotta keep going on this brief. How about tomorrow after 10:00? Get your paralegal to pull the files from archives. Study up so we can get right to specifics, Okay?"

With colleagues there's no need to apologize if you must postpone. And it's OK to insist they do their homework first.

Scenario #4: Assign the Next Few Steps to Move Things Along

DROP-IN PEER: "Got a minute?"

YOU: "Actually, I'm really jammed up. What do you need?"

VISITOR: "There's some confusion about the architect's rendering and she's out of town all week."

YOU: "And . . .?"

VISITOR: "And our proposal to the bank is due on Friday."

YOU: "Well, I'm just not in a position to pull away right now. Did you ask who's covering that architect while she's away. You might check with Art Macklin, too. He sat in on the discussions and he knows the bank people. I'll get back with you if I get any more ideas. Meanwhile, you can make some headway."

If you supervise newcomers, you owe them your help, along with frequent access so they can't stray far. But with more experienced workers, you must insist that they do their own legwork. Once newcomers gain some experience, you can make them reach higher with questions like:

* "Who else have you asked about this?"
* "What answers do you have so far?"
* "Why not construct a good solution and run it by me in the morning?"

Control the Urge to Hand-Hold

Here's a scenario where you may not be the right person to help, however kindhearted you feel.

It's late afternoon, and you are plowing through some deadline work when Marianne, your PR copywriter, appears in the doorway:

MARIANNE: "Got a minute, Boss?"

YOU: "Only if it's really quick. What is it?"

MARIANNE: "You suggested that I gather background on the City Council budget before I start on this press release. I'm finding it hard to fathom the numbers."

YOU: "Let's give it fifteen minutes tomorrow morning."

MARIANNE: "I think it would take more time than that."

YOU: "That's going to be problem. Remember: the budget data should only impact the closing paragraph of the release. So polish up the body of the piece, and do all you can to parse that budget data with the financial team so we can clean up the final draft in that fifteen minutes. Got it?"

If you are her boss but not a financial expert, Marianne may wake up and realize which colleagues she needs to ask, other than you—or which favor she needs to call in—to educate herself before she visits you again tomorrow.

Renegotiate Your Own Optimism

Sometimes, a task that looked like a cakewalk turns out otherwise. If, after a few minutes, you see a threat to your available time, you might say to a subordinate, "Stephanie, forgive me. I thought this was going to be easier to figure out. It's clearly going to take quite a while. I have a ten o'clock deadline coming up, so would you mind putting this off? Frankly, I'm out of time now."

Stephanie may be disappointed—but she may now put more effort into chasing down the facts so your later session will be productive. It's her issue: she must chase it.

Teach subordinates they must prepare well, to waste less time for those whose approvals they need. Her next boss may be tougher on that score than you.

SET YOUR RADAR TO
REDUCE RANDOM ACCESS

Many workers, surrounded by congenial teammates, may keep up an unconscious patter of friendly chatter to lighten up their otherwise strenuous days. And who would want to deny them? But read on to see what one team learned by noticing habits.

> After a Time Management seminar with Alec Mackenzie, one hospital administrator and his top-flight team gained so much insight about their habits that they ran a Time Log exercise for one week. They discovered they were spending nearly two hours a day in "door jamb" and hallway conversations. They had always gotten along so well, they hardly noticed their habit of randomly interrupting each other, whenever a good idea or a question occurred to them.
>
> Amazed at what they found, they decided to exchange total "openness" for "accessibility." They did not mean to cut the duration, but only the *randomness* of their contacts. So each person started batching non-urgent questions, and covering them in a couple of shorter sessions per day.
>
> Within two weeks, the time log showed their chat times dropping to only thirty minutes daily, and with far better follow-through, too.
>
> Next, they agreed to allow each other "closed door" times when they could work on priority tasks, undisturbed. Soon, they achieved 50 percent more issues settled and sent onward for action.
>
> Nurses' stations and lateral departments noticed they were getting their orders and answers more promptly because the executive team had abandoned "fly by" communication.

Monitor Your Physical Setup

The majority of mid-level workers don't even have a door. If your cube lies in the path to the break room or copy center, you'll get more than your share of visitors. If you can't move, or you can't close a door, you can, at least, create some visual barriers or sit oblique to the traffic, so passersby can't catch your eye or read your screen, en route.

Consider, too, whether extra chairs, candy jars, combat games during breaktimes, and personal coffee makers are luring the lonely to your lair.

Use Body Language and Graphics to Cue a Close

If someone visits for a valid reason, then stays to chat, allow this only for as long as you can afford. Stand up to signal "time's up." Or start shifting from your relaxed slump to a more upright, alert position, reach for a folder and say: "Now, let's cover this one last item before you go," or "Thanks for letting me know about that application. I'll try it, but now I need to . . ."

If the interrupter persists with another conversational tidbit, you could say: "I'd like to hear more about that, but could we continue after work? Right now, I need to get going on this customer call."

Your daily written plan or project pie chart, posted in plain view, can be your ally here. You can point to it while ushering your visitor out.

Head Them Off at the Pass   If you see a long-winded gossip-lover heading for your cube, stand up, greet the visitor and invite the person to walk down the hall with you to wherever you were apparently heading, anyway. You can say "Walk with me and we can talk for a few minutes on the way to Accounting."

Usually, gossip-mongers prefer a cozier arrangement—and will go bother someone else.

Put Visitors to Work

If drop-ins blithely ignore your every signal, put them to work. We met one man who developed this ingenious technique. He kept a folder in his drawer containing tedious chores he could give to a colleague who simply wouldn't take a hint.

"Before we can talk, I have a couple of jobs to finish up here," he'd say. "Since we're sitting here, would you mind collating these? Let me show you how."

This visitor would soon recall another appointment elsewhere.

Be a Pal But Protect Your Priorities

If you're part of a group standing around the water cooler, enjoy it. But when it's time to disengage, you could say something friendly and non-threatening, like: "Well, I guess it's back to the mines for me. See you guys later."

Some people have the knack of exiting a group, discreetly, even when the group is all worked up about something. They smile, shrug their shoulders as if to say, "I wouldn't know what to do in that situation, either," and they simply turn and move away.

When the Visitor Commands Respect

If the person sinking so comfortably into your chair is your boss, be gracious. But if you've got deadline work (for that boss or another), move toward a wrap-up. Success will depend on your rapport with the boss, of course. Make sure your body language says "busy" while your words say "help":

"June, can we continue this later? I want to know more, but I'm running late with this project for you . . . and I know you'll need it for the noon meeting. Forgive me for not saying so when you came in."

Your boss may either break off or extend your deadline. In either case—you've bought time.

When *You* are the Visitor

If you are in the boss's office when the conversation drifts off into trivia-land, say: "I've held you up too long: forgive me; I enjoy chatting so much, I forget the time," or "I have some other things for you on my desk that I really ought to get back to."

Then, stand up and scoot.

For Business Owners and Consultants

It's tough to gauge how much is too much socializing with clients. Often these informal chats are building the rapport that will earn you the next year's contract. As with your other skills (forecasting, planning, networking, marketing), socializing is a skill you improve with experience. Just as consciously as you plan your other strategies, you should examine your socializing and networking skills.

Awareness is key, so you may need to keep a daily log of the time you are devoting to socializing, especially as your business grows and your time gets heavily committed.

Schedule Regular Times for Staff Development

If your direct reports know they can depend on getting twenty-minute blocks of time for their questions or concerns, morning and afternoon, they'll work harder to consolidate their issues. Then, you can coach them in a context.

Experiment with Team Quiet Hour

When some companies install "Quiet Hour" across the whole organization, they get dramatic gains in productivity. Insiders make a formal agreement that internal calls and drop-ins are barred for that hour, which is reserved for uninterrupted planning and execution. If Quiet Hour is scheduled at a time when traffic is low anyway—and if a good cover person takes the few calls that do arrive—your customers and other outsiders never realize that Quiet Hour is on.

But, like all innovations, a few people (usually insiders) begin to undercut the system ("It's just me and I only need a minute . . ."). So Quiet Hour can gradually break down. Don't be discouraged. Even if you must periodically refresh and revive Quiet Hour, don't abandon it without a fight.

Add Floating Backup Service for Customers   If your whole team opts for Quiet Hour but your customers don't comply, you can opt for rotation duty, where one staffer covers the traffic for all—handling questions or making callback appointments so customers know they will get serviced shortly, without needing to recall or repeat their initial request. Establish a fair rotation system so no team member is disadvantaged.

LAST-RESORT DEFENSIVE MOVES

Have you regretted coming in early, staying late, or going without lunch, just to get a few minutes of thinking time? Beware these sacrificial methods. Once people see your car in the parking lot, early and late, they start arriving early, and staying late (whichever is more convenient for them) in order to usurp your time. They are many; you are only one! Instead, try one of these options:

Drop Boxes   Drop boxes were mentioned earlier (in Part I, Chapter 5), but they are such a simple mechanical solution that they deserve a second mention.

- Install a drop box just outside your cube with a well-marked slot where people can leave paperwork and packages. On that drop box, state your promised hour for clearing the box, so people know when to expect attention.

- Install a locked drop box that allows people to "hand-deliver" sensitive materials without needing to see you. One manager, afraid that any such box might be spirited away, asked the maintenance department to cut a slot in his outer partition, connected to a metal receptacle inside to receive sensitive materials. Fewer visits saved time for both the manager and his contacts. The documents remained safe.

Protect Your Turf and Time   Some senior professionals accept all their appointments on the requester's turf. That way, they can leave when they must, without having to dislodge a visitor.

Try Hiding Out   There are times when you'll jeopardize a deadline task unless you can find an empty office to hide in while you work. At those times you can leave a voice message on your phone and a sign on your door, saying when you will be available and whom they can consult—but not where you are (behind your closed door or working incognito in an empty office)!

A few years ago, when I visited the newly built offices of Intel in Rio Rancho, I noticed they had installed a simple deterrent to random interruptions. At the entrance to each open-door cube was a brass chain that could be drawn across the entrance and clicked closed. In the middle of the chain was a handsome brass medallion that said "15 minutes, please." When workers needed fifteen minutes of quiet to concentrate, they simply clicked that chain in place, and passersby complied. People told me that no one abused the chain by keeping it up all day; however, they learned how effectively fifteen minutes, uninterrupted, could accelerate problem solving.

Of course, you may say that your employees are not so self-disciplined.

HUMAN COMEDY

Andrea Ladanza, Director of Seminar Operations at AMA, hears a lot of stories at AMA's conventions, about the mind-set of chronic interrupters. She tells us:

Of course, in the cubicle world, drop-ins are a perennial issue. One administrator reported that even when she put up police tape, crisscrossed over the entrance to her cube so she could deal with an emergency, some intruder crawled under it, whispering, "It's only me."

CHECK YOURSELF

How do you score on escaping the socializing trap? Rate yourself on the following; then repeat the process thirty days from now. Simple Yes/No answers will suffice.

Questions	Today	30 Days
1. I keep my door "semi-closed" to socializing but open for business by posting "open times" for my team and giving appointments to most non-emergency visitors.	———	———
2. Whenever possible I complete the task, or put a placeholder there before focusing on an interruption.	———	———
3. Before entertaining a walk-in interruption, I ask what it's about so I can assess its relative priority and duration.	———	———
4. I set a time limit on interruptions when time is scarce, then give my undivided attention for that brief span.	———	———
5. With all but the newest subordinates, I ask what effort the interrupter has made on self-help before seeking my advice.	———	———
6. I ensure that my workstation is placed to minimize random eye-contact interruptions.	———	———
7. As a supervisor, I suggest team Quiet Hour, where one person covers phones while the rest focus on work for an hour. We crave that 4-to-1 payback for uninterrupted time.	———	———
Total	———	———

CHAPTER

19

Attempting Too Much

If you were born lucky, with high ambition, energy, and intelligence, you've probably been the darling of management recruiters, and a favorite of bosses with a lot of work to off-load. Your strengths may sustain you until the end of your career.

But these same virtues, extended too far, can expose you to the final time trap in our series, attempting too much. Unless you apply deliberate effort, you may find it hard to control your urge to overdo, embedded early in your time personality and cemented by praise from parents, friends, bosses, and customers.

GETTING TIRED?

Have you reached a point where people take your superior service for granted? Do you make everyone happy but yourself? Do you allow important priorities to get buried by convincing yourself that "it all has to get done, anyway"?

Keep your eyes open for the day when the overdrive that began as a virtue can morph into a vise drawn ever tighter around your time and your life.

How Long Has This Been Going On?

In the third edition of *The Time Trap*, Alec Mackenzie opined that the ways we manage ourselves and our time, for better or worse, are tangled up in a complicated kaleidoscope of interconnected actions and reactions, only vaguely understood by each of us.

When burdened by too many demands, the dedicated worker grows disorganized. Deadlines get missed. Delegation attempts fail because there's no time to train anyone. Those who attempt too much keep losing ground.

But if your assignments are too many, too ill-defined, coming from too many sources, you may say yes until you bring on your own collapse. If you are both ambitious and service-motivated, you'll be constantly torn, asking yourself whether you should serve their needs, or your own priorities.

Most likely, you'll opt for theirs—*and* try squeezing yours in, after hours! Once you believe that everything has to be done! Now! By *you!*— you will have entered the trap of attempting too much.

BEWARE ATTEMPTING THE SUPERHUMAN

Managers of both genders fall prey to overambition. It's not a male preserve. In the third edition of this book, Alec Mackenzie wrote:

> The "Superwoman" must be hostess, partner and mother in her hours
> at home, while competing at work with male counterparts who have
> the advantage of longer experience, a network of advocates and
> supporters, and rampant favoritism. She must work twice as hard to
> reach half as high for a third less pay.

Those are Alec's words, not mine. But most women recognize the situation as their own.

REAL VOICES

Andrea Cifor, Process Manager, sees youthful ambition through a sharp, personal lens.

> *My father died when I was about eighteen. He always talked about
> aspiring to various things he looked forward to doing when he retired.*

Then he died, suddenly, three months before retirement—never having taken the opportunity to do those things at all. That drove me to overachieving: I made sure I did everything I ever wanted to do, or else I worked full-tilt, toward achieving every goal. I never really slept much; this meant I had plenty of time to fill.

I set lofty goals for my life and I had hit them all by the age of forty. Ironically, this brought on a sort of mid-life crisis. I felt somewhat unbalanced and wobbly as if I had no foundation.

That life crisis, coupled with a devastating car accident, may have been the best thing ever to happen to me. The accident aftermath put me in near-death situations a few times. What a catalyst for assessing the value of your life. I looked back on my accomplishments with no regrets: none!

But the allure of overachieving for its own sake faded away. After the accident I had new breakthroughs to achieve. I was told that I would not walk again. Yet, I am walking again.

Superperformers, women and men, must beware spending themselves as if all goals were equally compelling. Life is short and full of surprises.

Too Much Work in Too Little Time?

Constant time pressure hikes your stress. If you work late today, only to correct errors made when too tired last night, your frustration will soon wear you down. When stress escalates, your health deteriorates invisibly but inexorably while you stew.

If your company feels forced by competition or other conditions to keep pouring on assignments week after week, you will be unlikely to recover simply by using the company gym. A brisk workout can tamp down your symptoms without relieving the causes at all.

You may try undoing the damage with coping techniques—counting to ten before responding, walking off your stress, playing soothing music, taking your blood pressure pills as directed. But all these moves, while helpful, may merely postpone an inevitable explosion.

How much better it would be to turn your energy to stress prevention. No, you can't eliminate pressure entirely. But you can notice and stem those behaviors in yourself that you tolerate out of blind habit: the notion that no amount of work is good enough; the notion that working hard is a goal in itself.

Calm the Need to Keep Proving Yourself

A very successful and hardworking salesperson showed up at one of our seminars (encouraged by her husband and possibly her boss as well). For years, she had worked from 7 A.M. until 7 P.M.—then dragged herself home feeling guilty about all the work she had left behind. But she learned the principles of setting priorities, and began to practice them, somewhat cautiously.

Not too long after the workshop, she looked up from her desk at 5:00 P.M. and saw that her staffers were leaving for the day. She looked at her own daily plan, saw that she had completed five of the six goals she had set, and said to herself: "That's good enough. Time to go home!"

But anxiety crept over her as she prepared to leave, so she started filling her briefcase with the sixth job. She stopped again, asking herself "Why am I doing this? It's my lowest priority; it can wait."

When she arrived home—on time, minus her briefcase—her husband asked "Anything wrong?"

"Absolutely not," she glowed. "Everything's great. In fact, why don't we go out for dinner? We've earned it."

So they dined out, and enjoyed the evening. Recounting this story later, she told Alec that she felt better that evening than she had in years, except for the initial flutter of guilt. For her, it was a turning point.

Optimism: A Virtue Overextended

A second executive fared less well. Take heed of the following:

> Another friend of Alec's, a business owner, was also president of a transnational association in Europe. He allowed this nonpaying but prestigious appointment to take most of his time, including time he should have been devoting to his profit-making business. He enjoyed the honor and recognition attached to this presidency, but he looked forward to the end of his tenure when he could return to growing his own business.
>
> However, when the time came, no strong candidate appeared. Friends prevailed upon him to serve another term. Appealing to his loyalty and his ego, they pleaded that only he could save the organization.
>
> Sure that his energy and experience would help carry him through, he agreed to stay for another term. Too late, he began to see that he was

attempting too much at the wrong time. His business, already declining from neglect, fell seriously behind the competition. In the end, he was forced to give it up altogether, and start earning again in a related field. His trap was overconfidence, his conviction that he could do it all, simply by trying harder.

LET'S LOOK AT PERFECTIONISM

In fact, let's stare—but briefly. You can probably blame your upbringing for this one, too. Attempting perfection may be ingrained, but it is also taught by word and example. You've heard the classic rule: "If something is worth doing, it's worth doing well."

If you're trying to save your sanity, change that to: "If something is worth doing, it's worth doing as well as it deserves."

The first version, combined with your secret sense that no one can do a job as well as you, may compel you to persevere in your exacting standards. Loosen up on this idea. It will lead you to micromanagement, and ultimately, to failure.

Learn to love the second version. Accept reasonable, adequate quality on items of lower impact so you can reserve astounding quality for your high-end offerings.

The day you learn this the hard way is the day that your boss or customer ignores or trashes your carefully calibrated work because whatever risk it was designed to control has ceased to matter to them, or the project has now stepped down from premium position.

Four Hazardous Habits of Mind

Once you've thought deeply about your early life and school days, you may get the same insights reported in our after hours chats at seminars. People confess:

1. "I needed to keep excelling, even under pressure, to keep up my sense of self-worth, but others were clearly indifferent about the results. They tell me I'm overdoing it, even to this day."
2. "I'm reluctant to delegate, either through lack of faith in others, inadequate practice in delegating, or discomfort about my earlier, failed attempts to let go."
3. "Almost daily, I overschedule myself, with unrealistic notions on how much can be done in a day."

4. "Perfectionism drives me to lavish attention on minor details and to keep reworking everything. If my name is on it, it has to be perfect or I can't release it."

Execute Four Escapes

What can you do to change your mindset and behaviors?

1. As we discussed in earlier chapters, you must dump the myth that you work better under pressure. People don't work better under pressure, they work faster! And that can lead to errors, discovered too late.
2. Don't assume that "it all has to get done"—at least not by you. Discriminate between high- and low-priority tasks. Then, assign and teach a low-priority task to a delegate. Allow for learning and refinement time. Realize that the consequences can't be too high if the priority is actually low.
3. With your team, build a standard lead time menu showing commonly repeated tasks so requesters learn to make reasonable demands. Post the menu on a shared Web site. Teammates and requesters will consult it before bothering you.
4. Finally, save your perfectionism for those tasks that warrant it. Make a conscious decision about how good a result must be. Build your quality standards for vital tasks; then set up your computer to flag any variables from that acceptable range. Your computer will keep an eye on things.

REAL VOICES

Kris Todisco, QA Director for an investment firm, has taught herself to chase the vital tasks. She offers:

From my full to-do list, I extract my "short list"—those items that must be done before my day can end. This helps me hold focus. If my day ends with that short list accomplished, then I go home with a mind at ease, and time to do the things I love most. Sometimes I just have to unplug and let the chips fall where they may. The funny thing is, I'm the only one who seems to worry about it. My senior managers have never complained. On the contrary, . . .

BOSSES: TAKE CARE OF YOUR HARD WORKERS

Many who jokingly refer to themselves as workaholics deserve much kinder labels.

They come in two classes:

The Entrepreneur

The first type of so-called "workaholic" is the entrepreneurial type, even though he or she is not yet self-employed. You will find many of them in your office, perhaps at the next desk—or even, perhaps, in your own mirror. Do you share their following characteristics?

- They work long hours.
- They love their jobs.
- They are dedicated to a "mission."

They are not workaholics at all! Though all workaholics work long hours, there are many who work long hours, without the other two motives—love of job and mission.

The Honest Bill Payer

The second type of faux workaholic is a solid citizen, fighting to stay afloat, financially. In today's economy, many workers seek significant overtime or a second job to make ends meet. The second job may start out as a "temporary measure"—but the burden often becomes permanent if conditions fail to improve. If they do manage to outrun the wolf, they feel triumphant, even when denying they're dog-tired.

Members of both these high-achiever groups have amazing staying power, although the entrepreneurs appear to have an advantage here. They certainly work long days, but with very little visible fatigue. With self-imposed stretch goals, they seldom show fatigue or boredom. They seem to have fun involving themselves in a wide range of interests, both professional and personal. They eat well and sleep well. And, their high energy attracts willing disciples to whom they readily delegate, officially or not.

RECOGNIZE A WORKAHOLIC WHEN YOU SEE ONE

Workaholics, by contrast, have a dreary time of it. Their compulsive behavior (like alcoholism, drug dependency, gambling, or any other addiction) drains and depresses energy rather than nourishing it. To satisfy the compulsion to stay busy, workaholics bury themselves in tasks that are mostly routine and time-consuming. They pride themselves on company loyalty but give little thought to the actual value of the work that takes them all day to perform. They expect unflagging loyalty in return, as if the time spent—not the results achieved—were the company's target.

What Bosses *Can* Do

Managers must resist the urge to practice psychiatry without a license. Whatever the unconscious motivations of workaholics, the outward behaviors are the sole area where you—as the person's boss—can try to help. The outward behaviors are easy to spot:

- Putting in ultra-long hours to achieve unimportant results.
- Denial or resistance when you offer advice or help.

In our many talks with frustrated bosses, we've heard complaints about the downside of this addiction among team members. Some tell us:

- Workaholics put in more hours than are required—or even allowed in some instances. We don't want people working in a dark, empty building. It's a security risk.
- They keep on with detailed perfection, long after the job has ceased to need it. That level of scrutiny is excessive.
- They still busy themselves with minutiae, keeping themselves unavailable for new assignments.
- Still hooked on the paper-pushing that built their early reputation, they refuse to delegate anything.

Perhaps this awareness has led executives to a gradual shift in defining hard work and loyalty. No longer do they see dedication in the employee who takes home a loaded briefcase every night, or who comes in on weekends to tidy up. On the contrary, such a person is now looked on, not as a fast-tracker, but as a drudge, likely to miss opportunities for the company, because he or she stays focused on the wrong things, hoards work, refuses to delegate, and fears training or developing junior employees.

Sure, senior managers still value employees who'll stay as long as it takes to solve a rare crisis. Good bosses have pizza and desserts brought in for the late-staying crew. They appreciate a team that "goes for broke" to get an outstanding result. They publicize and reward such efforts.

But good bosses also know that fatigue can breed embarrassing mistakes followed by tedious repairs and deflated pride.

So, many a leader will say—when the hour is late: "Come on, Everybody. We're outta here! Get some rest. We'll start fresh tomorrow."

NOTE TO BOSSES: If an employee is prone to "attempt too much," your influence and example can go a long way to encouraging balance. Use your power as a caring coach to focus "overdoers" on results, not hours invested. You'll reap the pleasure of seeing loyalty enhanced, and energy ignited afresh!

Congratulations, Readers!

You have worked your way through the last of the time traps; you've completed Part II. In Part III, you'll read about life lessons learned by our Real Voices correspondents, and you'll get some heartfelt parting advice from Alec Mackenzie and me.

In Part IV, you'll find quick solution summaries to keep you alert to any of the traps that may try to reassert themselves during the next thirty days, or thereafter. Meanwhile, here's your final time trap checkup.

CHECK YOURSELF

How do you score on escaping the trap of attempting too much? Rate yourself on the following; then repeat the process in thirty days. Simple Yes/No answers will suffice.

Questions	Today	30 Days
1. When I (or the team) get overloaded, I ask myself how well our methods meet objective standards for quality/quantity.	———	———
2. I check priorities and deadlines before signing on for new work.	———	———
3. We seriously question activities that contribute nothing to objectives: we postpone or off-load them.	———	———
4. "Whose emergency is this?" we ask ourselves when pushed into bumping authorized work for unplanned work.	———	———
5. I sketch out two lists: tasks that merit perfectionism, and tasks that can now be handled with looser standards. Making those choices forces me to differentiate between task values.	———	———
6. When I achieve my top goals for the day, I allow myself to go home knowing that fatigue breeds errors.	———	———
7. As a manager, I resist "psychoanalyzing" workers, and instead, coach them on the basis of observed behaviors.	———	———
Total	———	———

PART THREE

Parting Advice

Life Lessons in
Time Management

As you've been reading this book, how many memories have swept through your mind, called up by other people's stories? How often could you relate to confessions about those "bad habits," that our survey respondents had struggled to correct?

From the moment those responses began coming in, we were struck by heartfelt comments about the "good habits" people had brought with them to business—habits instilled early by their parents and grandparents, teachers, coaches, and bosses. Those gifts were not wasted. On the contrary—those good habits are now inspiring countless others, as they are passed down to new generations in their own families and shared with incoming generations at work.

What's so amazing is the fact that none of these respondents ever met the others. None of them will learn what the others had to say until they read this book, just as you are doing. So these magical comments were all spontaneous, straight from the heart, sent to us by e-mail, in just the form you're reading now. (You, too, can join the dialog by responding to the survey at the end of this chapter.)

One last thing: we invited all respondents to define themselves as they truly see themselves—especially in relation to time management. You'll remember them from some of their earlier responses. Now, you'll get to know them better as people.

INHERITED GIFTS

First, you'll notice how parents and grandparents instilled time management tools and critical thinking skills into the young minds of these businesspeople and professionals whom you've come to know from their commentaries in earlier chapters.

The Question: "How important is time management in your life?"

KRIS TODISCO: Wife and mother of two teens. Avid Girl Scout Leader, molding tomorrow's leaders today. Director of QA in a major investment firm.

Time management overarches every aspect of my life. As a mother and full-time employee, I'd never survive without time management skills. The question reminds me of what my grandmother Helen always said, "If you want something done, ask a busy person."

When I was in middle school, I had many a discussion with my other grandmother Elizabeth, about life and what I liked/disliked about my situation at that time. I can clearly remember her advice in response to my complaining:

"Nobody is going to be as motivated as you, Kris, to make your life better. If you don't like your life the way it is, then change it."

That advice did change my life; I began to imagine the "end state" results I wanted in various situations, and I set plans in motion to achieve them. Fortunately, I became a fairly skilled planner, which has translated well to my career in Quality Assurance.

ROGER NYS: Regional Manager, Howard Hughes Medical Institute. "Older parent" seeing the world again through the eyes of a five-year-old.

At home, time management is important—especially with a five-year-old at home. Planning seems to be in my DNA. I like to do things in an orderly way, almost linear-fashion. As an example, learning to fly an airplane and getting a pilot's license was easy for me, because I have always loved checklists and doing things with logical "if-then" thinking. I hope I can pass those skills on.

BART DENISON: Proud father, lifelong student, and Operations Lead for a major software manufacturer.

I'm a full-time employee, full-time student, and parent of three wonderful and highly energetic children. My wife and I constantly find ourselves struggling to manage the time available to us.

I just completed my first bachelor's degree and have reenrolled for a double major. Once I have both degrees, I'd like to pursue an MBA in technical management. Yet, I've been able to make agreements with most of my customers and managers that none of my team should be working more than forty-five hours a week on a regular basis.

LORRAINE SERGENT: Busy mother of three, grandmother of two, friend to all. Systems Analyst in banking.

Time management is extremely important both at work and at home. I have no special secret, but I'm naturally adept at multitasking. I get personal satisfaction from a job well done—and I like staying busy. I think I get both traits from my mom.

TERRY SPENCER: Executive Assistant. Grandmother and caregiver to her precious grandson. (Both his parents are facing serious health issues, currently.)

How important is time management in my life? At work, I have good systems in place for juggling daily priorities for three bosses.

At home, time has become more essential than ever, since our five-year-old grandson, Daniel, has been living with us for almost a year. Routine and consistency help us accomplish what has to be done in the evenings: dinner, bath, movie time. He's a movie lover with quite a DVD collection, and he loves his bedtime stories, too.

I try to instill in him that time constraints apply at night, yet I want to give him choices as well. If he's watching a movie and wants to go beyond the time to get ready for bed, I give him a choice of "continue the movie" but "no book." Inevitably, he chooses a book!

I use "choice" on weekends as well, when we're getting ready to visit his Mama. If he's dilly-dallying, he must make a choice that gets us out the door on time.

Daniel entered kindergarten this August. As the school year progresses, his grandfather (bless him!) has been taking Daniel to extracurricular activities—getting him off to school, taking him for dentist or doctor appointments while I'm at work. We're among an emerging "grandparenting" population, learning to juggle time and pushing retirement far out on the horizon. So far, so good.

The Question: If you are a lifelong planner/goal-setter, how did you learn this?

TERRY SPENCER:

I learned a lot from my mother; she was a single mom who worked full-time and often had a second job. I don't know how she did it, but I learned from the best.

TOM STOTESBURY: Captain, U.S. Merchant Marine. Geologist, linguist, and country-boy nature freak.

I learned planning and goal-setting from taking the consequences of failure to do so. A daily to-do list is with me at all times, to keep my focus on priorities and the immediate task.

VICKI FARNSWORTH: Executive Assistant to a team of physicians and executives, HealthAlliance Hospitals, Inc.

As for planning—I've been in administration all my career, so I've used every kind of tool—from integrated electronic tools, in Outlook, to reminders and tickler files. I use them all to keep us on track with date-driven planning.

I've learned from past membership in IAAP (the International Association of Administrative Professionals) and I keep up with lots of business reading. What I learned from Pat Nickerson's previous book, Managing Multiple Bosses, still comes in handy.

RICHARD SHIRLEY: Civilian IT Manager working for the military in San Diego.

I don't consider myself a lifelong planner, but I do set movable goals. I've always been taught to keep moving forward, not staying complacent with any level of success. Courtesy of the Jesuit priests of St. Joseph's Prepara-

tory School in Philadelphia, I've been taught to advance by working harder, doing better. That serves me well in the Information Technology field, especially for the military, where there is very little room for error in critical situations.

Some successful people still wrestle with planning and goal-setting:

KEN MAYO: Web Coordinator/Photographer for the Catholic Health Association of the United States.

I'm not a lifelong planner. When I change my priorities suddenly, I find it hard to stay focused. Having to do the same thing twice frustrates me, whether it's personal or professional. It happens because I'm tired or rushed. So integrated to-do lists in Outlook are helping me improve, and I use them at home as well as at work where I can hear myself saying aloud: "Focus, focus, focus!

The Question: How do you maintain work/life balance?

Most respondents report making deliberate and conscious decisions about this:

LORRAINE SERGENT:

For balance, I rely on patience, coordination, helpful team members, and loving agreements with family and friends.

RICHARD SHIRLEY:

At home it's a collaborative effort between my wife and me. We both share the same interests when it comes to our home, and making that a place that suits our family. If there's a project that only one of us is interested in, the other will support it. If it's a joint project, then we discuss what needs to be done and express both our ideas on how to get there. We then pick the one method that makes the most sense, or blend both ideas. The priority order starts with safety first . . . then the "must haves," and finally, the "want to haves."

TERRY SPENCER:

I have learned over the last year that I need some "me" time, so I've just started to set aside time to read, have dinner or a movie with friends, or go shopping just for fun."

MEL NORTHEY: President/CEO of Mel Northey Company, Houston, Texas. Church Elder, mentor to others seeking to establish small businesses.

Spending time with family and friends, either at home or traveling, helps with work/life balance. Our big family enjoys going on cruises together. But, we're just as likely to spend a quiet evening at home with a good book, as a change of pace from our travel to trade shows and site inspections with our international contractors.

LINDSAY GEYER: VP Human Resources, Port Blakely Companies. Devoted family member and friend. Avid gardener. Performing arts fan.

How do I maintain work/life balance? My husband works from home, so he takes on more of our chores there. But, when he travels, I take up the slack. We do this so that we'll have higher quality time together whenever we're both home. This also allows us to travel to see our families, since none of them live nearby.

ROGER NYS:

For me, work/life balance is easy. I follow a rule of not taking work home and not working on weekends. I tell my direct reports to follow the same rule. Also, several times a week, I run four to five miles at lunch.

A few still struggle with the work/life balance issues:

CATHY WILBER: Single mom, full-time pediatric occupational therapist and clinical manager. Serious yoga student, amateur artist, nature lover.

I try to find time for yoga, two or three times a week; I do vegetable gardening, and take nature walks. Currently, I'm trying to set a schedule for these things but I find my taste for unstructured spontaneity makes it hard to imagine relaxation as something I should schedule.

TOM STOTESBURY:

As for work/life balance and getting time to relax—I don't do it very easily. It takes a lot of discipline for me to commit to the relaxation part.

Typically, when I do take time to relax, the time seems to get shortened quite early in the process. It seems like some sort of guilt comes over me, as if I am not worthy of relaxation.

Others came to work/life balance the hard way:

ANDREA CIFOR: Process Manager. Overachiever, workaholic, and world traveler/adventurer.

I learned the value of work/life balance when I quit my career for a while and traveled randomly around Europe in a car with no maps. After a fateful road accident left me with a severe head injury, I returned to corporate life with renewed dedication to "me" versus just my career. I made time management on the job more important than ever, to allow time for "life."

My head injury left me with a sequencing disorder. This wiped out my chronological memory backwards from the two to three week mark. Dates mean nothing; days are not seen as twenty-four-hour buckets. Occupational therapy taught me something that has become my primary method for managing time. Unless a task is written into the calendar, it will most likely be forgotten, so I manage all my deliverables through the calendar:

- *I start each day by identifying all ad hoc items, assessing their worth and associated time footprint.*
- *If these items are few, and will take less than fifteen minutes, they are addressed immediately through a to-do list.*
- *If the items will take more than 15 minutes, I assess their priority, stack them against my other commitments and make them earn a slot.*
- *I also write in follow-up appointments triggered by e-mails or phone calls.*

While this leaves me with the appearance of being highly organized, the reality is that I am just dealing with a handicap and by doing so, I'm managing my time well.

When we did a series of seminars for the State of New York, we met a man (let's call him "Jerry") whose career involved helping troubled youths who were heading for a "third strike." Jerry's comments in class showed his dedication and wisdom, but his obesity, bitten-down finger-nails, and razor-burn rash told me he was also seriously stressed.

Once he started using a few time saving techniques from class, I sug-gested it might be good to enlist his family in helping him get some R&R. Though a little defensive, he promised to think about it. A few weeks later, he came to the Monday session and told this story.

"JERRY": A social worker with the State of New York, who simply couldn't master work/life balance unaided.

Last Friday night, my wife drove into town, picked me up from work, took my loaded briefcase out of my hand and locked it in the car trunk. She then informed me that she had dropped off our children at her mother's, and was 'kidnapping' me for the weekend. At first, I laughed, until I realized she was on the freeway heading away from home.

I must confess, I felt a bit peeved. I had a lot of work I wanted to do. When we checked into the resort she had reserved, I felt even more annoyed, but tried to cover it as best I could, plotting how I would cut this adventure short on Saturday. But on Saturday, she said she had com-mitted the car keys to the hotel safe and would not reveal the combination. She told me I needed to see how it felt to actually stop.

Well, I can tell you, it felt weird! I realized that stopping made me very anxious. That stunned me. My wife suggested that we not discuss it, not talk about anything serious, not worry about the past or the future. Instead, we would walk the grounds, we'd take a swim, we'd get some sun; we would linger over lunch. We'd browse the local shops with no er-rands in mind. So we did all that.

I started to feel myself simmering down. It was amazing how strange it felt. By Sunday, I realized that this single weekend could not cure it all; it simply made me aware. Because it felt so bizarre to stop, I saw that I had allowed my work to obliterate my life. Even my boss had tried to warn me: "Jerry, you can't personally save every delinquent kid in Albany." But I had judged him to be less dedicated than I wanted to be.

Whew! I'm still processing this, but I'm going to keep coming to class, and I'm going to keep listening to my boss's warnings—I'm going to take my blood pressure more seriously, and I'm going to let my wife kid-nap me again whenever she thinks I need it.

A Take-Home from "Jerry"   When overworking for a stretch of days, resolve to leave the office on time on a Friday, without your briefcase. Take a minivacation in your own backyard, or visit the mall or the movies. Get a loved one to help you reduce your addiction to worrying.

LIFE LESSONS FOR ALL OF US

Why should we all save time? Why banish our comfortable habits to open up one or two spare hours per week? What will we do with the time saved?

Perhaps we will savor a few more nights when we can leave work exhilarated instead of exhausted. Perhaps we'll open our front door at close of day, ready to greet the evening with the energy to enjoy life and the people in it. Perhaps we'll win back our weekends. Perhaps we'll take some of that vacation that's been stacking up, unused.

Until we can do some of those things, take a look back at the "Check Yourself" pages at the close of each chapter in Part Two. And for every question you can answer with a Yes, think gratefully of the people—from your parents, to your teachers, coaches, senior military officers, or bosses. Allow a healthy glow of gratitude to flood your consciousness. It will help you persevere.

If you'd like to contact us, you'll find the questionnaire mentioned at the beginning of the chapter reproduced below. We'd love to hear from you.

SURVEY FOR EDITION FOUR: THE TIME TRAP

Reply to Pat Nickerson at timetamer@sbcglobal.net.

1. How important is time management to your life? At work, at home?

2. If you are a lifelong planner/goal-setter, how did you learn this?

3. What time wasters irritate you most? (Your own habits, and other people's?)

4. What's your favorite time-saver tool?

5. How do you set and keep priorities:

- At work?
  - To-do lists?
  - Integrated electronic tools? Outlook?
  - Low-tech white board?

- ○ Filtering e-mails and calls?
- ○ Other?
- At home?
  - ○ Lists on the fridge?
  - ○ Cell phone, alarms?
  - ○ Other reminders?

6. How do you hold your focus or return to priorities once interrupted?
7. If you are a multitasking champ, what's your secret?
8. How effective are you at delegating? At work, at home?
9. How do you maintain work/life balance and get time to relax?
10. What's next? What could arise to challenge your best time skills?

Finally, please tell us how you would like to be identified in the text, e.g.:

MATTHEW SMITH, Chancellor, XY University, coach of his son's softball team, and wooden boat enthusiast.

SALLY WYATT, Program Manager at YZ Systems, single parent of teen twins, and serious gardener of three acres in Charlottesville, NC.

We'll introduce you as you see yourself. Thanks for your comments. They'll help make any future book more real and more fun for all our readers.

CHAPTER

Where Do We Go from Here?

Before you embark on your new time-rich life, here's Alec Mackenzie's advice on getting started.

BUILDING YOUR ACTION PLAN

Perhaps your time logs showed you the truth about where your time has been going. Now, you need an action plan to confirm and consolidate your resolutions about upgrading time management.

Many people, when first introduced to time management, pounce on a specific idea or two—and off they go to reform their practices without a thought about the overall patterns of their lives, or the ripple effects of one time management trap on another.

Maybe they come across an idea in their reading or in conversation with a colleague. But, when a challenge arises, they may or may not recall that good idea. If they do recall it and try it, they may not get good results on the first try. So the good idea drifts away.

Expect the Tug of Old Habits

On their own, few people can analyze the causes of their difficulties with time management or understand the invisible habits that cause the problems. Instead, they jump at quick and easy solutions, then wonder why the cure didn't take. In a few weeks, the old ways are back.

Long-term success demands a coordinated approach, one in which you recognize your persistent patterns of behavior and form a systematic plan, sketched out and posted where you can see it. Then, it must be followed, daily, to get you past disappointments.

So don't limit yourself to exploring a few "whats". Instead, work to understand the "whys"—the habits of your lifetime. Then, you'll find it easier to adopt behaviors that conserve time for the people and the passions you value at work and at home.

Set the Stage for Strategic Action

Decide which particular time traps you want to work on, based on what you learned from your logging exercises. Review the ideas you highlighted in reading about the traps.

Reexamine the Check Yourself questionnaires that close each of the trap chapters in Part II. The more Yes answers you were able to make, the stronger chance you have of escaping that trap, for good.

Next, locate the traps on which No was your most common answer. You might try running a narrow, specific logging exercise on your worst diversions from your top priorities to see what traps keep snaring you. For example—if you find yourself frustrated, again and again, with a project you should not have been doing in the first place, you might ask yourself:

- Was that a "failure to delegate" issue?
- Inability to say no?
- Poor focus on priorities?

Then, use the Quick Solution Summaries (in Part IV) to remind yourself what tools and techniques could help you root out any stubborn underlying habits.

Plan Your Attack

Some people like to start with their toughest trap to get a dramatic gain. Others, sensing the danger of fatigue, prefer to start with an easy-to-solve problem, ensuring a success to spur them on. The route you choose is entirely up to you.

But decide on one trap and tackle it with daily practice. Then, check your progress, thirty days on. Record and celebrate your progress. If you grow impatient with yourself, check the relevant page in the Quick Solution Summaries charts to see if you're feeling the same tug of resistance that stalled our anonymous commentators. Be encouraged.

You might keep tabs the way one seminar veteran did:

Time Trap	Cause	Solution
Slow to delegate.	I think I can do it better myself	Give up ego trip. Put training plan together today for Eric.
Micromanaged Eric today.	Was afraid Eric would miss something vital.	Stop the "teach-in." Let Eric play back his plan . . . say how *he* will handle the problem.
Took call on matter I should have passed to Eric.	Told myself it saved time. Not so. Not paying attention.	Confirm to the caller that she should talk to Eric about this.

Note how the solutions on this chart are tied to the causes, not the traps. As we said at the start of this chapter, you will solve your problems when you understand the "whys" and match your solutions to them, not to the time trap itself.

Here's another sample, based on a different set of traps and their causes:

TRAP: Drop-in visitors.

CAUSE: My vague application of our "open door" policy.

SOLUTION: Redefine my own open door policy. Decide how to announce the change without hurting people's feelings.

Don't be too conservative. Allow yourself to brainstorm; crazy ideas may open you up a little. Later, you can always edit.

Here's a range of suggestions for anyone with the open door dilemma:

1. Talk to HR. Rephrase the company's official statement about "open door."
2. Hang a Red Zone sign on your door when it must remain closed.
3. Charge a toll to anyone who ignores the Red Zone sign.
4. Angle your desk to face the window, not the door, so people don't catch your eye so easily.
5. Propose a "Quiet Hour" policy for your team.

Once you choose an idea that's workable, set a start date and begin.

TEACHING YOURSELF NEW HABITS

Old habits are well-entrenched. So, to reinforce any new behavior, recall the plan suggested by the great American psychologist William James:

1. Think big. Launch your new ideas strongly. Set up a new routine that contrasts vividly with the old. Create visual prompts. Announce the plan to others and enlist their help. A public declaration can motivate you to stay on track.
2. Work out a buddy arrangement with a colleague. You agree to check in regularly on each other's progress. This will help you avoid backsliding.
3. Practice the new habit often. Seize your first opportunity to act out your new routine. Resolutions install themselves in the brain—not when you think about them, but when you accompany them with motor action. Repetition—not resolution—will ingrain the new habit.
4. Practice the "no exceptions" rule. Allowing a lapse is like trying to manage a skid in your car. It takes much more effort to recover control than to maintain it. Exceptions can dampen the energy of all future attempts. Whenever you say, "I'll make an exception just this once," you begin to chip away at your fragile newly improved practices. You lose the momentum you worked so hard to gain.

TIME MANAGEMENT: A TEAM SPORT

You are in charge of your time, but your time-based decisions will impact on others. One woman was so enchanted when she first heard about Quiet

Hour that she put it into practice for herself without explaining to anyone why she was closing her door every morning. Her boss was puzzled and her colleagues felt shunned. It's not that she needed their permission, but she did need their understanding.

So let people know what you're doing. Enlist their help, and return the favor by sharing the time-saving techniques you learn. Lead by example. Few business development ideas are more team-friendly than good time management.

Good luck to you—and your team—as you build greater mastery of your time, for your life.

PART FOUR

Quick Solutions

TRAP 1: MANAGEMENT BY CRISIS

Issues	Better Approaches
My boss can't tell a crisis from a minor blip. He loves an uproar!	As a team, study your projects/processes to rank risks by consequence. Prove you deliver on Red Zone risks (Part 1, Chapter 5). Help boss defocus lower-level risks
A crisis blindsided us. Now we feel vulnerable.	Chart both *likelihood* and *impact* of threats. Build trust with lateral groups for mutual early warning system.
Firefighting is our life!	Focus on *preventing* new fires. Use only necessary force to quell old ones. Prevention outguns repair every time.
Faulty time estimates caused crises and overloads all year.	Murphy's Second Law says that things will take longer than you imagine. Examine previous lead-times. Add 20 percent cushions for a realistic standard lead time menu.
Poor reporting processes keep us blind to issues.	On a template, set interval targets to be met. Check off items completed and keep your own records, locally.
Team overreacts to VIP requests: All seem #1!	With demands from above—establish *what* is needed, *why*, and *when*. Illustrate *choices* and *risks*. Negotiate, using the Two-Column To-Do Chart (Part 1, Chapter 2).
I feel panicky when bullied by the boss.	Count to ten. Unless the place is under mortar attack, buy a moment to think. Go graphic: chart options together.
Oops! We punished the messenger: now we're cut off by lateral peers.	First, apologize. When others deliver bad news, teach yourself to say "Thanks for this heads-up," and mean it, even when the news disturbs you.
When the crisis ends, I resist "lessons learned." I just want to forget!	Create a "task diary" so you can set clear expectations for next time. Wring some value from any disaster.
I got involved in a crisis way too big for me.	Think "referral" next time humility is called for. Get an expert second opinion. Then help, where you can.
Yours?	

TRAP 2: INADEQUATE PLANNING

Issues	Better Approaches
Who has time to plan? People are pounding at my door all day.	One hour of planning saves three to four hours of execution. Plan—before the pounding starts. Post priorities so "walk-ins" can see their "competition."
Some planning systems are too complex to set up and maintain.	Once set up, an integrated calendar/project list saves time, repeatedly—and keeps coworkers informed. Or—sketch a simple chart showing your top 20 percent tasks (ranked by risk and value.) Add a pie chart to show time allotments.
Few days are typical here. Emergencies occur to wreck our plans.	While emergencies may disrupt part of the day, you can minimize damage when a glance at your written plan returns your attention to priorities.
I keep my priorities in mind; no need to write them down.	No memory is infallible. No to-do list is complete until priorities are ranked, and deadlines set in writing. Besides, you can't expect bosses and teammates to read your mind.
Can't choose between long-range and immediate tasks.	Break long-range tasks into segments. Place all segments on a timeline—some early, others later. Now, all tasks for today (whole or segments) become "short range."
Everything is urgent.	Use triage. Validity and risk outvote urgency.
I try to do "first things first" but traffic is heaviest in the morning.	Earliest slots may not be "best." Put toughest tasks into slots when you have best "energy, access, and privacy." Then batch similar tasks: several *calls, math* for two or more projects, then several *writing* tasks. Ride the learning curve.
Team disagrees about priorities: what deserves our best attention?	Set up a Risk/Value Criteria Exercise: Rank items such as safety, cost, compliance, profitability, staffing, and accuracy. Then, weigh tasks against them. Highest scores win.
Three bosses compete for my prime time. I feel trapped.	Focus on *tasks*, not owners, when negotiating. Insist that risk/value (validity) must trump urgency in most cases. Don't opt out. Express your view on relative validity of tasks; then, offer best options and build a set of standards.
When key client fails to plan, we must jump to it.	Get senior management to hold repeat offenders accountable. Build in penalties to compensate for chaos. What you tolerate will continue and worsen.

TRAP 3: INABILITY TO SAY NO

Issues	Better Approaches
My desire for approval makes me cave in and say say yes too often.	If your clients and managers are reasonable, you can say yes 80 percent of the time. The trap lies in saying yes to that 20 percent of requests that may be unreasonable.
I fear offending with a "no."	Smart bosses and customers are not offended when you point out a risk *they* may face. Instead, you gain respect.
I'm blinded by pride in my capabilities; then I pay if I come up short.	Your scarce skill set may increase demand, making your services more valuable. Resist spreading assets thin. Focus on Red Zone priorities. Delegate or relegate low risks.
I feel a sense of obligation to all who ask my help.	Discuss roots of this feeling with family or trusted friend. Control any "godlike" delusions. Your own team and boss may resent your being called away too often.
Can't find words to beg off.	Count to five. If saying no repels you, say: "I see a risk in this" or "Let me point out a risk you would face." Then, sketch the risk on a notepad, to break eye contact.
What if I lack an excuse?	Most often, "no excuse" beats a poor excuse. Best exit is your own set of priorities. Keep your top 20 percent visible.
I've always said yes. How can I change that now?	Recall times when people poured on guilt, to get a yes. Once you did the work, did you feel thanked? Or used? Know when the time has come for courteous assertion.
I can say no to everyone but my boss.	Acknowledge the boss's privileged position with you. Then, show your priorities and request a trade-off. Workers can't stay mum, then blame their bosses for self-interest.
I said yes once too often to one of my peers; then my temper exploded, hurting us both. I apologized, but— what next?	Consider a conditional approach: "I can do X for you only if you can do Y for me. Our working relationship has become lopsided. Are you willing to even things out?" Rehearse this with a friend (not from your company) until you can do it comfortably.
I fear angering a boss or client if I opt out of a task on ethical grounds. in our global firm.	Hold to your values. But avoid opening with "you." Instead, say: "I would not be comfortable doing that." or "That would feel indiscreet for me. We must find another way."

TRAP 4: COMMUNICATION

Issues	Better Approaches
My boss dumps hasty instructions (e-mail or "live")—and rushes off without clarifying.	Respectfully, point out any gaps in your understanding. Illustrate graphically, checklist style, so the boss can reply quickly, without needing to write any text. Provide an extremely convenient way to respond, then press for it.
We must write project plans so fast, I hit "Send" with a sense of dread.	Don't hit that keyboard, yet. Spend seven minutes doing a SMART Chart (Part 1, Chapter 3). Get team accord on *specifics, measurables, achievables,* and *resources.* Your write-up will then affirm a plan you can all support.
People barge in, all upset about something minor, insisting on instant satisfaction and relief.	Unless you run an Intensive Care Unit, you can buy time. Acknowledge that you understand the issue. Ask them to jot down what they need, focusing on what is still possible. Suggest that fast fixes often prove unsatisfying.
A valued employee comes in, threatening to quit. I feel like "promising her anything" to quiet her.	Don't quiet her. Value her. Listen without interrupting. Ask questions only to confirm understanding. Observe body language, noting what is not said. When she falls silent, ask her to work with you on a lasting fix, not a hasty one.
Stonewalling, resistant behavior by subordinates brings out the beast in me.	Don't press resisters: they've had more practice than you. Use friendly silence to reduce the voltage (mostly yours). Tell them the next ten minutes are all theirs. Then, listen.
It's tough to be assertive with someone aggressive.	Avoid linking the word "you" with anything construed as a judgment. Instead, say, "Here's what *I* need." Then say, "Tell me what *you* need." Go from there.
When people whine about fairness, I get miffed. But I can't say: "Life isn't fair."	Admit that any new policy will benefit some more than others. Address the luckier ones, asking how they could reduce pain for the others. People can be surprisingly kind.
Differing value systems and customs cause interpersonal foul-ups in our global firm.	Study the customs of your partners' cultures. Read some books on global business etiquette. Others have taken the trouble to learn our ways. Take the time to reciprocate!
We're all so busy, none of us has time for pep talks.	Post team victories "on the wall." Focus people on the next big push. Work to win them rewards that matter to *them.* Graphic targets motivate: graphic mileposts sustain energy.
Best communication rule?	Focus on the future. It's all we have left.

TRAP 5: POORLY RUN MEETINGS

Issues	Better Approaches
If there's no news, why hold team meetings? Is the boss lonely or something?	News can be e-mailed, but team cohesion can't be. At meetings, we get two-way idea exchange and nonverbal reactions. We meet to celebrate, to quiet anxieties, and to build trust by observing consistent behavior.
Our rule is: No Agenda- No Meeting!	Agreed—for scheduled meetings. For emergency meetings, creating an instant agenda becomes Item One. Agendas help all participants to prepare, stay on track, and write minutes.
Too many of our meetings are called prematurely: no one is ready to vote.	If a meeting helps teams to argue complexities, thin out the options, and explore emotions *before* voting, it's a good meeting. Try agreeing: "No vote today." People can then listen calmly.
Wrong people invited.	Meeting organizer should set date suitable to key players. Others can attend or send an authorized voter.
Late start-late finish! We're held hostage!	Facilitators: don't wait for latecomers—it rewards the wrong behavior. End on time or expect people to "bail."
While some take part, others play games on their smart phones.	Some companies confiscate electronic devices at the door. Why? Secret sneering by IM texters can damage teamwork, especially with overseas attendees who cannot see, but can sense skullduggery in the teleconference.
Interrupters are allowed to pull players from room.	Set policy so messages are held until after the meeting, unless there's a major emergency.
Leader permits departures from agenda.	Require respect for the agenda. If a leader fails to control it, the members must! Point wanderers to a "side issues board" to post items for later. Rarely—vote to allow the item.
The "minutes" issued long after the meeting do not reflect what happened there.	Produce "living minutes," laptop to screen, or post them on flip charts, using a simple list format. Everyone can assent at once. No surprises later.
Some people criticize, or dominate, or hijack others' ideas.	Teams who meet often should post etiquette rules. Facilitators can take the ball away from dominators. If you don't want your idea hijacked, stand up, post it to a chart as you talk. Then, invite others to join in.

TRAP 6: THE WORLD GONE VIRTUAL

Issues	Better Approaches
While doing legitimate Internet searches, I get sidetracked for hours.	Run a time log and measure your time investment. Next, set narrower search criteria for better focus. Then, delegate certain searches to interns, less pressed for time than you.
I hate the learning curve required by each new release of software	Yes—but you'll love the time saved by integrating your calendar with tasks, projects, assignments, and deadlines. Once you set your Preferences and practice a little, your new software can do everything but the laundry. Read the latest *Dummies* books or take classes to catch on, fast.
Despite firewalls, I get a ton of unwanted data.	Control your own Internet activity. Set Preferences to block traffic by topic or sender. Ask IT what more you should do.
My boss complains if I visit personal and game sites during work hours, but often, I'm on break.	Better to log and control your use, than goad your security team into monitoring you. Log to see how often and how long you "stay to play"—then put yourself on a diet. Latest freeware now let's you clock all your time investments.
My laptop was snatched recently. My password protection failed, and I took a credit card hit.	Talk to your IT department about the best approach to creating passwords, changing them frequently, and otherwise protecting the company's data and your own.
How much credence can I put into data researched on the Internet?	The Internet is free. No controls. No editors. No required differentiation between facts and opinions. Some sites strive for credibility. Check multiple sources including data from print publishers (who are still answerable in court).
I let my big brawling family e-mail me at work. Their "dueling e-mails" were seen by IT and my senior boss.	What e-mail address did you give your family? An address belonging to your company—or your role there? Bad idea. Fix it now! Expect some noticeable damage to your career.
Should we treat the Internet as some sort of villain?	No. We have met the enemy, and they are us.

TRAP 7: E-MAIL MANIA

Issues	Better Approaches
My boss says my tone on e-mail sounds harsh.	Ask a trusted friend to read your text aloud: you'll hear any terseness. Don't open sentences with the word "you" except for "Thank you" or "You're right."
Can't get teammates to stop forwarding junk mail.	Make your reasons clearer. Filter incoming mail by subject or sender, if all else fails.
I can't resist opening e-mail, even when busy.	Turn off the signal. Set specific times of day to open e-mail. Then dare to lengthen the intervals.
Giant attachments crowd my inbox.	Agree with the team to post large documents to a shared site. Outline main points in your e-mail: include a link to the full document.
Old subject lines no longer apply.	Update subject lines to suit the current state of play. Or change only what follows the colon, e.g.: (*original*) ABC Visit: Budget; (*update*) ABC Visit: Postponement.
Long "threads" run back months, with no or conflicting conclusions.	The "owner" or project manager must consolidate the data at intervals, delete the old, and write a new summary. Invite fewer commentators, too.
People get criticized on e-mail; discord results.	Indiscretions always leak. If you supervise the sender, then coach, counsel, or discipline. If customers or vendors are the victims, expect repercussions.
My innocent e-mail was misinterpreted.	Set your spell checker to flag "flamers or blamers." Words like *wrong, neglect, mistake, ignore,* or *fail* tend to upset receivers. If angry, don't use e-mail at all.
People use e-mail and IM, even in the same room with others.	E-mail is great for speed over distances. Otherwise, it does isolate us. Use face-to-face and phone chats for two-way talk. Allow nuances and silences to aid understanding.

I find myself re-reading e-mails without acting on them.	Set up an efficient system such as:
	• *Not my business?*
	  Refer, Reject, or Delete.
	• *My business: easy?*
	  Read, Respond, Act, then File.
	• *My business: complicated?*
	  Read, acknowledge receipt, announce time needed. Then, research, decide, respond.

TRAP 8: THE UNTAMED TELEPHONE

Issues	Better Approaches
Hooked on smartphone technology, I buy fun new "apps" daily. It's like eating popcorn: I can't stop!	People who couldn't walk past a rotary dial phone booth in the old days can't pass up a phone gizmo now. No need to track the time you're spending; you'll see it on your monthly bill! If ready, find a "cell phone addiction" support group.
I feel obliged to take calls from customers or bosses even when rushing to meet a vital deadline.	First, reserve time for vital work in your Red Zone, free of calls. Then bracket each Red Zone with contact cushions so people can reach you and you can respond. Give them any time except Red Zone time.
In a service industry, we must take all incoming calls no matter the value.	Use caller ID. Set up a system to refer mid-value calls to live help. Bump lowest-value calls to voice mail with a callback promise or other help. Prioritize: then provide.
We've had a change in procedure that will drive a lot of internal phone traffic.	Don't take calls one at a time on big changes. Set up "clinic times" when people can gather in groups to ask questions and get answers. Post illustrated instructions on a shared website. Support change through several media.
My biggest customers tend to phone at heaviest traffic times, getting queued up.	Treat such customers to a graph showing heavy traffic. Find a "privileged slot" when you can service them properly. Customers may still call at will—but at least some of their service will be top-notch and reliable.
Requesters leave so little data on voice mail, I have no idea what they need.	On your voice mail greeting, say: "Please leave your name and number, and a brief message about what you need so we can get back to you with an answer."
If I fail to respond right away, some callers will leave repeated messages on voice mail.	Again, your voice mail greeting can head this off. You say: "Please leave a message about what you need. I can begin returning calls at ___ o'clock. If that would delay you, please call ____." (Set up a referral service person.)
Some callers just drone on.	It's OK to cue a close. Example: "Kim, before we hang up, I want to be sure we've agreed ..." or "Before I head to my meeting, have we covered everything?"
I sometimes fail to get to the point, myself.	When you know someone is busy, say so. Try: "Hi Louise. This is Jeff. I know you're busy, so here's one quick question." Then, say what you need. She'll be grateful.

TRAP 9: INCOMPLETE INFORMATION AND THE PAPER CHASE

Issues	Better Approaches
Our team can't decide what info we really need.	Your team could answer the eight questions on page 176 to determine what you do need. Then build a set of request templates to help your info-sources supply the right data.
We're still paper-heavy, with poor filing facilities. Can't seem to store it, find it, or get it moving.	If buried, get help from a trained administrative assistant, at least to dig you out. As for moving paper onward— pencil your reactions into the margin, so you need not reread the original. Store incoming paper vertically— never stack it.
I'm constantly interrupted by people dropping off essential paperwork, but it's confidential stuff.	Provide convenient vertical "drop boxes"—well-labeled for easy slotting. Provide lock-boxes for confidential drop-offs.
Lateral groups deliver data we asked for—too little, too late.	Begin early. Say *why* you need it. For heavy requests, use the two-step method: First, ask confirmation on feasibility and deadline. Then, press for the data itself.
An info-source fails us, then acts defensive at complaints.	Don't *ask why* something's late. Ask *what* it would take *now* to expedite the request fully. Take it forward.
Lateral groups request data with no deadline or priority.	Create a request format that requires specific data including specs, deadlines, and priorities. Make compliance easier.
Straggler managers fail to OK action reports.	If the majority have voted, seek boss's OK to close your memo with: "Unless we hear from you by _____, we will assume you are willing to join the majority vote."
My own boss is slow to OK action on reports he pressed me into writing.	Don't make the boss wade through the whole text. Instead, e-mail a list of points needing approval, with links to the text. Make it easy but be firm about deadline.
My journal-reading load is brutal. Can't get through it.	Rotate duty among staffers; give credit for good summaries. Switch to electronic journals; scan with AutoSummarize.
I put off letter-writing until too tired to write.	Keep a file of best phrases from earlier letters. Adapt and reuse whenever you're too tired to write well.

TRAP 10: CONFUSED RESPONSIBILITY AND AUTHORITY

Issues	Better Approaches
How does responsibility differ from authority?	Define responsibility as duty: authority as power to perform it. List your duties and powers, side by side, to clarify.
There's no written description for my job.	Write your own, in list format. Open each entry with a verb, e.g.: *supervises, buys, appoints, selects.* Get this description approved. Update it before each performance appraisal.
My job overlaps others.	Of course, large workloads will often justify several players with the same skill sets and titles. Simply negotiate areas where work might be duplicated wastefully.
A teammate muscles into my area, confusing others whose help we need.	Without apparent rancor, clarify with the boss to eliminate confusion and avoid conflicting instructions. Illustrate consequences already occurring, as objectively as you can.
I've been made responsible without the authority I need.	Before acceding, find out whose cooperation you'll need. Help draft a notice for the boss to send out, authorizing you to expect the usual support.
Our job titles do not reflect what we actually do.	Titles convey authority, and assure at least minimal respect and cooperation. Check the *Dictionary of Occupational Titles* for ideas on accurate titles. Talk to your boss and HR.
Our organization chart is completely outdated.	Every organization with more than one layer of authority needs an org chart. Failing that, get approval to sketch out task ownership and hierarchy, at least, locally.
Our evaluation format is unrelated to job descriptions.	Well in advance of your next review, add a column or overlay that ties your actual performance factors to the evaluation format. Your boss may welcome the clarity.
I'm a busy research chief. No one on my team has time for written review nonsense.	The annual written review is seen by most organizations as a legal right, even for highly educated and motivated teams. Neglect could haunt you later if disputes arise. At least, let no employee be the last to know that he or she is in trouble.
My boss has me write my own annual review	Negotiate. Whoever writes the review can also set raises and promotions. I bet your boss will come around.

TRAP 11: POOR DELEGATION AND TRAINING

Issues	Better Approaches
I hesitate to delegate—mistakes could be costly.	Accept some risk as inherent to delegation. Overcome it with smart task selection. Then recruit and provide rigorous training and frequent follow-up.
It's quicker to do it myself.	True once, but not repeatedly. Choose repetitive tasks so competence can build. Your cost/hour is too high for repeats.
I'm not ready to train; we have no tools in place.	That's okay. You need to prepare training tools well ahead of trainee arrival. Write an index card for each task segment. Organize the cards for easy learning, a few at a time.
With previous attempts, I micromanaged the poor newbie—drove him crazy.	Teach at a "learner's level"—not your veteran level. Set reachable targets; get feedback reports at agreed intervals to prevent yourself from "hovering."
My trainee said she "got it": then she fumbled badly.	First, you train and demonstrate. Then, the learner repeats and demonstrates. That playback is vital. Withhold any critique until the trainee runs the full set of steps. Retrain if necessary. Let learner show you again, until you are secure.
I enjoy some jobs too much to delegate them.	You got your credits when you stabilized that job. Now that it's safe to delegate, it's going to take newer, more challenging tasks to make you famous.
Even my most seasoned people call me a control freak.	When supervising people with deep experience in a task, you must focus on results, not rigid rules and methods. Measure outcomes, not activities. Loosen your grip.
I can't delegate; everyone is overloaded, and we're in a hiring freeze.	Trade off with a fellow worker, each using best strengths to save time. Form temporary partnerships. Or get approval for outsourcing at lower rates per hour.
Confidential or proprietary work must stay with me.	Negotiate this. Can your management prove that some age or experience level signals readiness to handle confidential or proprietary work? Warn them against bias—or create a way to mask confidential data, yet delegate routine support work.
Lacking budget, we all put in excess overtime to the point of exhaustion.	If you're a nonprofit, seek volunteer help. Paper the district with flyers about your worthy mission. If you're profit makers, use flex hours to attract students or skilled retirees.

TRAP 12: PROCRASTINATION AND LEAVING TASKS UNFINISHED

Issues	Better Approaches
I don't notice I've been dragging my feet until someone accuses me of it.	On late starts, humbly ask a coach to "call" you on it, every time. If you're "failing to finish," just check those "late" flags in Outlook or on your project time line.
People say I enjoy the drama of leaving things to the last minute.	If it's true, give up the "hero" role. Impending lateness, kept secret, will irritate bosses, and embitter peers assigned to last-minute rescues. They'll take their revenge some day.
I've really bought into the notion that I work better under pressure.	No. You work faster, at the expense of quality and safety.
I do the stuff I enjoy first, leaving less time for the dreary or difficult stuff.	You needn't "*do* priorities first," you must "*slot* them first" so their on-time completion is assured. Best work gets best slot. Keep your fun stuff out of the Red Zone.
But, it all has to get done, doesn't it?	No. The vital or urgent work has to get done: very high consequences flow from it. But minor tasks, postponed, may get forgiven or easily caught up.
Other people's faulty deadlines cause our tardy starts, late finishes.	Use your own standard lead time estimates, or insist on seeing their estimates, up front. Then, waste no time renegotiating if the task proves harder than advertised.
The workload is so big, I grow weary and lethargic.	Look into objective standards for your job title. Measure your actual output against norms. If you can prove overload, then negotiate. If not, do you need a smaller job with more modest rewards?
I admit, I'm lousy at self-discipline.	Use electronic or written reminders, a list, wall chart— any vivid visual cue. Jolt yourself into action before your boss or customer finds someone better.
As a researcher, once I "crack the case" I lose interest. Hence, I don't finish the details.	If you can prove your role as resident genius (and you'll have to), your organization may provide you with a whole troop of qualified "finishers." Gladly.
If I try to multitask, my memory blurs on the tasks I left in midstream.	Sure, finish brief tasks in one go. For large tasks competing over months, check "Mind Mapping" Web sites for formats that keep all tasks creatively and colorfully, in view.

TRAP 13: SOCIALIZING AND DROP-IN VISITORS

Issues	Better Approaches
As social animals, we need a change of pace from our drudgery ... so why not drop in on colleagues?	Sure, we'll drop in on friends, but we should look before we barge in. Avoid breaking another's concentration just to relieve your boredom. Find less busy pals at the break room, cafeteria, or water cooler when you want to socialize.
I warn that I have only five minutes to spare. But they overstay.	Tell the visitor that your five minutes are all theirs. Don't return the volley; it lengthens the conversation. At minute four, start moving toward your previous obligation.
I dare not throw visitors out for fear of offending.	Be candid about your deadlines. Express regret and suggest a later time, and possibly a different place.
As a subject matter expert I must stay available to all.	Set up some open times, when those who need your help can rely on your full attention. Don't cut contact time. Just cut randomness.
I micromanaged my new hires: now they're "trained" to bother me for every little thing.	Maybe it's time to teach "exception reporting." Invite warnings about deviations from plan, but ask them to keep notes on your advice and consult those notes next time. Otherwise, set regular, not random, check-in times.
Chatty friends—among them my boss—tend to tarry too long.	Stand up when it's time to wrap up. Foreshadow the end of the chat: "Is there anything else we need to cover? I've got a tight deadline. It's for you, Boss."
My office sits in a traffic pattern.	If you can't change the location, at least seat yourself obliquely to the passing throng. Don't catch their eye. Find a remote hideaway when concentration is crucial.
People must interrupt me to deliver highly confidential reports into my hands.	Position a secure slot or lock-box near your office or just inside, so people can deliver packages without interrupting you.
Friends with too little to do settle in for long visits.	Jokingly threaten to put them to work. If the work is not "classified," do as you threatened, with a smile.
I see socializing as a trust-builder, an investment in the future.	Good. Everything in moderation. After a lengthy visit, make a note of the time spent; be honest about the point of diminishing returns. Go for brevity with no less warmth.

TRAP 14: ATTEMPTING TOO MUCH

Issues	Better Approaches
My family complains I work too much. Despite my high energy, I do feel burned out lately.	If work feels endlessly dreary, if you awaken tired after a night's sleep, you may be in early burn-out. See your physician for a stress checkup. Take that vacation time you've racked up. Write a plan for balancing work and life.
I'm an entrepreneur, and energetic workaholic. But my personal life has evaporated.	If you love what you're doing, and hardly notice long hours (business owners easily do eighty to ninety hours a week), then good! Focus on results, simplify work. Decide how long you can do this. Is your bio-clock ticking? Is your health strong? In any case, when tired, stop for the day. Fatigue breeds mistakes.
But it *all* has to get done.	By you? Alone? Today? Chart high risk/high value work. Get that done. Check upper mid-value work. Get that done next. Calculate benefit of lower-value work. Postpone it.
I'm a perfectionist in all things.	Be a perfectionist in many things, but not all. For example, rough data is enough for a "go/no go" decision. Fine-tuned figures are required only if you decide it's a go!
Work pals say I overdo it, but I take pride in hard work.	You'll do better taking pride in outstanding results. Hard work is not a virtue in itself.
They've folded two jobs into one. I took it on, and it's a killing load.	Find data (objective quality and quantity standards) for your blended job title/description. Search industry reports; talk with your opposite number in related firms. Find out if you are carrying two jobs for one paycheck. Do a time log, and negotiate for money, time, help, or task reduction.
As a boss, I worry that the whole team is overworked.	Help them build realistic time estimates for their work. Focus people on productivity (high payback for energy invested). Then, get them the part-time or temp help they need to dig out of a temporary or seasonal overload.
As a boss, I'm blessed with a dedicated team; they'll sometimes work until exhausted, though.	If they're cleaning up a real emergency, stay alongside. Know when to feed them, when to tell them they've broken the back of the problem, when to send them home. Say: "New day tomorrow!" Then, make your thanks public.

INDEX

assertion as time saver
  mutual assertions for increased comfort, 118
  non-assertion leads nowhere 119
  one choice to avoid, 118
  showing risks diplomatically, 98
Attempting Too Much (Trap)
  four escapes, 256
  four hazardous habits, 255
  optimism, perfectionism, 254
  recognize a workaholic, 257
  the urge to prove yourself, 254
  what bosses can do, 258–259
Authority and Responsibility (Trap)
  authority defined as power, 191
  caution: mismanaged authority, 202
  clarify with an "org chart," 197
  five ways to clarify, 194
  fuzzier lines with matrixes, 44
  the harsh sound of "no," 97
  job descriptions done right, 196–197
  mapping gaps in authority, 194
  negotiate: don't opt out, 54
  political savvy in meetings, 135
  responsibility as duty, 192
  the right title is important, 195
Autosummarize tool: Microsoft WORD
  for e-mail thread control, 156
  for journal reading, 188

body language saves time
  ignored by demanding people, 240
  observe with compassion, 123
  power of subliminal signals, 117

power of the eye, 18, 121
read and react to gestures, 117
use to enhance messages, 117
use to hurry visitors along, 245–247

Checking Yourself on Escapes from the Fourteen Time Traps
  Trap 1: Crisis Management, 81
  Trap 2: Poor Prioritizing, 95
  Trap 3: Can't Say No, 108
  Trap 4: Miscommunication, 124
  Trap 5: Meeting Mania, 138
  Trap 6: World Gone Virtual, 150
  Trap 7: E-Mail Use & Abuse, 162
  Trap 8: Untamed Telephone, 174
  Trap 9: Info & Paper Glut, 190
  Trap 10: Confused Authority and Responsibility, 203
  Trap 11: Poor Delegation and Training, 220
  Trap 12: Procrastination, 237
  Trap 13: Over-Socializing, 250
  Trap 14: Attempting Too Much, 260
choices
  choices for logging time use, 62
  choices in crisis management, 77
  choices: your focus, your time, 10
  criteria for validating tasks, 48–49
  entertain fewer: save time, 3
  in call screening, 164–165
  in declining a request, 99
  in handling conflicts, 120
  myths: delegate or not, 207–210

Cifor, Andrea (Real Voices)
  de-randomize response, 15–16
  decision dumping at meetings, 128
  driven youth; maturation, 252–253
  minding one's own business, 80
  three communication rules, 110
  work/life balance, 269
Communication (trap)
  eight secrets: skillful sending, 113
  focus 80 percent on future, 109
  focus on what is still possible, 123
  giving feedback to bosses, 112
  listening: eleven avenues, 113–114
  passive/aggressive playbook, 119
  Positive Vocabulary Chart, 121
  radar: reduce randomness, 244
  robust receiving, 113
  technology hikes speed and volume,
    110
  verbal scenarios, 111
  winning cooperation from insider and
    lateral teams, 177–179
conflicts
  administrative negotiating, 102–103
  among multiple bosses, 50–55, 102
  among varied disciplines, 50
  between Urgent & Important, 99
  conflicting priorities, 45
  conflicts made graphic, 38, 83–85
  in your to-do list, 25
  inner or interpersonal conflict, 120
  listening, despite conflict, 118
  passive-aggressive games, 119
  supporting staffers in matrix, 107
Crisis Management (Trap)
  crisis as good thing, 74–75
  don't make a mountain, 72
  five simulations/solutions, 73–74
  prevention: seven options, 75–77
  recognize a killer crisis, 72
  recovery: four options, 77–78
  what to avoid: three cautions, 79–80

deadlines
  deadline dementia, 51
  deadlines can't trump impact, 91
  deadlines in task diary, 229
  deadlines versus meetings, 134

  handle multi-tasking, 89
  insist on estimates, 52
  reminders to lateral teams, 177
  rushing to risky decisions, 232
  state "drop dead" deadlines, 76
  when: less vital than what, 178
Delegation and Training (Trap)
  corporate barriers, 216–217
  five myths that stall us, 206–209
  five-part task definition, 210
  task selection criteria: value, stability,
    repetition, 209–210
  ten-step hand-off, 211–214
  two items you can't delegate, 215
  ways to recruit staffers, 217–218
  why we hesitate, 205
Denison, Bart (Real Voices)
  gaining life-work balance, 269
  hold focus when interrupted, 239
  prioritize with bosses, colleagues, 50
the "do it now" delusion, 46

E-Mail Mania (Trap)
  how speed drives expectations, 140
  overuse and abuse, 153
  perceived political necessity, 153
  team-wide etiquette reviews, 161
  tone issues, lack of privacy, 152
e-mail: ten worst issues and suggestions
  1. high volume, 154
  2. oversized load, 155
  3. long threads, 155–156
  4. junk e-mail, 157
  5. indiscretions, 157
  6. subject line neglect, 158
  7. reply-all, 159
  8. message misinterpreted, 159
  9. e-isolation, 160
  10. e-mail procrastination, 161
estimating task time
  predicting lead time, 76
  respecting staff estimates, 106
  standard lead time menu, 53
  unrealistic estimates, 16
  work estimating chart, 52
executive assistants, administrators
  administrative skills, 180
  coordination (hospital setting), 170

handling interruptions, 249
how assistants built a spin-off, 184
negotiating "fly by" demand, 102
phone screening scripts, 168–170
planning: central to career, 266
stemming the overflow, 154

Farnsworth, Vicki (Real Voices)
administrative planning, 266
legitimate priority conflicts, 55
using technology with fellow assistants, 170
feedback (see also listening)
the delegate's burden, 193
instant performance review, 200
offering: to faltering bosses, 112
once-a-year not enough, 202
providing tools for, 124
soliciting feedback, 113

Geyer, Lindsay (Real Voices)
on effective multitasking, 230–231
on technical time-savers, 148
on work/life balance, 268
goals and objectives (see also planning)
driving self-management, 23, 27
goals worthy of focus, 7
why we resist setting goals, 28–29
goals to objectives to priorities
alternatives for reaching, 81
as first phase of planning, 95
as part of daily plan, 234
blocked by crises, 71
the cascade process, 29–30
celebrating attainment, 236
CFO example, 37
conference calls to set goals, 165
focus on the right goals, 50
goals and mid-life crisis, 253
goals in performance reviews, 202
the honest bill payer's goals, 257
interim goal setting, 228
large-scale industrial example, 36
launching team objectives, 52
leader's role in team goals, 33
linked to validity, 233

long- and short-term, 229
Objectives Chart (illustration), 38
planning flexible goals, 229
simple homegrown goals, 33
specific, measurable goals, 197
ten vital questions on goals, 66–67
workplace cascade illustrated, 36
going graphic
posted for multi-task teams, 51
to aid team thinking, 47
to highlight red zone tasks, 60–61
to maintain good habits, 223
to prompt new habits, 276
to propel action, 76
to retool thinking, 18
to settle project conflicts, 102
to teach risks at NASA, 32–33
to validate tasks, 232
to-do lists, 24
visual cues aid listening, 115–116

"Handle Paper Only Once"
boss view: human comedy, 186
co-delusion with "Do It Now," 46
Human Comedy
cell phone abuse, 164
deadline dementia, 57
flash cards for interrupters, 241
paper handled only once? 186
phone addict in the O.R., 173
when visitors duck in, 249
human habits
allowing distractions, 66–67
back-grounding your team before leaving town, 111
changing permissive habits, 68
cure habit of pile-scanning, 182
five faulty assumptions, 19–23
habit of irrational rescuing, 79
habits of random responsiveness, 17
how denial delays progress, 223
impeding progress, 19
interwoven tapestry of, 18
reinforce change: break teams of ingrained habits, 198
teaching yourself new habits, 276
use time log to spot habits, 245

Iadanza, Andrea (Real Voices)
    handling drop-in visitors, 249
    negotiating fly-by requests, 102
important vs. urgent (*see* priorities)
Information (Trap) (*see also* e-world and
        paperwork)
    administrative solutions, 180
    anticipate needs: eight points, 176
    converting paper to data, 183
    criteria for filtering, 13
    delegating searches for data, 188
    design of search criteria, 149
    info overload, *xiii*, 12–13
    managing paper, 181–186
    options to ease cooperation, 177
    requesting data with tact, 176–177
Internet: World Gone Virtual (Trap)
    avoiding Internet scams, 146–147
    cool tools, 145
    data security, 141
    drowning in information, *viii*
    e-learning curve, 140
    hardware security, 142
    how crucial is connectivity? 4
    how technology saves time,
        147–148
    inhibit e-addictions, 143–144
    Internet evolution and future, 149
    Web conferencing, 135, 141
Interruptions
    antidote: a written plan, 88
    chart: red zones with cushions, 61
    control e-interruptions, 154
    defend your right to focus, 239
    don't interrupt learner recitals, 213
    drop box and self-help options, 62
    interruption-free zones? 15
    last resorts, 248–249
    log to check frequency, 59
    logging self-interruptions, 82–83
    maintaining concentration, 10
    phone interruptions rank 8th, 163
    random interruptions worst, 18
    reduce random calls, 167
    returning to focus, 11
    seen as beyond one's control, 17
    systems for "live" service, 164–165
    using high-tech trackers, 63

valid interrupters: new priority? 60
validating interruptions, 86

job descriptions
    done right, 196–197
    job titles: why they count, 195, 201
    reduce wasteful overlaps, 197
    regular updating, 220
    timely change announcements, 198

logs (*see* time logs)
leadership
    conferring power: obligations, 191
    four consequences, 192–193
    how one manager helps teams focus on
        the possible, 122
    risks for the newly-appointed leader, 192
    taking care of best workers, 257
    teams follow clear objectives, 43
Lee, Ivy, Management Consultant, 85–86
Life Lessons
    a social worker learns balance, 270
    gaining life/work balance, 267–270
    ingrained goal-setting, 266
    inherited gifts in time mastery, 264
    new feature: edition four, *xiii*
    parent/grandparent exemplars, 264
    Time Trap Survey for your use, 271
listening (*see also* communication)
    bad habits in virtual meetings, 135
    eleven avenues, 113–114
    good listening takes less time, 114
    how "no" can stall listening, 97
    listening exercises prove it, 115
    listening to resistant people, 117
    visual cues aid listening, 115–116
    when tempted to say yes, 103

Mackenzie, Alec
    acknowledging Alec, *vii*
    advice on easy time-logging, 57
    building new action plan, 273
    his original ten Time Traps, *ix*, 16
    on communication, 109
    on corporate paper cleanup, 185
    on giving feedback to bosses, 112
    on over-social hospital team, 245
    on phone control, 172

on poorly run meetings, 125
on self-management, 252
only 1 in 10 writes a plan, 235
thanking Alec "live," *viii*
written daily plan a must, 88
Mayo, Ken (Real Voices)
counterproductive, 5
tools for holding focus, 267
meetings
Admiral Rickover's agenda, 133
create a critique card, 129
decline meetings four ways, 134
etiquette rules: wall signs, 137
five good reasons for, 128
for planning at mid-level, 87
how to beach a red herring, 132
how to break a stalemate, 132
keeping good order, 136–137
liberate contributors, 132
mutuality a must, 127
needed for multi-disciplines, 50
politically savvy time savers, 135
recommended types, 125
timed agenda for control, 130
unmanaged, 14, 16, 110
virtual meeting options, 135
multitasking
among multi-disciplines, 50
becoming adept at, 265
for multiple bosses, 85
graphic plans for, 51
in the military, 10
keeping "plates in the air," 230–231
makes written plan a must, technology
for, 141
may invalidate "Do It Now," 86
newly appointed managers and team
multitaskers, 192
organization charts: clear roles, 197
time-saver or waster? 4–5

NASA (Houston)
tool: clarifying requirements, 32
trajectory team gambit, 33
voice mail on priorities, 171
negotiating
based on patterns of demand, 47
in customer service, 93–94

integration tools for, 24
quantity, quality, time, 11
showing risks, options, scope and deadlines, 55,76
to enhance cooperation, 177
to protect your team, 107
to select tasks, 209
to validate importance over urgency,
230–232
trade-offs pie chart, 102
two generic rules for, 92–93
updating conflicting schedules, 89
Northey, Mel (Real Voices)
keeping objectives flexible, 229–230
maintaining work/life balance, 268
Nys, Roger (Real Voices)
controlling e-mail and paper, 187
delegation: lifelong lessons, 219
easing work/life balance, 268
frustrating calls and v-mail, 166
good linear-planning habits, 264

objectives (*see* goals and objectives)
open door policy
needs redefining, 245, 275
Outlook: Microsoft Office application for
to-do lists, reminders, 10, 63, 87,
201, 148, 267
creating pre-sort rules for, 157
flags for team follow-up, 141, 266
recalling errant messages, 158
task/calendar integration, 19, 22

paperwork management
better screening and filing, 185
converting paper to data, 183
cut outgoing paper five ways, 189
don't defend your "heaps," 181
dots detect wasteful riffling, 182
the dreaded in-tray, 181
drop-boxes for routine delivery, 248
handle once if simple, 186
logging flow against priorities, 67
offering handy drop zones, 184
re-use regular report formats, 189
read once: note decisions, 87
still with us despite computers, *xiv*
take paper vertical, 182

Pareto's Law: The 20/80 Law
    adaptation of, 109
    illustration of, 47–48
    making time for priorities, 230
    overturns "do it now," 46
    prioritizing with, 88
    required for prioritizing, 45
performance evaluations
    five suggestions for use, 201
    instant review card, 200
    metrics for, 195, 199
    once yearly, not enough, 201
planning
    anticipating needs: checklist, 176
    daily plan: show what matters, 85
    in a crossfire of bosses, 93
    involving team early, 204–206
    key to partnering colleagues, 93
    mid-managers' time chart, 86
    pre-determine fallback options, 89
    put off by pressure, 13
    seven options in a crisis, 75–77
    to enhance decision making, 94
    to plan calls and callbacks, 166
    with SMART charts, 40–43
    X-factor: contingencies, 67–68
priorities
    access and privacy, 86–88
    best time: based on energy
    clarifying with appointees, 192
    closed door a necessity, 245
    criteria for setting, 91
    criteria for validating tasks, 92
    don't opt out: show risks,
    drawn from goals, objectives, 28–36
    fate of mid-to-low priorities, 231
    options and your preference, 93
    prioritizing with colleagues, 93–94
    scenario: using your "gift hour," 7
    survivability, not scheduling, 30, 91
    three barriers to maintaining, 90
    top managers need screening, 169
    visual reminders, 18
Procrastination/Tasks Unfinished (Trap)
    the eight usual excuses, 224–225
    keep the day plan visible, 235–236
    only reds can bump a red, 234
    possible causes, 224

procrastinator/boss script, 226–227
propel action with graphics, 76, 233
seven ways to break a spell, 228
six ways to hold momentum, 228
task diary for re-start, 228
the task tower, 233
three reachable remedies, 223–224
three stimulants for startup, 222

Q-Card (graphic tool)
    to show risks to requesters, 106
Quick Solution: fourteen summaries,
        280–293
    1. Management by Crisis, 280
    2. Inadequate Planning, 281
    3. Inability to Say No, 282
    4. Communication, 283
    5. Poorly-Run Meetings, 284
    6. The World Gone Virtual, 285
    7. E-Mail Mania, 286
    8. The Untamed Telephone, 287
    9. Incomplete Info/Paper Chase, 288
    10. Confused Authority, 289
    11. Delegation/Training, 290
    12. Procrastination, 291
    13. Socializing/Drop-Ins, 292
    14. Attempting Too Much, 293
quiet hour policies
    antidote to "open door" abuse, 276
    floating backup for customer service,
        248
    quiet hour for teams, 248
    your closed door time, 245

randomness and responsiveness: double
        trouble
    flaw in phone handling, 167
    random access as fatal, 244–245
    seen as virtues, 14–15
reading time
    Alec Mackenzie advice, 187
    nine time savers, 188
    tech hint, 188
Red Zone (top three tasks daily)
    both important and urgent, 232
    bracket with contact times, 60, 167
    diversions from, 59
    kept in a three-day log, 68

no phone in red zone, 166
protected in daily plan, 235
red versus mid-risks, 231
red zone illustrated, 233
time allotment questions, 234
time chart sample, 61
when to close the door, 276

sales
hiring administrative help, 180–181
logging protects priorities, 58, 64
make peace with production, 93–94
overtime cut by goal tracking, 254
quell customer phone games, 171
use of standard lead time, 53–54
show risks (instead of saying no)
five reasons to decline requests, 99
five-step softener, 97
giving reasons not excuses, 104
harsh sound of no, 96
how to rescind a hasty yes , 103
non-assertions to avoid, 100–101
risk reduction Q-Cards, 106
setting a conditional yes, 104
showing risks w/diplomacy, 98
turning down "roles," 105
scheduling (see planning, priorities)
Schwab, Charles (when president of
Bethlehem Steel), 85
senior executives
appoint stand-ins for meetings, 130
let your team turn you down, 106
protecting your turf, 249
reading practices of, 187–188
setting goals and objectives, 29–30
supporting key players, 76
time budgets (chart), 83
untamed tasks: your province, 208
what senior managers value, 258
Sergent, Lorraine (Real Voices)
on effective delegation, 214
on life/work balance, 267
on staying busy, effective, 265
Shirley, Richard (Real Voices)
on lifelong planning, 266
on matching people to tasks, 219
on triage, 10
on work/life balance, 267

on workflow software, 148
on x-factors: the unexpected, 67
small business owners, consultants
delegating: two gambits, 218
going global, xiii, 145
learning integration tools, 24, 140
seeking administrative help, 180
self-employed socializing vital, 247
setting goals/objectives, 37
staffing: full and part-time, 218
task diary: lessons learned, 229
S.M.A.R.T. (see planning, templates)
Smith-Hemphill, Deborah, Ph.D.
(Real Voices)
on curtailing long threads, 156
on info "hide & seek," 149
on Internet evolution, 148–149
Socializing and Drop-Ins (Trap)
five ways to manage drop-ins, 240
four tactics: deal, postpone, refer,
assign, 241–242
last resort defenses, 248
overlooked unless logged, 57
physical setup adjustments, 245
protect your right to focus, 239
when visitors command respect, 247
Spencer, Terry (Real Voices)
life-lesson: grand-parenting, 265
on lifelong goal-setting, 266
on work/life balance, 267
Stotesbury, Tom (Real Voices)
on planning/goal setting, 266
on work/life balance, 268
supertraps, three (source of all others)
distractions, expectations, urgency, 4
Survey Questionnaire, 271

task validation
end-of day checklist, 10–11
for mid-managers, 9
for senior managers, 8
seven criteria for accepting work, 7
team time
case: team reorganized, 204–206
cross training in teams, 198, 218
How teams gain clarity, 32
meetings must be mutual, 127
planning team priorities, 89

team time (*continued*)
  preventing team fatigue, 258
  Project Acceptance Form, 31
  project teams, matrix teams, 107
  quick "stand-up" meetings, 125
  quiet hour coverage, 248
  shared web site for team, 155
  Team Criteria Chart, 47
  team threat assessmentprocess, 75
  team-wide e-mail policy, 161–162
  teams unified on objectives, 49
  three-stage team deployment,
    29–30
  win lateral team loyalty, 177–179
Telephone Untamed (Trap)
  avoiding phone addiction, 172–173
  clinics, callbacks, and cushions, 167
  conference call savings, 165
  customers crave live coverage, 164
  four service upgrades, 168
  plentiful "killer apps," 163
  premium callers get "privileged
  screening for senior execs, 168–169
  smoother sign-offs, 172
  time-saver options, 170
  time-slots," 167
  voice-mail greetings, 171
Templates and Tools for You to Use
  Admiral Rickover's Agenda, 132
  Chart: Decide or Delegate, 210
  Criteria for Setting Priorities, 49
  Eight Objectives for a Year, 38–39
  Instant Performance Review, 200
  Make Me a Request Board, 123
  Meeting Critique Card, 129
  Meeting Room Rules, 130
  Pareto's Law Illustrated, 48
  Percentage Goal Completion, 66
  Pie Chart for Task Tradeoffs, 102
  Positive Vocabulary Chart, 121
  Q-Cards on Risks, 106
  Red Zone Interrupted Chart, 61
  Red Zone Task Chart, 59
  Risk/Value Criteria for Projects, 92
  SMART Charts, 41–42
  Task Restart Diary, 229

Team Threat Assessment Tool, 75
  The Task Tower: Red Zones, 233
  Time Pyramids: Manager Levels, 84
  Time Trap Diagnosis Chart, 275
  Two-Column To-Do List, 25
  Work Acceptance Template, 31
  Work Estimating Chart, 52
time logs
  analyzing your log, 66–67
  barriers: boredom, inaccuracy, guilt,
    56–67
  five cautions, 63
  log red zone tasks, 59
  low- or high-tech choices, 62
  one logger's Q&A, defenses, 64–65
  selectivity: top three tasks, 58
time management
  cure: two-column to-do chart, 25
  false assumptions
    mere common sense? 20
    work best under pressure? 20
    death of spontaneity? 21
    too busy to learn? 22
    one tool is enough? 23
  least manageable resource, 26
  team sport, 276–277
Todisco, Kris (Real Voices)
  on Blackberry and Outlook, 141
  on delegating details: making time for
    decisions, 216
  on short-listing vital tasks, 256
  on two grandmothers' advice, 264
triage (*see also* priorities)
  distinguish importance from urgency,
    10,14, 44, 46, 62, 84, 111, 230, 232
  field hospital model, 9, 91
  procrastination and urgency, 291
  survivability, not scheduling, 91
  to validate urgency, 9
  when everything seems urgent, 281

urgency, *see* priorities

Wilber, Cathy (Real Voices)
  on self-discipline challenge, 21–22
  on work/life balance, 268